WHOLE LEARNING

Whole Language in the Upper Elementary Grades

PAT CORDEIRO

Richard C. Owen Publishers, Inc.
Katonah, New York

Library of Congress Cataloging-in-Publication Data
Cordeiro, Pat, 1944–
    Whole learning : whole language and content in the
upper elementary grades / by Pat Cordeiro.
       p.   cm.
    Includes bibliographical references (p.   ) and index.
    ISBN 1-878450-15-8
    1. Language experience approach in education—United States.
    2. Language arts—Correlation with content subjects—United States.
    I. Title.
    LB1576.C727   1992
    372.6—dc20   91-39407
                                                           CIP

Richard C. Owen Publishers, Inc.
135 Katonah Avenue
Katonah, New York 10536

9 8 7 6 5 4 3 2 1

10·27-93 - 1668936

This book is dedicated
to the memories of
Jim Locke, my father
and
Ben Grotz, my student—
with so many others,
they taught me and I learned.

Foreword

In *Schools of Thought*, Rexford G. Brown offers a definition of literacy that "goes beyond basic skills and includes enhanced abilities to think critically and creatively; to reason carefully; to inquire systematically into any important matter; to analyze, synthesize, and evaluate information and arguments; and to communicate effectively to a variety of audiences in a variety of forms" (1991, xiii). This literacy of thoughtfulness "involves both the exercise of thought and a certain amount of caring about other thinkers in past and present communities."

As I read *Whole Learning: Whole Language and Content in the Upper Elementary Grades*, Brown's definition came alive. Pat Cordeiro's students engage daily in the kind of learning that provides opportunities for students to become thoughtfully literate. In her book we get to see her view of learning and how she goes about her art of teaching. There is none of what Brown calls "talkinabout" in her classroom—"talkinabout" reading, "talkinabout" writing, "talkinabout" science. Instead, she and her students read, write, observe, experiment, predict, record, and so on. Her students don't just learn the facts but instead have acquired a language of learning—a way of thinking about their learning.

Pat knows herself as a learner both past and present. She acknowledges that her elementary/secondary schooling was not always a positive experience. When she began teaching she relied on her early learning to help her teach. But as she observed her students and tried to make sense of what they did, she eventually made a conscious decision *not* to teach as she had been taught. As she works towards an understanding of her own learning, she makes clear decisions about what her students should learn and how she'll go about teaching it. Her role as teacher is closely connected to herself as a learner. She takes herself seriously as a learner and expects that her students will take themselves seriously.

There are many other reasons for Pat's success. First of all, she never says she can't teach the way she believes she should teach because she doesn't have time or there is so much curriculum to cover. She accepts the givens of her school day and curriculum and asks, "Now, how can I do what I think is best for my students?" Problem solving is what she and her teaching are about. You will see how she restructured her day and didn't try to "cover" each subject each day.

She doesn't cite her students' lack of commitment to learning, lack of intelligence, or their less than ideal backgrounds as reasons why she can't teach in the ways she believes students best learn. Instead, she believes they can **all** learn and she works towards engaging students in meaningful, authentic learning experiences.

Evaluation systems don't stop her. She acknowledges that her instructional practices are different from other teachers, and therefore she must work towards an evaluation tool that matches what she values about what her students learn and how they go about doing it.

Pat also shows us that she doesn't just learn from language arts educators (too numerous to mention). Although she keeps language at the forefront of her thinking about learning, she goes beyond and learns from experts in other curricula areas who view learning as a process too. She borrows freely from their ideas and incorporates an abundance of appropriate children's literature across the curriculum.

Whole Learning shows how one teacher envisioned the practical implications of the diverse ideas of researchers and theoreticians. She shows with great detail and insight how she went about her teaching. Her ideas can serve as prototypes for the teaching of other concepts and themes. In this respect, Dr. Cordeiro's book itself is truly generative. Teachers can't help but to read it and say, "Tomorrow, I think I'll try . . ."

Mary Ellen Giacobbe

Brown, Rexford G. *Schools of Thought*. Jossey-Bass Inc., San Francisco, CA. 1991.

Preface

This is a book about what worked for me. During the 18 years that I taught elementary school, between 1965 and 1990, I was always allowed to learn and grow, to take time to discover what worked. I came to teaching well prepared. I was, on my mother's side, a product of a long line of successful teachers and missionaries and, on my father's side, blessed with curiosity and the ability to solve problems. Both sides cared a lot about people. An unbeatable combination for a teacher.

I came to whole language through process writing. In 1980, I went with school colleagues to hear Dr. Donald Graves speak at Harvard University about first graders and their writing processes. After years of invention and what could best be called "jury-rigged" strategies, Don's work gave me the direction I needed. I took a leave of absence, enrolled at Harvard and there met Mary Ellen Giacobbe. Through work with her and Dr. Courtney Cazden, my advisor, I began to define what teaching meant to me and came, eventually, to this book.

Looking back, I see myself always moving toward being what I now call "a whole language teacher." I always found myself more taken with children's ideas than my own, more involved with listening to them than to my carefully plotted lessons, more sure that each learner would react in a different way. I was always willing to let the schedule go and give time to things my students and I thought were important, to link and connect. Together, we were always willing to explore.

This didn't always make me successful, nor did it sit well with some educational philosophies. But in the long run, my persistence paid off for me. My belief in following the lead of each learner, no matter how long it took, served me best. Over my years of teaching, I had class sizes from seven to 35 but I always tried to focus on children one-by-one.

When I implemented a process writing workshop in my third grade in 1982, I began to formalize classroom practices that before had been random for me. I asked learners to tell me what they were thinking and I wrote down what they said and what they planned to do next. I showed them how I learned things and talked with them about it. And I followed all the way through on long-range projects. As a teacher, I learned the theory behind my practice.

And as I moved through the 80s and up through the grades, I extended these formalized, theory-based practices into all the subject areas. I found that after spending a dynamic hour in the morning interacting for writing, no one—especially me—wanted to switch to "teacher talk," the old paradigm in upper elementary content instruction. So we kept on conferencing, thinking out loud, and sharing ideas and plans. We began to look at the process of learning everything in a whole way.

This book is about Whole Learning—whole language philosophy embedded in all processes of learning, across content areas linked thematically. Whole Learning has a broader meaning and application than the term "whole language," relating various areas of curriculum, making content relevant and "whole," and highlighting skills as they serve the context.

For many years I taught in an unusual school, one not afraid to take risks, a school that allowed teachers to be full-fledged educators. That ideal school environment is the one I'll be describing as I plan out some of the ways whole language can work itself out once children can read.

This book is for teachers of intermediate grade children, grades three through six. I will primarily be focusing on all-day, self-contained situations where one teacher is responsible for all major subjects, where activities link learning across whole days and more.

But whether teachers have students in a self-contained classroom for all day or only for a short length of time, developing a sense of wholeness and integration is possible. For teachers in departmentalized settings, planning for whole learning is across weeks, may extend to other classrooms and other teachers, and must be focused firmly on developing a sense of continuity and community.

This book describes competencies achieved by whole language students in the primary grades and what we as upper-level elementary school teachers can do with those competencies. There are thoughts on building a community, engaging students in problem-solving, and amplifying assessment and evaluation. There are strategies for using informal writing and reading as tools for learning in the content areas.

This book is divided into three general parts, modeling how I went about building a whole learning classroom. Part I is about my "Thinking and Planning." It explores *why* I proceeded the way I did, the broad scheduling decisions I made, how I developed a curriculum with room to move, who the learners are, and what kind of classroom climate supports and nourishes them. These are the things I thought about every August.

Part II is about "Doing." It is arranged to reflect the flexible schedule that characterized my Whole Learning classroom. I start with writing time, because that is how class time started each September. As the year progressed, we continued to focus the day's beginning with writing time, but the nature of the writing tasks shifted, as each content area "took its turn being first." Our work with social studies often began early in the day because much of the schoolwide, thematic work centered around broad, social studies topics. So social studies is the second topic in "Doing."

The order of the other content areas, science, math, literature, reflects their "turns at being first." Science sometimes started us off, especially when the moon was visible in the morning because we collected data on the near universe and watched for days when we could see the earth, the sun and the moon all at once. In late September, we began our charting and graphing of natural events, so math/science activities soon began the day and lasted into the afternoon. In the early spring, we explored "big ideas" in mathematics, devoting several days to talk, activities, and reflection.

Readers' workshop is next, because on rainy days, we sometimes, in my students' words, "just read," from early morning on, stretched out on the rug, curled up in our chairs, talking, writing, and reading to each other, working with literature. Reading went on all day, as did writing, especially in content. As the year went by, I introduced strategies for informal and formal reading and writing in content. So reading and writing with trade books and a variety of subjects, reading and writing to learn in content areas, completes this section.

Part III is about reflecting, assessing and moving on. "Taking Time to Do Philosophy with Kids" is in this section, a time when students reflect on living and assess themselves and their values. This is followed by "The Theory behind the Practice," a chapter on theoretical perspectives for the ideas in this book. For me, this is the place where I am ready to think theoretically in a study like this: I have done some effective practice and now I want to think more deeply about what my beliefs about learning are and how I should extend and deepen them in practice. I need some theory. There is also a chapter on how learners and teachers together can enhance and clarify the "Assessment and Evaluation" of learning, both formally and informally. Part III closes with "Moving On," a look at what happens to teachers who continue to grow and change, as seen through my own growth lens.

As Dorothy Watson (1987) points out, all things whole language are designed to be starting points. And if they aren't working for us at some point, we must feel free to modify or replace them. Extending that thought across content, this book is mainly about helping teachers to think and plan for themselves, to put into action those things they are convinced will excite them and their students, to enjoy, be creative and to organize variations on the Whole Learning theme for their own classrooms.

Acknowledgements

There are so many people to thank for the production of this book that it's hard to know where to begin. If I forget any names, please consider yourself properly thanked. I'm very grateful to you all.

First, thanks go to the teachers, students, and parents of Veteran's Memorial Elementary School in Provincetown Massachusetts, a very special place. I'm grateful for all the learning we did together over the years from 1968 to 1990 while I grew up as a teacher. My friends and past colleagues at that school gave me many good times and shared many thoughts and experiences. They are second to none in their dedication to teaching and learning. And now, the teachers there and the principal, soon-to-be-Dr. Elliot Tocci, are doing exciting work on portfolio assessment with Dr. Howard Gardner's Project Zero at Harvard University. Once again, Veteran's Memorial Elementary School is on the cutting edge of the very best in education.

I thank the students who worked with me and the parents who supported me over the years. My students showed me what young learners are all about through what Michael Armstrong calls "their seriousness of purpose . . . their high intent." That seriousness, that high intent, made this book possible and my life a very rich one. I owe them all a great deal. Special thanks go to Helen and Maria Grotz for permission to use Ben Grotz's name in memory of his young life.

I'm grateful to my early readers who told me I should keep going, that the effort was worthwhile: my friends, Bobbi and Jim Fisher, and my friend, Linda Squire, who read the first forlorn scribbles and helped this writing process to move forward.

Grateful thanks go to Richard C. Owen, my publisher, whose encouragement, questioning and suggestions have carved out the main body of this text. Richard's vision for education sustained me through my long process. Many people at Richard C. Owen Publishers showed great care in the production of this book. I appreciate the hard work and fine tuning of Susan Goldberg who copy edited so carefully and made many excellent suggestions. Thanks also to Kenneth Hawkey for the invaluable expertise he brought to the design of this book. And, of course, much thanks to the reviewers selected by Richard, Dan Powers, Ann Ziegler, Susan Stires, and Joan Van Braymer, who spent endless hours laboring over drafts of this book and sent me pages of helpful and insightful comments which guided me through the main body of the text. Thank you all for your hard work and for your encouragement for my ideas and stories.

My thanks to my friend, Mary Ellen Giacobbe, for writing the Foreword to this book. We've thought together for a long time and watched ideas grow. I'm very pleased you're part of this project, Mary Ellen.

Thanks to Sally Wilson, Dr. Greg Knisely, and Dr. Pat Davidson for reading chapters and making many useful suggestions. Thanks to the support of my friends in the Whole Language Teachers Association who helped me to really understand whole language. And thanks to my new colleagues at Rhode Island College who have encouraged me in the last stages of this book with their interest and good wishes.

Much thanks goes to my mentors and friends, Dr. Courtney Cazden of Harvard Graduate School of Education and Dr. Pat Davidson of University of Massachusetts at Boston. They taught me how to really think. And an extra thanks goes to my friend, Bobbi Fisher, for her continuous interest in our collaboration. I count a lot on your feedback, Bobbi. Together, we create a thinking environment that helps us both learn.

Finally, thanks to my family whose love and support sustain me as I rush through life: my husband, Marty, who gives me the help I need to do the things I think are important and who shares my pride in our accomplishments; my mother—artist, writer, teacher, linguist—whose talks with me help me think things through and who has always given me that rare thing, unconditional support; my sister, who shares my history and whose fine mind helps me to see other sides; and, of course, the memory of my father, who continues to whisper in my ear of his great pride in his family and his love for the life we live. Without all of you, these great things would never happen.

PC

Table of Contents

Foreword by Mary Ellen Giacobbe   v

Preface   vii

Acknowledgements   xi

PART I: THINKING AND PLANNING   1

Chapter 1   Whole Learning   3

How I started   3

Why we need Whole Learning   5

What is whole language?   7

What this means to upper elementary teachers   9

Learners with a history   11

Chapter 2   Blending a Scheduled Day   13

Thinking it through   13

Fall daily schedule   14

Across the subjects and through the day   16

Strategies for linking through the day   17

Blending the day   22

Things that help blend   23

Keeping a schedule in my mind   25

Chapter 3   Moving toward a Whole Learning Curriculum   27

Growing a classroom   27

Literacy as a means to an end   28

Levels of curriculum   29

What is a generative curriculum?   29

Portugal: A simulation in a generative curriculum   30

A word about learning centers   33

Changing as teachers   35

Chapter 4   Living in a Whole Learning Climate   36

Classroom climates   36

Essential element: Community   37

Essential element: Authenticity   40

Essential element: Appropriateness   43

A word from a climatologist   43

PART II: DOING   45

Chapter 5   Start the Morning: Writing Time   47

Remembering writing time   47

Writing process in action   48
Advanced writing process in action   50
When do we find time?   52
What writers know   54
Starting out in writing time with learners
with a history   55
Working with writers in process   60
Experienced writers and their planning   61
Writing and problem-solving   65
The things they write   68
Books to help   69

Chapter 6   Integrated Learning: Social Studies in Context   73
Remembering Social Studies   73
Problem-based thematic simulations   75
The Westward Migration   77
The Royal Archeological Institute of Cairo   85
Everyday life in early America   96
Working within simulations   112
The Mantle of the Expert   114

Chapter 7   Integrated Learning: Science Lab   115
Remembering science   115
Whole Learning and science   116
Charting and graphing   118
Special projects   123
Moonwatching   128
Doing what scientists do   134
Books to help   135

Chapter 8   Mathematics Lab   136
Remembering mathematics   136
Computation in a concrete way   139
A climate of trust   141
Problem posing   143
Writing in mathematics   145
Exploring big ideas in mathematics   147
Mathematics as Whole Learning   153
Books to help   154

Chapter 9   Readers' Workshop   155
Remembering teaching reading   155
Drifting away from basals   158
Writers who read: Having Author Dialogues   159
Readers' Workshop: choice reading   161

Literature Circles   164
Books to help   168
Reading content material   168
Chapter 10   Content Learning with Trade Books   175
Remembering text books   175
"Dense print" books versus picture storybooks   176
Picture storybooks for all ages   177
Picture storybooks as text models   178
Picture storybooks as models of creative products   180
Picture storybooks as a way of learning how to learn from books   186
Picture storybooks with a difference   192
Sources and booklists for picture storybooks   194
Chapter 11   Strategies for Informal Writing in Content   196
Remembering academic writing   196
Freewriting in content areas   198
Informal versus formal writing   205
Jotting things down   206

PART III: REFLECTING AND ASSESSING   209
Chapter 12   Taking Time to Do Philosophy with Kids   211
Remembering philosophizing   211
Doing philosophy   213
Philosophizing about topics like "honesty"   214
Reflections   217
Chapter 13   The Theory Behind the Practice   220
Developing theory   220
Developing a theory of conditions of learning at upper elementary   221
Brian Cambourne's Conditions of Learning   222
The adult performance model   224
Comparing and contrasting the models   227
Applying both models to upper elementary learners   229
Learning from Lev Vygotsky   231
Inter- to intrapersonal learning   232
The zone of proximal development   232
Spontaneous versus scientific concept development   234
Vygotsky and integrated school learning   234
Chapter 14   Assessment and Evaluation   236
Reflecting on assessing   236

Portfolio assessment   238
Self-evaluation   244
Ongoing evaluation   247
Books to help   247
Putting it all together   248
Chapter 15   Moving On   251
What happens when we move on   251
Teachers and their moving on   253
Listening for surprises   255
A new view of my faults   256
I move on   257
Bibliography   259
Bibliography of Picture Storybooks in Content Areas, 1991   267
Appendix   271
Index   283

THINKING
AND
PLANNING

Whole Learning

How I Started

I started teaching in 1965, first grade, 35 children, and we all sat in our desks all day. I sat behind a very big desk, the biggest I ever saw. Most of the children could just see over the top of my big desk from where they sat in their small desks, islands separated from me and from each other.

We each worked away at our own projects at those desks. I reproduced the entire twelve days of Christmas and colored them in at my desk, to make a bulletin board. They worked on their papers and colored them in, to develop fine motor control, as we called it. I taught them the way I had been taught. We were very far apart. No one moved around.

I don't really know how they did. I was young and I left, and from those small students, I moved up to teach sixth grade, the big kids, and we all sat through the day, too. Except that now I sometimes stood at the board and talked and pointed. They sat and wrote.

That sixth grade year I found long division very hard to teach. I wasn't able to help kids who were stuck on what to do with all that stuff that hangs down in a long division problem—I didn't know what it meant either.

So I moved to second grade. And gradually over the years I have worked my way back to sixth grade. Now we all move around and talk to each other. Now I do pretty well with long division because over the years as I came up through the grades, math manipulatives came into my school, and I learned a lot, moving around and talking.

Math manipulatives are materials used to help children understand abstract mathematical concepts in a concrete way. They are usually objects that are purchased as sets, like Cuisenaire rods, pattern blocks, attribute blocks, chip trading, base ten blocks, and centicubes, or things that are collected like rocks, shells, or bottle caps. Little children learning to add one and one in a program that uses manipulatives will first handle two objects, putting them together, perhaps on a chart designed for working with adding objects, to help them understand that two separate objects put together make a set called "two." Only after they have worked with the manipulatives will they move to an abstract representation of the problem, perhaps with pictures and numbers, showing $1 + 1 = 2$.

As I learned how to work with students and math manipulatives, I was able to explore processes in math for the first time myself. I learned what was really going on in a long division problem. And I applied what I learned to teaching.

All through my teaching career, I have found that most of what I taught was just like my experience teaching long division. The way I was taught to do things did not help me to teach them. In fact, sometimes the way I was taught stood in my way.

Somehow, the way I was taught never allowed me to explore the learning process I was going through. So I was never able to do that with my own students. What I've discovered is that helping students to understand means helping them to undergo a process, helping them to reflect meaningfully on what they are doing and how they are learning.

For instance, students learning about the American Revolution could simply be asked to read and memorize facts from a textbook. Or, they could use the study of the Revolution to think about how they might learn any body of content, to reflect on and improve all of their learning process. To an observer, the difference between these methods would be demonstrated in the nature of the classroom talk.

In the first instance, students and teacher would discuss only the subject. The talk might be primarily by the teacher and student talk might be limited to the "fill-in-the-blank," or "guess what the teacher's thinking," type of response.

In the second instance, where the subject at hand is seen as a way of understanding the larger process of how we find and acquire knowledge, the classroom talk would often be about learning and the questions would be authentic, asked for a real purpose, using the American Revolution material as a case in point. Students and teacher would talk about how information is located and interpreted, how we decide what is important to learn and remember, how we solve the problem of learning about something like the American

Revolution. The instructional intention in this case is to provide students with the tools and the insights needed to acquire any body of knowledge. Teachers of this kind of learning interaction are concerned with enhancing students' awareness and understanding of the learning process they are experiencing.

And so Whole Learning has evolved for me as a way of teaching meaningfully. It is not at all the way I was taught, nor is it like some of the trends and movements I tried out in my younger career. It is not a concept in isolation as individualized reading or new math was, nor is it a reading strategy like language experience. It is not a teacher-centered concept like the open classroom movement, dependent on teachers' abilities to team closely together.

Whole Learning is more than all of these. The result of a continuing spiral in education, it connects changes that have gone before to conditions and freedoms as they are today. It honors the empowerment and practical knowledge of teachers and students and recognizes that learning exists in context. It encourages teachers and students to take risks, to try new things and to learn together. Whole Learning is a comprehensive philosophy, linking students and their curricula, redefining the teaching-learning relationships, and extending literacy across content.

As a result of all of this, my classrooms now look and sound very different from the way my first-grade classroom did, so long ago. Now we are all teachers and learners. We sit together—when we sit—so that we can all talk to each other. Knowledge is transmitted in all directions across the classroom, not just from the front to the back, not just from me to them, or from them to me. We are willing to try new things, to pursue subjects that interest us until we are satisfied, to talk together about how we did something, how we thought about it. I am a classroom resource, another learner, "the journey-maker," as Dorothy Heathcote puts it. My primary interest is no longer what I will do, but how we did what we did, and how I can help students to make optimum use of their own learning processes. As Bobbi Fisher says in her book, *Joyful Learning*: "I trust the children as the authorities of their own learning" (p. 1).

Why We Need Whole Learning

8:00 Bell rings; kids come in; day begins
8:05 Everyone settles down; writing time begins as usual with writing and reading of writing plans
8:15 Two kids finish collecting lunch money; I check it
8:16 Everyone writes

8:20 Art teacher comes in to change art schedule

8:22 Archie and Annie get ready to leave for band rehearsal

8:23 Media specialist comes in to see if we have the library's Bank Street Writer disk

8:25 Several students begin discussion of reader's expectations in Mable's story; discussion grows

8:28 Bert and Waldo gather materials to take with them to remedial reading

8:30 Discussion grows; samples are brought out; we all gather on the rug for intense head-to-head thought session

8:35 Migrant teacher arrives to take Mitzie and Cy for forty minutes; nurse takes Sophia, Emily and Max to have ears and eyes checked; Charlotte and Zelda get ready for instrument lessons; secretary comes in to check on breakfast ticket money

8:38 Discussion deteriorates; everyone up and around; Teacher reorganizes

Sound familiar? As I talk to teachers, I hear the same concern: When do I teach *everyone*? When does something that feels whole happen in my classroom?

Teachers care. Teachers ask caring and difficult questions: How can I "de-compartmentalize" my self-contained classroom? How can I deal with everyone else's agenda? How can I teach a large curriculum in a meaningful and effective way? How can I have an "integrated day" in a disintegrated schedule?

Pulling it all together for myself was the starting point for what I call Whole Learning. Whole Learning at upper elementary begins with the philosophy of whole language and extends literacy development into content areas with a focus on process. Here, learning is viewed as a process, occurring actively. In active, process learning, there is a primary emphasis on the processes taking place and a secondary emphasis on the content being used to focus the learning. Teachers in process learning episodes concentrate on the learner's process both for instruction and assessment. The underlying assumption of process learning is that if a learner understands a process thoroughly, then many areas of content can be mastered using that knowledge of process.

Whole language and Whole Learning are not teaching methodologies, sets of lesson packets, instructional gimmicks, and never what Dorothy Watson (1987) calls "anemic routines." Rather, they are exciting and energizing concepts. Teachers up through the grades are renewing themselves and their students through working with language in a whole way and the literacy events that give language life and meaning.

As Ken Goodman pointed out during a talk in Rye, New York, isn't it unusual that people are surprised to learn that teachers are excited about what they are doing, that they believe in their ideas and they are willing to fight for them? David Hornsby, a principal from Australia and coauthor of *Write On* and *Read On*, tells how moved he was by meeting U.S. teachers on the brink of retirement who said, ''I can't retire this year—I've discovered whole language—I need one more year.''

What is Whole Language?

The basis of Whole Learning, whole language is a philosophy which has had far-reaching implications in modern education. Courtney Cazden (1991) describes the whole language movement as having an environment in which ''children learn what they live, what they hear and try to speak, in a context of meaningful, functional use with people who care about them and have confidence that they will learn'' (p. 8). Connie Weaver, in her book *Understanding Whole Language: From Principles to Practice*, emphasizes that whole language is ''a philosophy, a belief system about the nature of learning and how it can be fostered in classrooms and schools'' (p. 3).

Bobbi Fisher describes her whole language-based beliefs with this list:

- Children learn naturally.
- Children know a lot about literacy before kindergarten.
- All children can learn.
- Children learn best when learning is kept whole, meaningful, interesting, and functional.
- Children learn best when they make their own choices.
- Children learn best as a community of learners in a non-competitive environment.
- Children learn best by talking and doing in a social context. [p. 3]

In their brochure, the Massachusetts-based Whole Language Teachers Association records a set of principles of whole language. Starting by writing that ''Whole Language is a term commonly used to encompass many complex concepts,'' they include the following:

All children are capable learners. They learn by active participation in their own education as they think, make choices, create, take risks, and solve problems.

Children and teachers are empowered as they share self, community and culture in the classroom.

The ideal conditions under which children learn to talk can and should be replicated in the classroom.

The bonded relationship between the teacher and the child is crucial.

Children learn in a supportive environment by:
- observing authentic demonstrations by bonded individuals
- engaging in joyful participation
- initiating and sustaining self-regulated practice
- sharing, through performance, newly-acquired skills and knowledge

Reading builds foundations for lifelong literacy.

Children learn to read by reading and to write by writing. Readers and writers construct their own meaning based on prior knowledge, experience and interactions with others.

Children need to read and re-read a wide range of high-quality literature, including both fiction and non-fiction.

Skills are always best taught in context.

Grouping is flexible and always temporary.

Assessment is ongoing and most effective when it documents what children **can** do rather than what they cannot do.

Learning is a lifelong process of moving from approximation to competence.

Literacy and learning are joyful causes for celebration.

Whole language environments keep language whole. Don Holdaway (1979) describes whole language strategies as ''an attempt to set up the conditions of (oral language) 'acquisition' in classrooms'' (p. 10.). As children learn to read and write in the same way that they learn to talk, educators observe ''literacy without tears.'' Here, children learn by focusing on whole texts before becoming involved with the parts, the grapho-phonics, the words, the sentences. As Don points out, traditional instruction begins with parts and ''often ends with the study of parts.'' In such learning, students never get to the whole—writers never write a real story, readers never read whole books. Learning is fragmented, disjunct, partial and decontextualized. Whole language tries to keep learners always in touch with the ''main road,'' even when they ''take a detour'' (Clay & Cazden 1990) to look closely at a part.

Whole language classrooms actualize Brian Cambourne's (1988) optimal conditions for learning. Based on principles of oral language learning, these conditions describe learning environments where: learners are *immersed* in what they are learning; *demonstration* is available from more able peers and adults; there is a positive *expectation* that learning will take place; learners are actively *engaged*; a learner's *approximations* of standard form are accepted; *response* enables self-correction; there is ample opportunity for *use*; and, learners are granted *responsibility* for how learning takes place. When these conditions are in place, learners can take risks, secure that the classroom is a safety net providing a haven for growth.

Whole language environments are child-centered. In a child-centered, or learner-centered, classroom, you are as likely to see the children standing and talking as the teacher. In whole language classrooms, children and teachers engage in learning cooperatively, sharing reading, writing, and speaking. They participate in genuine communities, bonded by common goals, arranged around authentic literacy events.

Whole language experiences start where the learner is. Learners approximate, or give their version of the standard form, as when an infant says "Baba" for "Daddy." As learners approximate, they fine tune themselves toward competency, relying on self-monitored feedback from those around them.

Whole language impacts on teachers. Jackie Finn, of the Whole Language Teachers Association writes: "Whole language teachers believe that their framework, theory and practice form a dynamic whole. The framework changes with new knowledge and the continued observation of children in the process of learning" (personal communication, 1991). Ken and Yetta Goodman and Wendy Hood (1989) call whole language a "grass-roots movement among teachers" who "integrate oral and written language with conceptual learning."

Whole language environments are safe havens for growth and change. In her new book, *Invitations: Changing as Teachers and Learners K-12*, Regie Routman offers this far-reaching "invitation":

> Whole language is about all learners feeling whole and able and part of a community of learners. It is about belonging and risk-taking and feeling successful as teachers and learners. It is about the power of collaboration to break down the isolation of teachers and to establish communities of belonging and learning for all students and teachers. (p. 4)

What This Means to Upper Elementary Teachers

Teachers at grades four, five, and six want to incorporate the principles of the whole language movement in their classrooms but are frustrated by the literature's apparent emphasis on emergent literacy—beginning reading. Much of the literature and training associated with whole language has been directed at teachers of kindergarten and first grade.

Once I was at a "book share" with teachers grade two and up. As we exchanged picture books and Big Books, we talked about our mutual experiences in teaching for literacy, and what was happening with our colleagues. We agreed that for a while we had all steered clear of anything "whole language" because we connected the term with emergent literacy.

Typical of the problems that upper elementary teachers have with the mismatch between current whole language literature and the nature of learners in upper elementary school is reflected in the whole language movement's use of the term "child-centered." Classrooms which are good whole language environments are said to be centered on how the **child** learns and are said to start where the **child** is. One of the first things I had to monitor myself for as a teacher when I moved up through the grades was how I talked to my students and what I referred to them as. Students above fourth grade do not welcome being referred to as "children" and I had to check constantly before sentences came out of my mouth. I taught myself to refer to them as "people." "Boys and girls" was even considered insulting by my sixth graders. I used the term "ladies and gentlemen."

Upper elementary teachers will be thinking about how to make their classrooms "learner-centered," a term which begins to move away from the concern with emergent literacy and young children. They will be looking for literature which talks within the framework they do, which is designed for working with learners of all ages. And that will affect their translation of Brian Cambourne's conditions of learning.

Whole language learners are growing up and upper level teachers are ready to move into this exciting realm, too. But the literature is trailing behind the interest. Upper elementary teachers will find these works specific and useful to their level, available as of 1991: Three essays in Ken and Yetta Goodman and Wendy Hood's *Whole Language Evaluation Book*; Nancie Atwell's *Coming to Know: Writing to Learn in the Intermediate Grades*; essays in Tom Newkirk and Nancie Atwell's *Understanding Writing: Ways of Observing, Learning, and Teaching*; Linda Rief's *Seeking Diversity: Language Arts with Adolescents*; Carole Edelsky, Bess Altwerger and Barbara Flores' chapter called "What whole language looks like in the classroom, scene two" in their book, *Whole Language: What's the Difference?*; parts of Linda Crafton's *Whole Language: Getting Started Moving Forward*; and, a book with potential for downscaling the ideas for use with upper elementary, Carol Gilles, Mary Bixby, Paul Crowley, Shirley Crenshaw, Margaret Henrichs, Francis Reynolds & Donelle Pyle's *Whole Language Strategies for Secondary Students*.

Lacking more comprehensive guidance in what whole language means to them, intermediate teachers want to know how they can maximize what children already know, what competencies they can rely on, and how they can adapt whole language early learning practices to upper level advantage.

Bobbi Fisher, who teaches first grade in the Sudbury, Massachusetts Public Schools, and I have been giving a whole language workshop called, "Help! Here Come the Whole Language Kids! What Do We Do Now?" In it Bobbi describes what children learn in whole language kindergartens and I describe how those competencies play themselves out in sixth grade. Teachers appreciate the opportunity to see connections across grade levels in terms of shared competencies.

These teachers want to create literacy events in all areas of their curriculum. They want to apply a whole language philosophy to all learning and move beyond an initial concern with developing reading. Intermediate teachers want to explore how they can build whole language tenets into a framework that includes all areas of learning. They want to know how to adapt strategies for fostering learning in young children to working with older children, learners with a history. They want to provide what Carole Edelsky, Bess Altwerger and Barbara Flores describe as "content-rich curricula where language and thinking can be about interesting and significant content . . . subjected to critical analysis" (1991, p. 9).

Learners With a History

A special aspect of upper elementary is that teachers at this level work with learners with a history, learners who have been around learning and classrooms for quite a while. Sometimes these histories are positive, sometimes they are not. How experienced learners feel about the classroom affects how conditions of whole language are introduced and implemented when this is new for them. When learners have a negative history, teachers may have to engage in some "catch-up" work to repair damage done by earlier learning experiences. Learners with a negative history may not trust a hasty application of positive expectation and may need reassurance that they are trusted to take responsibility for their own learning. For these learners, the safety net must be very secure and very obvious before they can return to an earlier, more trusting model of learning.

At the upper elementary, with our learners with a history, we will not be able to unqualifyingly apply a model of learning which is drawn from learners with no history. We *do* have differences. In Chapter 13, "The Theory behind the Practice," I have developed more fully how I see these significant differences.

Upper elementary students are also learners on the edge of adulthood, learners who are looking more toward the life of the adult world than the life of the preschooler. How learners envision themselves in the world affects the kind of environment they take to. Knowing that I'm working with people who think they're adults and who try to do what they think adults do has been a strong position for me. I can help these "nearly grown up" students practice what they will need soon.

Learners on the edge of adulthood want to take responsibility. If I set up conditions that allow them to work like adults, to pretend that they're grown up, they will try to work as hard as they think grown-ups might. And that all fits in very nicely with my use of Brian Cambourne's optimal conditions for learning.

Blending a Scheduled Day

Thinking it Through

When I first started teaching I wondered how I was ever going to organize the day. All the kids had reading during the first hour so that was taken care of, but I wasn't quite sure what to do after that. And since I was teaching in an outpost, in a small building near the church, no one came near me to tell me what to do.

So what I did was structure the day by page numbers. We did spelling page 14 for however long it took, and then we went on to math page 15 until it was finished, and that was followed by the time it took for science page 16.

Teachers develop a sense of "lesson" length. That's the usual length of time it takes to tell students how to do the something the teacher has in mind, get most of them through it and then collect the products. And it just about perfectly matches how long it takes most children to do the typical workbook page. One begins to reinforce the other.

These lessons are all teacher-directed, teacher-conceived, and serve the teacher's need for organization and control. For we do need to feel like we have a handle on the day we are in charge of. Nothing frightens a teacher as much as the thought of a classroom out of control, one proceeding from moment to moment by chance, with no sense of direction or underlying structure.

But to let the underlying structure be directed by page number without carefully thinking about why we are doing it is to organize the curriculum by default. And when I started thinking about it, I found that I didn't like my reasons for doing it. They all came back to expediency.

What I'm after is a schedule and a structure that truly enables the students to be the center of the classroom. This means that any schedule I write down must be tentative enough so that when students say, "But we're just getting started—we need more time," there *is* time to spare. What I gave up when I took this stance was being so sure that I knew best what had to come next. What I gained was confidence in knowing that my instincts about learners were right—in the end, I really **did** "know best." What I knew was not what everyone absolutely **had** to learn next, rather I knew that if I followed their lead carefully by listening, watching and interacting, they would show me what **should** be learned next.

I believe strongly in the need for unity and connectedness in learning. And I believe that people learn best when they have responsibility, choice, and control over how that learning takes place. Thus, I relate subjects, as much as I can, through theme or concept, and I link experiences. I try to listen to the learning going on around and within me.

Fall Daily Schedule

Here is a schedule, one that was generally kept only in the fall. From early in the school year, many variations and changes occurred. We must remember that a schedule such as this, kept rigidly, reinforces the decompartmentalization of the self-contained classroom and works against Whole Learning. Blurring of content material across the designated times was my eventual goal, so that Readers' Workshop in the spring became a vehicle for dealing with content material in the same way we dealt with student-selected fiction in the fall, and writing time moved from publishing fiction to publishing many kinds of writing and research.

In the following chapters, the different subjects will be discussed. Here I will give brief descriptions.

8:00–9:00   Writing Time
            • Writing Process Workshop
            • Infused "Language Arts"
            • Infused Spelling
            • Infused Vocabulary
            • Author Dialogues

9:00–10:00	Readers' Workshop
	• Reading Process Workshop
	• Choice Reading
	• Reading Journals
	• Literature Groups
	• Author Dialogues

10:00–11:00	Math Lab
	• Independent Math Work
	• Thematic Studies
	• Problem-finding, Problem-solving

11:00–11:25	Science Lab or Social Studies
	• Charting and Graphing
	• Simulations
	• Special Somethings

11:25–11:55	Lunch
11:55–12:20	Silent, Free-choice Reading
12:20–12:50	Recess
12:50–2:00	Science Lab or Social Studies, or "Special Somethings"
	• Charting and Graphing
	• Simulations
	• Performance Time
	• Special Somethings—of all sorts

This fall schedule was arranged to allow an organized flow of information through the day. In the fall, I spent some time teaching procedures—where things were (like all the materials for writing and publishing) how we could move and interact in this setting, what I expected the students to do and what we all would expect me to do. The students, in turn, shared their ideas about how they would like learning to go in this classroom. I established only one central rule: We would all act reasonably. Beyond that, the detailed rules were a negotiated settlement. I don't think it's up to me to set the rules. After all, I'm not the only one who has to live in the room for a year.

Writing Time was first thing in the morning because students who are writers know what to do and are able to go right to it. Many come in with writing in their heads all set to be recorded. Also, I had found over the years that if I left writing time till last, we never got to it.

I set up the early morning this way because, as many teachers know, things don't always go the way you plan first thing in the morning. There can be many interruptions. I believe it is important to have a routine in place that permits organized, significant learning to happen from the beginning of the day. In my early days in teaching before I had writing time, I found myself assigning busy work that students could do alone so that I could deal with the problems that cropped up first thing in the morning.

Having writing time first solved that problem. During writing time there are many "teachers" in the room—everyone is able to help in some way. And writers often want to be left alone to write. Once our routine for beginning writing time was established, the day began without me calling it to attention. When the morning started this way, it said that we all came to school to learn and we automatically began when we got there, by writing.

The schedule I set up in the fall was not the schedule I kept by the end of the year, no matter what grade I taught. It wasn't even the schedule I had in January. And, over the years, as my curriculum became more flexible and my program more thematic and integrated, it wasn't even the schedule in place in October. By that time, in recent years, we had already adjusted our schedule to fit our needs.

What is the point of a schedule, if not to fulfill the needs of the students and teachers? Back when I first started, I knew that I had to cover all the subjects, but it never occurred to me that I didn't have to cover them all in one day. I never thought about working as long as we needed to on one subject one day and then not doing that subject the next day. And it never occurred to me to relate subjects to each other through concepts in common such as problem-solving, presenting them together.

We need all the subjects. Each school subject contributes its own piece to the overall development of the learner, as the Soviet psychologist, Lev Vygotsky, concluded. None can be left out. But how we choose to work with them is the choice we as learners have.

I chose to work with them by seeking opportunities to blend them together, to demonstrate their connectedness through themes and concepts, in common, so that learners could experience learning in a whole, united way.

Across the Subjects and Through the Day

Linking across different content areas is helped by having continuity in learning processes, expectations and procedures. For instance, it helps if the way writing time is conducted is basically the same from kindergarten through the exit grade. In this way, upper level teachers can count on and make use of students' prior knowledge of these matters. I believe we lose more than a month of school when we must reteach procedural matters and expectations each year. It takes a long time to help students know the teacher's ways. And students, as those of us who have been students know, spend most of the beginning of the year trying to ''psyche out'' the teacher, trying to figure out what this particular teacher thinks is important—will she/he worry a lot about handwriting and spelling, students wonder as writing time begins. Will this person care about my ideas? Will I be able to talk things over? Can I open my desktop when I want to? What kind of a person is this who's in charge of me for a year?

When we look at it this way, students don't have much power. The beginning of every year is rightfully frightening and unknown for students when all that they have learned about how classrooms and communities operate must be laid aside to make way for a new person's agenda. I was fortunate to work in a building where all agreed that continuity across the grades was important. Thus, some procedures we worked with were put in place in kindergarten and were kept constant. This was one of the greatest strengths of our work with children. We worked to make the school and the curriculum a coherent whole for both the teachers and the students.

Strategies for Linking Through the Day

Here are some strategies and processes that can be used throughout the day and in a variety of subject areas. These help to strengthen the sense of wholeness in the learning.

Themes To the extent possible, all subjects revolved around the same theme, such as Egypt or the Westward Emigration, or the same concept, such as justice or infinity. ''The extent possible'' means that the theme or concept is followed *within the bounds of authenticity*. I once had a principal who color-schemed the classrooms and I had the avocado room. My bulletin boards were supposed to be avocado—and changed every month, I might add— regardless of their educational content. That is not thematic instruction because it is not authentic to the learning going on, but is forced and extraneous.

Bess Altwerger, in a talk at the C.E.L. conference in Winnepeg, Canada in 1988, pointed out that thematic instruction is also not ''The bears' birthday party.'' In classrooms driven by the ''bears' birthday party,'' there are bears everywhere, on the walls, on papers, on children. Books and stories about bears are read and written, and math word problems are full of bears. In such a setting, the impression is that the teacher got hung up on bears, for the theme has nothing authentic to do with the curriculum and has been imposed from the outside.

Themes arise from two sources: the ongoing curriculum and children's interests. Often themes arise from a combination of the two, the result of ideas generated during classroom activities. When my class and I were learning about Portugal, and pretending to travel to Portugal, students developed a strong interest in American immigration laws. So we "sidestepped" to take an extended look at what's involved in traveling to other countries. In the process, we learned much about what it means to be an American. Themes thus are learner-centered because children have input into the path that the study will follow.

Themes are broad enough to include several subjects and to permit extensions, like the Portugal unit. Themes might involve concepts, like infinity, and might have a philosophic basis, like what it means to be free. Units built around themes "reflect patterns of thinking, goals, and concepts common to bodies of knowledge" (Pappas, Kiefer & Levstik 1990, p. 49).

Themes can be "Big Ideas in rich contexts," with topics like infinity or justice explored deeply, extensively, through as many interests as the learners can create. To qualify as a Big Idea, a theme must have three components: the Big Idea must encompass more than one case, be generalizable, and have implications across disciplines; the thematic work must begin with the teacher's intention to develop understanding of a concept; and, finally, the concept, the Big Idea, must be one that continues to intrigue the experts (Cordeiro, in press). Working with students on a concept like infinity is a good example of all three.

Rich contexts are classroom environments which are multi-textured, where learning is going on in many modes and not just through teacher-talk or textbook-digesting. In rich contexts, students make choices about learning from many modes. Many resources are available. Learners exercise options about concept development by exploring what works best for them.

Integrated day   To the extent possible, boundaries between subjects are broken down so that students can understand the connections between domains. Related to thematic instruction, integrating the day enables students to look at learning from many perspectives. When my students and I spent a month on and off working on the theme of "infinity," we lived on the boundaries of math and science from a literate perspective. And when we worked for several days on Gamow's (1947, p. 28) problem about the "Infinity Hotel" and the infinite number of mathematicians who want to stay there (Cordeiro 1988), we worked for a while in social studies and infinity as we considered issues of travel and social relations in an infinite context. When we "went West" in the westward migration simulation, pretending to be travelers in covered wagons crossing America, we did a lot of relevant and necessary math, like calculating how heavy our wagons were, how much food we had left, and how far we had to travel.

A linked curriculum in a well-knit day also can be strengthened by focusing on processes and awarenesses which help the student to unite various subjects. These can be used as learning themes in themselves–as when teacher and students together look at different subjects through a lens like "reliability of source," or what it means to be an expert, or is solving problems the same no matter what the problem. These processes can also be underlying long-term goals for higher order learning held by the teacher as a curriculum directive. These are:

Infused critical and creative thinking   When critical and creative thinking are infused into curricular areas, they are highlighted, instructed and discussed within the context of the subject (Swartz & Perkins 1989). They are not separated out on worksheets or for fifteen minutes in the afternoon. The infusion of these vital thinking skills and our working awareness of them provides tools to be used in learning rather than isolated subjects to be studied.

Infusion is an interesting word. Infusion is what happens to the tea in a teabag when it soaks into a cup of hot water. The "good" in the tea gets soaked out and blended through the hot water till the mixture is just right. Likewise, critical and creative thinking gets "soaked" throughout the day, through the program until the mixture of content and how to think about it is just right.

Thus, when students studying about Portugal got involved in classifying the kinds of geography found in that country, I called their attention to the fact that they were using a critical thinking skill, classifying. We took time to discuss what we do when we classify, how people can do it better, what other uses we might find for the skill.

Infused problem solving awareness   Because I believe that we learn and function through a series of processes of problem solving, we talk about how we do it as often as we can. In my classroom, as in many of the rooms in the school I taught in, we referred often during the day to a generic problem-solving framework (Rowe 1991) on the magnetic chalkboard, a model designed to be moved around on the chalkboard to help us understand where we were in the problem-solving process at any given time in any given problem.

This framework (*see* Figure 1) shows the stages we go through when we solve problems, with each stage written on a separate, laminated segment so that we could write details of our immediate problem-solving in washable magic marker.

In each segment, specific critical thinking skills that help at that stage are listed. If we were talking about classifying, we could all look at the problem-solving model and see that classifying was listed as useful at the stage of organization. Thus we were able to tie the infusion of critical thinking directly

FRAMEWORK FOR INFUSED CRITICAL AND CREATIVE THINKING INSTRUCTION

Problem-Solving • Decision-Making • Examination of Issues

Situation

Organization
- Fluency
- Flexibility
- What do we know?
- What do we need to find out?
- How can we find out?
- Recording
- Grouping
- Comparing/Contrasting
- Classifying
- Ordering
- Sequencing
- Prioritizing
- Patterning
- Originality
- Elaboration
- **Brainstorming**

Using one's thinking abilities

Data gathering
- Questioning
- Researching
- Observing
- Reading
- Interviewing
- Experimenting

Being open-minded

Assessing information and sources
- Reliability
- Assumptions
- Analogies
- Fact/Opinion
- Adequacy
- Accuracy
- Relevance
- Currency

Questioning

Question, issue, or problem generating
- Fluency
- Flexibility
- Causal Interference
- Identifying Cause/Effect
- Causal Chains
- Multiple Causality
- Causal Explanation
- Evidence
- Predicting
- Hypothesizing
- Generalizing
- Originality
- Elaboration
- **Brainstorming**

Risks

Seeking evidence

Question, issue or problem stating
- Asking/answering questions for clarification

seeking alternatives

Answer or solution generating
- Fluency
- Flexibility
- Causal Interference
- Identifying Cause/Effect
- Causal Chains
- Multiple Causality
- Causal Explanation
- Evidence
- Predicting
- Hypothesizing
- Generalizing
- Originality
- Elaboration
- **Brainstorming**

Answer or solution finding
- Evaluate criteria
- Value Judgments
- Reasons for conclusions
- Evidence

Evaluating possibilities critically

Plan of action
- Fluency
- Flexibility
- Considering alternatives
- Originality
- Elaboration
- **Brainstorming**

Action implementation
- Communication

TECHNIQUES
Brainstorming
Questioning
Inventing
Modeling
Summarizing
Using Analogies, Metaphors, thematic Stories

© J.W. ROWE, revised 1991
Provincetown, MA

FIGURE 1

to its role in problem-solving. And we often did this, moving the segments of the model on the chalkboard to focus specifically on the stage we were interested in at that moment.

We found that the most important section for us was the second section, organization. In this section were written three questions:

What do we know?

What do we need to find out?

How can we find out?

I have taught these three questions in other teachers' classrooms and one recently told me that when she wrote them on the board, a student immediately said, "We must be starting a new unit!"

Infused writing process in content   I'd like to have my students reading and writing all day long, so I have lots of little systems in place to enable them—and me—to use writing as a tool for thinking in content areas. We'll look into those strategies in Chapter 11 "Strategies for Informal Writing in Content."

Infused reading process   Many of the strategies and policies in place during Readers' Workshop were used throughout the day—choice reading, dialogue journals. We'll take a closer look at these in Chapter 9.

Math and science opportunities   Many of my best interchanges with students in math and science evolved spontaneously in the course of other investigations. They worked so well because we were all interested, the time was right for learning, and we had come to that intersection together, not with me deciding the summer before that everyone would like to learn this. I tried to be open to these opportunities and devise a schedule and a policy that both encouraged and permitted them to be fulfilled.

Thus when we were working on the study of the nature of infinity as a mathematical concept (Cordeiro 1988), we also studied astronomy so that we could discuss infinity as a scientific, astronomical possibility.

I also made use of several learning environment strategies to help students interact and integrate learning in a variety of areas. These are:

Independent study   Students are enabled to pursue topics they are interested in, to each become "experts" during the early stages of a thematic unit. I help them to choose topics which will be appropriate for them and which will advance their understanding—even if it means they miss some other things. I am not convinced that what I might have decided we must learn is always best for all students. Optimal conditions for learning (Cambourne 1988) require that learners have choice and a sense of their own direction. How can I encourage responsibility in learning if I am not willing to follow through by letting them learn when they need to, when interest builds? What I most want to do is build lifelong learners, people who know what they want to learn and who know how to go about it.

Ad hoc group work (part or whole)   I often worked with the whole group but sometimes small groups were formed. Groups were always formed in my room *for a time and for a purpose*. They were never permanent. Usually small groups were heterogeneous. I believe firmly in the power of interactions between students of varying interests and abilities. I find that students weak in one area are strong in another and bring that strength to the group.

I did have temporary, self-selected homogeneous groups, usually in Readers' Workshop. Students of similar backgrounds, interests and abilities sometimes were all interested in the same book and chose to read together. That was their choice for that book.

Collaborative learning   Lev Vygotsky, the Soviet psychologist, said, "All the higher functions originate as actual relations between human individuals" (1978, p. 57). My classroom was an interactive place with many rich occasions for shared literacy. I worked at promoting what I call "cooperative competitiveness," where we all helped each other to win together.

This takes a lot of talk and movement. When I was a student, I got in a lot of trouble for those two things. I can hardly remember a year when I didn't get a minus on my report card for the teacherly equivalent of "talks to friends too much." But after a while it came to me that my talk served a vital, personal purpose. I was either talking about things I was learning or else I was maintaining the social links necessary to talk about the things I was learning. I realized that I learn by sharing, by talking, by checking my ideas out with others. Now I give myself room to learn by talking and I maintain friendships that let me delve deeply into my ideas with others. I work hard to counteract the "silence the child" movement I was schooled in.

Blending the Day

One spring, my sixth graders and I did a math project for about two weeks, almost all day, every day. We were all very involved in it and luckily we had the freedom to pursue our learning thoroughly. We did math steadily for about two weeks, but for the two weeks before that we had worked on reading and writing in depth, and after the math project, we went to work on an in-depth social studies project.

How do we move from a scheduled day to a scheduled month? It usually began for me somewhere near the end of September, during writing time. By that time, the student writers were deep within the stories they were writing and were beginning to feel a need for more time. Usually, each year, toward the end of September someone said, "When can we have writing all day?"

I would explain the need for covering the curriculum and how we have so much to do that a whole day on writing is hard to find. But secretly, inside, I was pleased. I knew that learning was blossoming.

The students would then explain that writing time was just getting going when it was time to stop. They said it made them lose their stories and their interactions, since many of them collaborate on writing, and then they would patiently explain to me how it is possible to spend a whole day writing and then spend another whole day on math, making up the lost time. And we all knew that once we got going in social studies we would spend many whole days working only on that because that's how everyone did it in our building. And I listened and was persuaded.

It happened every year. They argued for longer periods of learning interaction and I was persuaded. That's how I encouraged these learners to take charge of their learning. I also tried, from the beginning of the year, each year, to demonstrate a willingness to listen, to be a learner, too. Since a major instructional goal for me in all learning environments is to promote in-depth learning and an understanding of how we each learn, I am pleased when my learners express the need for more learning time, when they know what they need to learn and how they need to learn it. I believe this is the greatest gift I can give them.

Thus, the day began to blend. Content domains entered each other's designated times. Writing for research work in social studies was done during writing time as well as during the social studies block. Reading talk and work with books went on all the time.

Things That Help Blend

Teacher-developed curriculum   A teacher-developed curriculum helps the blending and integrating effort because it takes into account the abilities, interests, and resources of the learning population. Although developing a personalized curriculum is hard work and takes much negotiation among teachers, it is well worth the effort and I highly recommend it.

Informed teachers and administrators   When interests flare and the opportunity presents itself, the teacher must be willing and able to follow the path. Maximizing a teacher's flexibility and creativity in part requires a school with an informed administration. But in the end it is the teacher who must know when to follow and when to lead.

Students who become experts   I have students learn enough about a topic so that they can find some aspect of it that interests them, and they become experts on part of the larger topic. In this way, we learn together in a reasonable length of time what it would take one person a long time to learn alone. This also fosters the idea of ''ownership,'' an essential component in the framework for creativity in the fields of writing and reading.

Appropriate use of materials   This program works best when textbooks are used as one resource among others and not as the ''guiding light.'' It is hard to develop appropriate curriculum when someone else's table of contents has been allowed to dictate sequence. In addition, incessant readarounds as the primary means of transmitting information will never make content areas exciting and captivating.

Furthermore, a program which is blended and integrated is nearly impossible to sustain if teachers must report what page the class is on in any given textbook to an administrator. Part of an older effort to make instruction ''teacher proof,'' reporting page numbers destroys teacher and student creativity, demeans teacher knowledge, and undermines staff morale by setting up a stratified teacher corps with those who must report appearing as professionally ''lower'' than those who get reported to.

Creative use of materials   Sometimes books are used comparatively to develop an understanding of reliability of source. For instance, we might read the section about Christopher Columbus in three or four different books and then compare how the facts and incidents are reported. In the process, we would evaluate the books and the information, perhaps charting or mapping a comparative study. Determining the best available source would probably send us off to do more research.

Students in upper elementary grades often develop an interest in why facts and incidents are reported differently in different books. This can lead them to investigate the historical and political climate at the time of writing and publication. Students also can develop an awareness of how and why textbooks are written the way they are, why readability formulas are used, and how that use controls and oversimplifies information by requiring a limiting vocabulary.

Searching for opportunities to link the day and the content The best way to promote linking is to be constantly on the lookout for intersections for literacy in context. By stepping back from the curriculum, we as teachers can help ourselves to see it as a series of opportunities for reading, writing, speaking, and listening.

Developing a curriculum and simulation in a content area required me be more literate, too, to do some reading and researching. The "Director of the Royal Archeological Institute of Cairo"—me—did have to know a little more about Egypt than the "visiting Fellows"—my students—at least in the beginning, in order to write the "invitation"—the first part of the study. But after that, we researched together. I personally have found that such research is not oppressive because I develop an interest in the topic, too, as I take on the role of "Institute Director" and assume the "mantle of the expert," as Dorothy Heathcote and Phyl Herbert called it.

I see these opportunities best when I also see my whole classroom pulling together as characters in a great play. Together, we become people at work in the world, learning to do things like reading, writing, speaking, calculating, negotiating, and thinking, because those things are necessary to get the job done successfully.

As I create the daily tasks, I draw on my students' sense of what needs to be done, and needs to be learned, the curriculum of the school, and new things I am learning myself. Tasks emerge as essential and exciting in the world we have created around us. Each time through is different.

Keeping a Schedule in My Mind

Although the schedule established in the fall drifted as the day and the curriculum began to blend, I *did* maintain a sense of the fall schedule in my mind. For I believe that there need to be particular times when the teacher is available to work specifically with writers on writing, with readers on aspects of reading process, with emergent mathematicians on conceptual learning. So, often, even though my writers were working on a variety of different things, I personally concentrated for the first work period of the day on their writing processes. And during the second work period, I focused my mind on reading processes. And so on.

Thus, I maintained a sense of continuity and control as subject areas and learning domains began to blur through the day. The schedule became my mental focus, but not necessarily the order of the day. And as we spent a day going deeply into a topic rather than trying to cover all the topics in one day,

I mentally looked at that topic through a series of content areas lenses. I tried to look in breadth, across many areas, while they looked in depth, down deep in one subject.

In dealing with topics in depth, we give learners time to "play" with a subject, to get involved, to "mess about" as David Hawkins puts it. This is how learning in depth really happens. We work with children in depth to help them understand and improve their own educational processes because we believe that learning how to learn is the most valuable education we can give them.

Eleanor Duckworth puts it this way:

> Teachers are often, and understandably, impatient for their students to develop clear and adequate ideas. But putting ideas in relation to each other is not a simple job. It is confusing; and that confusion does take time. All of us need time for our confusion if we are to build the breadth and depth that give significance to our knowledge. (1987, p. 82)

And so we spent most days after the first of October in broad periods of interactive learning. Not always one subject all day, but one subject blended with another subject for the length of time it needed. We tried to learn in depth to give ourselves time to mentally relate one thing to another.

Moving Toward a Whole Learning Curriculum

Growing a Classroom

Growing a classroom is like tending a garden. Both classrooms and gardens have growth paths of their own with separate and distinct patterns. Both benefit from the guidance of one who understands how to work with the development of organic things. Successful outcomes in both cases are the result of careful, experienced, and flexible planning.

Just as the caretaker in a garden must have plans, so the teacher must think out a structure in advance. Overall curriculum must be organized, boundaries must be made, and goals and results known. Just as a beautiful garden is the direct result of the time and effort of the gardener, so a successful classroom shows the skill and care of a thoughtful teacher.

But in both the classroom and the garden, nature plays a hand. The gardener's plans must take many divergent factors into account: weather, soil, plants, unexpected happenings, how the plants want to grow. The teacher's plans and intentions will only guide the classroom's organic growth as long as they, too, are compatible with a wide range of divergent factors. Any goals, plans, boundaries, or intentions made by the teacher must be flexible enough to account for individual development, variations from day to day, and life outside the classroom.

All teachers' plans are subject to these constraints. But this particularly affects those teachers at the upper elementary level, grades four, five, and six, the so-called "content" grades. These teachers are generalists. Within these grades, students should acquire a firm foundation in five major content areas: literature, math, science, history, and geography.

Literacy as a Means to an End

In Whole Learning, aspects of literacy are used as the means to the end. The end is the learned content, the means are the literate tools for exploration. The five content areas are couched in the context of extended literacy development, using writing, reading, speaking, and listening as tools.

Not yet independent disciplines, the content areas at grades four through six can become staging grounds for taking literacy beyond a merely "essential" status into a productive mode. Literacy in these grades can use content as a vehicle to attain its fully mature status as an "expressor" of learning rather than an end in itself. In kindergarten and grade one, and up into grade two, the focus is on learning to read and write. From grade three on, reading and writing begin to shift "downward" in consciousness, becoming more and more automatic as they become tools for learning. Just as competent talkers cease to concentrate on the "how to" of talking as they begin to use speech as a means to an end, so competent readers and writers are able to look away from the "how to" of those literacies and toward the information they reveal.

Literacy in the upper grades also serves as the thread that binds the five divergent areas together. Without this binding, all classroom participants are subject to what Don Graves once referred to as "the cha-cha-cha" curriculum—do a little of this, a little of that, over here, over there.

The primary effort of the upper grade teachers must be to bind the curricula together, to relate the disparate, to integrate the disintegrated. For this is how life is and this is how we learn. The need for some sort of an integrated day is a very pressing problem among dis-integrated teachers who are striving to build community between children who constantly come and go.

The philosopher David Hawkins (1981) points to the cognitive need, the learner's psychological need, for linking:

> The tree of knowledge . . . is full of cross-connections . . . Young children most of the time—and all of us some of the time—learn optimally by these cross-connections, moving fluently from one focus of interest to others . . . Slow can be fast and good teaching an art of indirection . . . Made absolute, as it so often is, the straight path degenerates—to coloring between the lines, painting by numbers, doing algebra by rote.

Levels of Curriculum

We could see curriculum as having a variety of levels, segregated coordinated, and integrated. In *segregated* curriculum, all subjects and content are separated and no attempt is made to relate them. Teachers traditionally write "advance lesson plans" when directing a segregated curriculum. This is the kind of curriculum under which I was schooled.

In *coordinated* curriculum, classroom activity, goals, and structure arise from one central source—a book or a topic, for instance. I call this the "mix and match" curriculum. If there is a beehive in a picture in the book we're all reading, then we might study bees, draw bees, read other books about bees—it all would be coordinated. Coordinated curricula are often developed by the teacher during the summer.

So-called *integrated* curriculum has so far been the teacher's best attempt at thematic instruction. All subject areas are integrated within a larger framework, perhaps stemming from a simulation or a topical interest. Teachers put a lot of time into producing integrated curriculum materials and activities. All cross-curricular activities and worksheets are planned in advance.

All three of these levels of curriculum are teacher-directed, teacher-constructed, and teacher-choice. Activities and lessons are usually pre-constructed and outcomes are pre-ordained. Little room is left for natural development and evolution. One bright child with a difficult question, a single divergence in expected outcome, even a mechanical glitch in the audio-visual equipment, can raise havoc with the teacher-planned direction of any of these three types of curriculum.

Don Holdaway has added the fourth level of curriculum implementation: *developmental* or *generative*. This implementation plan allows for input along the way as the curriculum proceeds. It requires a teacher and a classroom structure that welcomes flexibility, but it permits creative teachers and students to have a clear field for process learning.

What is Generative Curriculum?

To make Whole Learning work, we must understand the difference between traditional advance lesson planning and a generative curriculum. In advance lesson planning, teachers plan each "lesson" carefully, in some detail. Lessons are generally 30 to 40 minutes long and may or may not be connected to each other. Principals in the act of evaluating often look for "lessons."

Teachers in the upper, "content" grades have traditionally been taught to think in terms of teaching lessons rather than teaching children. These lessons are usually prepared in advance, rendering them theoretically immovable, unchangeable, carved in stone. This planning is supposed to assure the teacher and the administrator that planning has been done.

However, as experienced teachers know, advance lesson planning does not necessarily guarantee success. In fact, advance planning that fails to account for unexpected contingencies, that supposes an ordained direction incompatible with students needs, that ignores developing interests, will be difficult to fulfill and may fail.

In a "generative" curriculum—Don Holdaway's (1989a) term for the kind of curriculum that might work best—teachers map out a general plan using grade level curricula as a guide, develop clearcut goals and objectives, choose materials, and design beginning activities. Subsequent activities and linking of subject matter evolve as a result of the initial activities, the underlying structure, interaction with materials, and fortuitous interests and discoveries. Generative curriculum accounts for the process that teachers and learners are undergoing.

Some of us have wondered what kind of curriculum we were doing when we felt like we were "flying by the seat of our pants." Generative, developmental curriculum is what we were striving for. Because in this kind of curriculum, the goals, objectives, structure, and selected materials guide us in an overall way. The day-to-day activities are generated from the developmental needs of both teacher and learner. As Douglas Barnes (1976) puts it, in *From Communication to Curriculum*, "To become meaningful a curriculum has to be enacted by pupils as well as teachers . . . In this sense curriculum is a form of communication" (p. 14).

Portugal: A Simulation in a Generative Curriculum

In the generative curriculum development for my sixth grade unit on Portugal, I began my planning of a simulation, or role-playing involvement for all of us, with the following goals that I hoped to achieve by the end of the unit:

Students should augment their prior knowledge of researching and reporting content information.

Students should acquire general information on Portugal.

Students should develop an awareness of the categories of study available in a topic like Portugal, such as history of, geography of, life of present-day inhabitants, special problems, similarities and differences between

Portuguese culture and American culture. Some of these might become topics for individual research as students selected an area of study as they became classroom "experts."

Students should select a category and become an "expert" on it.

All students should experience success topically, socially and in literacy in the unit study, with these sub-goals:
- All should continue to grow in social and personal development
- All should continue in intellectual development
- All should continue to experience growth in self-esteem.

When we began the unit, the simulation, all that I had planned was the very beginning and the very end. At the beginning we would become travelers to Portugal and we would end up "in Portugal" at a fair. I knew that most of the simulation interaction would be in reading and writing, for although the content of this theme was primarily social studies, my agenda is always literacy.

This particular schoolwide unit was going to end with an outdoor fair with Portugal as a theme. This would be the culminating activity for a unit lasting about a month and a half in each classroom. In order to get ready for our part in the fair, I knew that we would need to acquire some understanding of Portuguese culture and customs, geography and history, so that we could decide on an activity, game, or display to bring to the fair as our contribution.

I wanted us all to experience a sense of traveling to a foreign country so I began the simulation by posting a notice that everyone in the room had been selected as travelers on a special venture. A "tour of Portugal" was being planned for selected "travelers and their families," and what they had to do was to notify the agency of who they were—I knew they would all pretend to be grown-ups—what their special interests and occupations were, where they lived, who was in their "family" or "traveling party" and why they wanted to go to Portugal. I put maps of America and Portugal up on the back bulletin board and sat back to see what would happen next.

Within a day, I started to get letters—in a special box on my desk, marked "Applications for Portugal Tour"—answering all the questions in the request. Students got excited and so did I. I thought it would be up to me to have to think of what would logically come next. But the next phase came from the students.

One nice thing about doing simulations with upper elementary students is that they slide in and out of it with no more problem than turning around. A student would approach the application box in character as if he were approaching a desk in a government office, saying, "Here's my application," and then would turn to me as the teacher and say, "You know, what we ought to do is make identification cards—like driver's licenses and credit cards."

And that's what we did. We got hold of some magazines and scissors and small pieces of cardboard and I emptied my wallet so that they could use real identification cards for models. After a while—several days, in fact, because they got very involved artistically—all the travelers were fully credentialed. We learned a lot about what people need to possess to show who they are.

The travelers continued to generate the curriculum. Because we were leaving the country, we had to have passports. I went down to the local post office and got passport forms to fill out. The "passport office" opened everyday at 10:00 A.M. The first few days, I was the "government official" but after that students took over.

Applying for the passports was a pretty complicated process. There's a lot written on the back of a passport application that travelers have to swear to, and that writing taught us a lot about America and its freedoms. We took a sidestep to think and talk about it. Understanding those freedoms, in fact, became the real agenda of the simulation.

My students enjoyed pretending to be grown-ups so much that they were, in the simulation, in the full swing of active, successful adult lives. They generated the paperwork for decent bank accounts for their mythical lives, had good lines of credit, even designed family trees and family albums.

One problem did occur for those students who had invented large families. When they faced the reality of traveling with many children—some had up to seven—it proved to be very expensive since they all had to have passports and tickets and traveling clothes. Several invented children suddenly suffered mysterious and fatal illnesses. Families shrank.

As students continued to generate their own curriculum, they moved in the direction of studying American civics. They became interested in how it is to live in this country, what's involved in traveling to foreign countries, how countries govern differently. It was up to me to fulfill this interest and also move us in the direction of studying Portugal.

We returned to the maps on the wall. The "travel company" asked the travelers to plan a written itinerary, telling why they wanted to go to each place in Portugal. They became experts on aspects of Portuguese life. And so the simulation continued. By the time the schoolwide fair rolled around, we were ready to take part with a Portuguese game that other classes could play.

In the process of accomplishing this long-range goal, the generative simulation allowed wide latitude for students to pursue their own interests while they worked on the mandated agenda. Had I laid it all out in advance, as I might have in my early career, we would never have uncovered the great interest in the workings of American government and culture. Nor would we have had time or freedom to pursue it.

By starting where the learners were, by listening to them, I was able to see the path as it developed in front of us. I still held to the long-range goals and introduced elements that moved the theme forward. But we were able to learn much more than I expected about topics that I thought would never interest upper elementary students, like civics. And in the process, I grew, too.

A Word About Learning Centers

In the late 1970s, learning centers were quite the thing. Many of us teaching then spent long hours putting together colorful, complex carrels of things to do. If we were really good at it, we had one for each content area. They all had charts for signing up and keeping track of which activity had been done. They had stacks of ditto sheets run off in advance or cards to write on or graphs to fill in. Sometimes they were thematic, but most often they were just decorated. They all had lots and lots of "stuff," all teacher-selected and teacher-designed.

These carrels were usually arranged around the room on tables and counters. The really complicated ones were free-standing. Some had little bookcases behind them. Everywhere there were lots of plastic baskets and trays in bright colors. They were all very colorful. Artistic teachers did well on their evaluations during the heydey of learning centers.

We all sat in the middle of this bright display, waiting for the chance to roam free, making choices. Eventually a time would come in the teacher-planned schedule when students could go to the centers and do work, but in a "fun" way, as opposed to the times when they had to sit and listen. Sometimes which students went to which centers was scheduled by the teacher. Usually everybody had to go to all the centers during a given time span. But my students thought that the best times were when they could choose where to wander.

When I look back on my classroom with the cardboard learning centers all around the room, I think of a mall. We sat in the middle like the people who sit near the escalators at the mall, waiting, resting, surrounded by all those centers.

The advent of learning centers coincided with the opening up of the class-room. They were the beginning of the decentralization of authority in the classroom, the beginning of free movement and use of the classroom as a place to live rather than just a place for desks. They were the beginning of choices for learners and concrete experience in tandem with teacher talk. They encouraged interaction between learners.

I guess what always bothered me about learning centers was that they left me out. They were designed to free me from supervising so that I could do—what?—have groups, work one-on-one, set up more learning centers? Like shopping at the mall, there was a depersonalization about learning centers. They were designed to be student-and teacher-proof, set up so that students could work independently. Sometimes they worked so well that I felt like I was intruding when I sat in on a learning center activity.

I felt like a lot was going on in my classroom and I wasn't in on it. I was supposed to be circulating around, taking notes, but I felt left out of the learning that was going on. And it bothered me that a crucial component was missing: my opportunity to seize on what a student was wrestling with and use it to take that student to a higher level. Lev Vygotsky calls this working in a student's "zone of proximal development," working with a student on the edge of moving up to new understanding. I felt like I was missing all those times.

The other thing that was troublesome was that the centers themselves were all me, with nothing of the students in them. They were extensions of how I thought students should learn certain things, planned and built sometimes before I even met the students. Now I can't imagine working that way. But for those of us just breaking out of the lecture model, they were a safe "halfway house" on the road to better teaching.

In the last five years, I haven't set up any learning centers. Some special centers developed because all the learners in the classroom found that they were useful for a specific purpose. Sometimes, I spent extra time organizing those special centers and making them look nice. Often, the students did as good a job as I would have at putting together their own centers for learning. I think they were tired of being left out.

Back in my old days, students were only allowed in for the last parts, using the center and cleaning it up. It's sort of like never being allowed to design or build your own house. Only being allowed to live in it and keep it tidy. Looking back now, I see that I lost half the learning, the planning part.

The learning centers I built in the '70s made my room look nice. They reassured me that students were being exposed to things I was supposed to cover. They provided time, choice, and movement in an environment just learning how to do those things. Beyond that, I'm not sure how much learning was going on. Sometimes I think that what my students mostly practiced was how to shop at a mall.

Changing as Teachers

In each of the chapters in this book describing activities during the day, we will be looking for intersections for implementing a generative curriculum. But just as each sentence in our language is a new creation, so each teacher's implementation is a new creation. We can only point the way to locating possible intersections. Which path each teacher chooses is the direct result of that particular day's happenings in that particular classroom. Thus, a generative curriculum must always start from the whole present day in each different classroom. The ideas in this book are designed to be starting points.

Growing a classroom is hard work and it takes a long time. Like making a garden, sometimes the hardest part is getting started. At home, I live on what used to be a meadow. It takes a long time to turn and shake the turf, preparing the ground for fertilizer and seeds. It's like that with classrooms, too. It takes a long time to turn over what's been there for generations, to take a new look at how learning might take place.

When I moved into the room where I taught sixth grade, there was a Bible in the desk drawer. It was very old and had been there for a long time. It reminded me of how different teaching and learning used to be in that very room, when teachers were required to read passages from it every day, for their own edification. We are tied to our past as educators but it is up to us to rethink how learning can best take place to prepare citizens of the future. We must grow our own classroom. Each teacher with each class does it differently.

Living in a Whole Learning Climate

Classroom Climates

When I taught first grade way back in the mid-sixties, the climate in my classroom was like a desert. Dry, barren, plain-colored—nothing moved as far as the eye could see. Once in a while it would rain in the desert, flowers would bloom, and for a little while there would be color and movement. Little creatures would come out of their sand-colored cubbies and move from place to place, smiling and laughing, enjoying the brief respite. And then it would dry up again. Creatures would pull back into their hiding places, colors would fade, movement would disappear from the horizon. The beige and grey of the classroom would return.

At the height of the short open classroom movement, the climate was quite different. In my open classroom, which existed for a little over a year, the climate was like New York City in the summertime. Hot, bustling, exciting, confusing, not easy to live in. Inhabitants of that climate rushed about, busy with many things, detached from me and from each other. Like in the city, much seemed to go on "at night," when the inhabitants were asleep. Supplies were restocked, new places opened up, major overhauls and cleaning went on, all done by the "city's maintenance crew"—me. The "open classroom city" had a night life that the inhabitants never knew about. Like commuters from the suburbs, they only came in to work.

It was hard to live in both of those climates. Neither had the essentials of the climate I try to live in with learners now. Now I like a climate that is more moderate, with a blend of essential elements. Sort of like New England in the spring and fall.

In New England, the spring and fall climates are reasonable. There is some rain and some sun, warmth in the day and cool at night, a balanced climate that is easy to live and work in. Like New England, a Whole Learning climate should be pleasant, with certain elements present but not oppressive. Such a climate encourages learning.

The classrooms I like to work in now are balanced, with elements that were mostly missing from my classrooms of old. I know I am in a successful Whole Learning climate when it has these essential elements in proper measure: community, authenticity, and appropriateness.

Essential Element: Community

Unlike the classrooms I studied in, Whole Learning classrooms are communally active places with groups of students working together. When I was a kid, I remember turning around to see the students in the back of the room. I must have been in fourth grade at the time. I remember thinking how many kids there were and how quiet they all were. No one I teach has ever had that experience.

Whole Learning classrooms are characterized by cooperative learning (Johnson, Johnson, Holubec & Roy, 1984.) Whenever possible, students and teacher sit in a circle so that everyone can communicate with everyone else. In my classroom, I sat in a student desk in the circle. The circle changed from time to time. Occasionally, we formed what my students appropriately called "islands," groups of students isolated from each other and from me. These island formations served whatever purpose was at hand, and then a whole-group community was re-formed as soon as possible.

We might, for instance, have broken out of our whole-group formation for several days during the time that "expert" groups were working together in a content-area topic, or when "wagon trains" needed more time together during a Westward movement simulation. But eventually, we would begin to miss talking to each other, some students would begin to complain about having to look over their shoulders all the time, others would begin to miss the faces of the people whose backs they were looking at. And so we would re-form the whole group into a horseshoe or circle, "circling the wagons," we called it one year.

No classroom is too large for a whole-group formation. I have worked with forty sixth-graders who formed themselves so that everyone could see and speak to everyone else. Eleanor Duckworth, Harvard professor of teaching and learning, formed a large class into an inner circle and an outer circle to facilitate and foster community. It can always be done.

Essential to the concept of community is the inclusion—and self-inclusion—of the teacher. Without this clear statement of intent to share learning, developing a true community of learners is impossible. So I used a student desk. The sheer massiveness of the traditional teacher's desk sets up an obstacle to community that I cannot overcome. Even sitting at a table put me above the height of my students, setting me apart, in an artificial way that impeded valid communication.

One of the most difficult obstacles I have faced in working in other teachers' classrooms has been the pre-established physical plant. When I consult, I often go into a classroom for a 45-minute demonstration—not enough time to create a new environment. In demonstrations of Whole Learning, I try to model how to enable students to share ideas with other students, what people do in a community. This is a new notion in many classrooms I visit.

In some classrooms students in the back of the room usually talk only to the back of other students' heads. Students in the front of the room usually talk only to the teacher. In these classrooms most students expect to share ideas only with me. And I am expected to be in that small, sacred area in front of the blackboard.

Once I substitute-taught in a small school in the northeast. I moved the kids around, chatted with them, and when we watched educational television, I gave them permission to move their desks together. They were incredulous. I often wondered how the teacher went about reestablishing the old order when she came back. The kids and I had a great time. That day, we did some whole learning.

I have found that teachers do not always appreciate dealing with the aftermath when I move student and teacher desks, or when I approach the students in a totally new way. For this reason, when I do demonstrations, I usually try to manage within the established order. But managing presents a real dilemma for me. How can I foster and share in a community when I am expected to dwell in the sacred spot?

Building community is a vital part of the Whole Learning philosophy. But at the upper levels, community building has specific differences from community-building at the primary levels.

In many schools, most upper level children have been together as students for several years before. Even though building a community may not have been a focus for children's teachers in previous years, nonetheless these children have been together in a variety of socially organized ways. These precedents have to be accounted for in any community to be built.

Some children may, for instance, be friends outside of school, or, if the school is in a small town, they may be related by family. Some children may take part in the same sports or classes and spend a lot of time together outside of school. In building community, these prior connections have to be honored and recognized.

Another factor in community-building at the upper levels is the pre-adolescents' evolving need for peer bonding. As the teacher strives to build a community involving everyone, the students may be striving to build a community which involves everyone except the teacher.

I once taught an upper elementary class where the students had always been together and knew each other well. They were the only class in the town at that grade level and had never been interchanged with other students. They were so bonded to each other, and their sense of community with each other was so strong, that working with them was like taking care of someone's very large family. They had a strong community before they met me and I was not part of it. Their essential loyalty was to each other, not to me, and only partly to the community I tried to build. I was moderately successful but never quite felt that I had grown the kind of classroom I strive for. I was able to get them to bond together with me for some activities some of the time but not all of the time and not for all activities. Their past histories and established social order was occasionally cause for classroom dissension and sometimes obstructed having us all work together.

Students at the upper elementary are also highly involved in developing sub-communities. We sometimes call these cliques; they sometimes call them teams. These sub-groups may move counter to a full sense of community and must be accounted for in classroom work. Thus, as I work to bond the whole classroom together, I give recognition to the various sub-groups. I might say to them that I know they usually compete on the ball field but here I need them to work together.

When we consider pre-adolescents as pre-adults, we can look at these differences in a new light. Adults also may be bonded to other special adults, may need very much the approval and comraderie of peer bonding, and certainly have sub-groupings which are strong, often formed of people who are alike in some way.

But when adults group together into communities to learn new skills, to apply a model of learning—as my mom and sister do when they go together to learn watercoloring or life drawing—they often become members of new communities, communities of people with different abilities and preferences. Applying this model in the classroom through the creation of adult-like performance situations gives students the same opportunity that adults have to move beyond their established communities and form new communities based on learning.

In Whole Learning, then, communities cooperate. Most often, they are whole group communities which are heterogeneous. This permits shared learning. Sometimes sub-groups are formed for particular purposes, but these are always temporary and "ad hoc."

Essential Element: Authenticity

When my sixth graders as "Westward pioneers" sat down at home to write a statement about why they wanted to move, many of them forgot for a moment that they were sitting in their own bedrooms, doing a homework assignment. Many of them became for a time the character they had chosen and wrote their statements from that character's point of view.

"Jenna Mingo" wrote:

> Dear Diary: Just the other day my husband told me we were moving to Oregon. He put me in a state of shock . . .
> My husband also said we have to sell everything, like toys and clothing. Let me tell you, I had mixed emotions about this trip. I mean, after all, I have my father to take care of.

Lost in her five page diary entry, sitting in her room, Alice brought much more to this assignment than was asked for. She, for that time, became Jenna Mingo and "lived" a real-life situation in her mind. Giving students the opportunity to participate in an authentic situation as they practice literacy and content enables a depth of participation not possible in traditional, text-book-bound instruction.

Many children often live in a make-believe world in their minds. Pretending to be someone else, usually a grown-up, and "playing a game" is the hallmark of childhood experience. "You be the———and I'll be the———" is common childhood chatter and the blanks are hardly ever filled with identities of other children. Most often children imitate and play at being grown-ups. Children are very good at this, at creating an imaginary world from nothing, at becoming someone else to see how it feels. This is how children rehearse for adulthood, practicing who they might be. Reality is a flexible thing for children.

Twice in my teaching experience, students brought imaginary playmates to school with them and both times it was upper elementary. When Ben Grotz entered my sixth grade classroom, he announced with a twinkle in his eye that he had brought his friend, Neddick, with him. We all complied, Neddick was given a desk, and for a while, we had fun with Ben's imaginary playmate.

In third grade, Maria brought a large, three-foot-high, W.C. Fields puppet to school one day. W.C. stayed with us for a long time and became a rather active member of our community. He had a desk, pencils, paper, and books. He was the only one in the class who wore a striped suit and spats. We enjoyed W.C.'s company a lot. He and his friends published *W.C. Fields, Part I*, a tongue-in-third-grade-cheek story of his adventures in and out of school.

When I had that same class again in sixth grade, W.C. came back to school. W.C. had grown in literacy, just as his classmates had. He "turned in" several assignments—with help from his friends of course—and eventually he and his friends published *W.C. Fields Part II*, a much bigger venture than Part I, with many chapters. Part II is dedicated to "all the people who helped out W.C. Fields." In a preface, his helpers wrote:

> There is a doll named W.C. Fields. (We) wrote this story about him. It is what he thinks and what we pretend he says. W.C. Fields was a comedy actor a long time ago. This story is just as funny as when he was an actor.

The rest of the book, carefully divided into chapters with titles like "Arguing and mean people," "Loving," "School works and smarts," "My trip to the barn," and "My best friend Charlie," was told from W.C.'s unique classroom perspective, but reflected many of his helpers' sixth-grade concerns. Like all the student-made books on the shelf, this book ended with a note "About the Authors." After telling what they were like, the authors were described as "very creative." I agree.

In authentic learning, we strive to create a discovery-based environment, one in which learners are engaged in decision-making and problem-solving. When we can, we make learning authentic in a real-world way: we write letters to real people, we collect oral histories of real people, we read and write in the real world. But we cannot always work in the real world. We cannot, for instance, "go West" or to Portugal or to ancient Egypt. We cannot study about all topics by writing letters to real people and collecting anecdotes from the surrounding community. Sometimes we have to create our own "flexible reality" by taking part in classroom simulations.

Simulations involve roleplaying, like the westward emigration simulation, and tap into children's natural sense of a flexible reality. Children will perform all sorts of academic tasks when they are in the service of accomplishing a larger, 'real' purpose.

As far up as sixth grade I played imaginary games. I was often an Egyptian queen living in a pyramid-palace. I knew a lot about the topic. I had read all the fiction I could find and had researched the topic as far as I was able. I created artifacts and costumes based on references I found. Had my teachers known how much work I was capable of doing when I was interested, I think they would have been surprised. They expected so little.

Even today, I live a certain amount of time in the world of the imagination, in a "flexible reality." As I travel through a department store, credit card in hand, I pretend I am rich. Reality continues to be what I make of it.

In Sir William Golding's *Lord of the Flies*, children entered an adult world through a a mix of fantasy and reality. Thrown back on their own resources, lost on a deserted island, a group of boys continued to "play make-believe" as they had at home. But the reality of the situation blended with the fantasy, to create a living, flexible reality. A movie version of this book advertises the theme like this: "We did everything just the way grown-ups would have . . . what went wrong?"

Children's ability to create an adult-like world out of a suggestion is an ongoing activity for many youngsters. And yet this knowledge of a flexible reality is a childhood strength rarely tapped by traditional schooling. Many students rarely get a classroom opportunity to pretend to be someone else, to practice the adult performance model and get credit for it. Few schoolchildren learn and master skills and concepts in situations that deal with authentic material.

Authentic material is that which is embedded in a 'real' situation, one which draws on the notion of a flexible reality to allow children to try out adult performance. Authentic materials are those which provide information for a larger purpose, accomplishing some goal or solving some problem. Authentic materials are never ends in themselves, but rather are literate means for accomplishing authentic learning.

Authentic learning always happens for a valid reason, not just to satisfy a grade. Authentic learning is accomplished so that the learner can satisfy a larger goal, one which often imitates what grown-ups do in a similar situation. When we do math, we try to tie it to real life. We do calculations because we need the information they yield, not because we have to complete a page.

At the upper elementary level, where everyone looks to the adult world to see how to act, Whole Learning uses the principle of authenticity to make learning real and meaningful. We make use of children's inborn sense of a flexible reality to let them dwell in a world both adult-like and authentic. We make use of authentic learning to enable a generative, discovery-based curriculum and to foster a classroom day which is linked and whole.

Essential Element: Appropriateness

In classrooms supported by Whole Learning, children see themselves as successful learners. The characteristics discussed so far provide this climate. In these classrooms, all children have equal opportunity for involvement in the process. Strategies and activities are appropriate, specifically designed to provide the opportunity for students to perform at their own developmental levels.

When all the students in my classroom became "Fellows at the Royal Archeological Institute of Cairo" they had to provide a "resumé." But what they provided varied greatly from student to student. They developed the format for their own resumé, often from information they had gleaned from adults outside of school. As the "Director" I received everything from a student-typed version of a full, formal resumé to a handmade copy of a job application. All were acceptable, all represented learning appropriate to each student.

Whole Learning classrooms have expectations, but these are supported by Don Holdaway's "high degree of positive prophecy" so that all students feel that they will succeed in meeting these expectations. And because the expectations for each grade level are founded on learning process, students at all levels can involve themselves in these processes to the degree they are able.

Appropriateness is supported by a high degree of trust. Students get immediate feedback through communal activities and guided self-correction which varies between content areas. Self-regulation occurs on an ongoing basis. One way that this is accomplished at upper elementary is through having students do most of their own correction, together as soon as they are finished.

A Word from a Climatologist

One year I was a Lucretia Crocker Fellow. That's a grant given to teachers by the Massachusetts Department of Education for a year of traveling around the state sharing programs, doing demonstrations and workshops. I went into fifty different schools that year, talking about writing to learn in content areas and I got a good chance to sample lots of classroom climates.

Climates are readily distinguishable by how the inhabitants live. I went into classrooms that were like deserts and a few that were like inner cities. I did find some that were like the best of New England in the fall and spring. "Rain" fell in many of them and the inhabitants were often happy and refreshed. In those classrooms, the inhabitants lived in groups and talked to each other.

But John Mayher and Rita Brause said it best in their article "Is Your Classroom Like Your Grandmother's?" They said, "Transmission instruction is still firmly bolted to the floor" (p. 619), referring, of course, to the old desks that some of us used that were, in fact, bolted to the floor. Those desks could not be moved, which assured those in charge that no one would be able to sit in a circle or in groups or face the back of the room. The climate of those classrooms had been decided by a furniture maker. It was impermeable, immovable, unchangeable—a dry, barren, and isolated way of life.

Whole Learning classrooms are flexible and learner-centered. In them we will find the teacher modeling and the teacher learning. But we will also find students modeling and learning. The climate is one which permits change and growth.

How does a classroom climate founded on community, authenticity and appropriateness benefit students? Listen to "Lady Marilyn Elizabeth Taylor" as she writes to "The Royal Trading and Exploration Company" requesting passage to the colonies, circa 1691. She might not have predicted she could write so well.

> I'm sorry to say that I'm a widow with a child of eight, Carol Anne Taylor.
>
> My husband passed on four years ago. With John dead, I started to help Johnathan Cobbert, a blacksmith in London. I've earned my living from him for a while now. I'm currently 30 and turned so just two days ago. He's written a letter of recommendation which you may read on the following sheet.
>
> I would like to move to Jamestown, Virginia, the reason being I have friends there who said I can stay with them until I save up enough money to support my child and me (although I have a pretty large savings). This has already been arranged.
>
> I'm so very thankful for this opportunity to make my child's and my life more pleasant.

Learners who live in temperate climates enjoy themselves and their learning. Their growth is measurable in words.

DOING

Start the Morning: Writing Time

Remembering Writing Time

I don't remember much about writing when I was in school. I remember very white pieces of paper, sitting alone trying to think, and an obsession with sharp pencils. For me, pencils had to be very, very sharp before they would produce good writing. In talking to other writers since I have grown up, I have found that some of them have the same obsession.

Even when I began writing on a computer, I found myself thinking about sharpening pencils. For a long time I couldn't imagine how I—and others—had developed such a bizarre writing habit.

And then I began to think about what I know now about myself as a writer and how it was when I wrote in school. As a writer now, I talk a lot before I start to write; I roam around the house doing small chores; I read a few things, some relevant to what I will write, some snippets of writing with a style I like. I call people on the phone and say, "What do you think of this idea I'm putting together?" I give myself a lot of space and time for ideas to grow and find response.

When I was in school we never moved around, especially not when we were supposed to write. Very much the lonely learners, we sat by ourselves with our assignment and a piece of paper—and a pencil. In my school days we only used pens when we were copying over perfect papers to put on the wall.

There we all were, stuck with that paper and very little time to drum up an idea and get it on paper before it was turned in. No one to talk to, no one to bounce ideas off of, no one's ideas to think about for variation, no opportunity to move our bodies around to get our minds going. But there was that pencil. That pencil, I believe, became our salvation.

Because the only way to move in those old, traditional classrooms was to go to the pencil sharpener. There, lingering in line, we might have an opportunity to talk to someone, to let communication and a sense of audience begin to develop. At least there was movement, a chance to get away from the paper for a moment, to busy one's mind with routine matters like sharpening a pencil so some automatic, intuitive process might come forward with a piece of writing.

Many of us who were schooled in the old way of writing developed such artificial systems for helping us to get going while composing. Once we were actually composing, we continued to use the pencil sharpener, I believe, as a way of taking a rest from the writing once it started. Writers often walk away from writing in progress to give it a chance to "cook," to incubate. In the old school, we got away from it for a while by heading for the pencil sharpener. It was much easier than trying to get permission to go to the bathroom.

Writing Process in Action

Students in process writing classrooms today don't have this problem. They are encouraged from kindergarten on to think of themselves as writers, to explore together what they do when they write, to collaborate on writing projects and to continually seek active oral and written feedback on works in progress.

Commonly called "process writing," today's classroom writing times encourage teachers and students to explore together the process that writers go through, to focus their attention not only on the writing but also on the writer. Writing time today assumes that understanding yourself as a writer is the best way to improve in the composing process. Don Murray (1984) writes,

> Students become writers when they read on their own page, in their own hand, what they did not intend to write . . . Writing—writing that is working . . . always surprises the writer. And the student, becoming a writer, continually seeks new surprises, new meanings, new lives of words. Students who believed you thought, then wrote, now write to think.

I was once asked to give a definition of process writing. I found it hard and I'm not very satisfied with the product. At best, it's an attempt to make something complex into something simple. But for what it's worth, here it is:

Process writing is
teaching and learning which focuses
interactively
on processes
available to a writer
when developing a text
which articulates the thoughts of the writer
and communicates them to a reader.

Working with the processes involved in writing is an interactive enterprise between communicating people and it has two parts: first, the writer clarifies thoughts, articulates them in print to satisfy what the writer wants to say; second, the writer focuses on making those thoughts stand alone so that they communicate with others. Vernon Howard and John Barton (1986) call this "articulation before communication." They believe—as I do—that writers always write first for themselves to discover what they know and how they can say it. This is the articulation stage. Only later may writers become concerned with how to make that piece of writing communicate with another.

This is not the way I was taught. My early writing attempts were always directed at communication—my thought was always on the reader. Thus my focus was on spelling, punctuation, topic sentences, neatness. Only recently have I learned to let all that wait until I am satisfied that I have said what I want to say.

When I work with writers, I model writing for "me first." In practical terms, this means that in the early chats or conferences that I have with writers about their piece of writing, I only ask them about its content: Have they told their story? Have they said what they want to say? What else can they tell about it? I say, "Tell me more about this part." This is easy for me to do, to stay "hands off," because I don't know their stories—only the writers do. My job is to help them pull the stories to the surface.

Only later do we begin to consider how to make the writing stand alone, a published piece. Writing that is published, that is "out there," must stand alone. It must communicate. The writer is not there to help the reader construct text from the written words.

As writers become experienced in working in this way, the articulation and communication stages begin to overlap. Writers in the early stages begin to insert more editing, express more concern with communicating. I think it is partly because they are becoming better readers of their own text. They need the communication part, too. Writers who use no periods begin to insert them to help themselves. Fluent authors with a poorly developed sense of sequence begin to search out the twists and turns in their convoluted plots because in re-reading, they get lost too. Given plenty of time to develop a concern for fully expressing their own ideas, writers develop a natural concern with communication. The key to this evolution is the feedback these writers are getting from other writers and readers of their texts and the evolution that occurs between the writers and readers.

Advanced Writing Process in Action

Two sixth graders, George and Gerry, had worked long and hard for several weeks on a story called *Shadow Fox* and were rightfully proud of it. Typed, it ran for four pages. They shared it with classmates informally and also read it to us all in a group conference. It was a story slated for publication. That meant it would be carefully edited, typed, and photocopied. Those copies would then be sewed into carefully designed books with cardboard covers and illustrated. One of the copies would become a ''shelf copy,'' joining the fifty or sixty others already on the display bookshelf.

The problem with the story was this: no one in the class could understand the ending. The writers, George and Gerry, were fans of the game, ''Dungeons and Dragons,'' and carried with them a supply of stock characters and assumptions which many of the rest of us did not share. The character of Shadow Fox was their unique creation from their experiences with Dungeons and Dragons characters.

As we all listened to the story, we followed with excitement the tale of how the wizard helped the rebels recapture the castle from the evil Shadow Fox and his army. The story ended like this:

> It took two days to reach the castle. Some even died because of the traps that Shadow Fox's army had put in a long time ago.
> Finally they reached the castle and the wizard did as he had promised. He opened the huge door into the castle.
> Then all the rebels charged all of the fat and ugly monsters.
>
> The battle was long and a lot of blood was spilled. But after seven days the rebels took over the castle and got rid of everyone. But Shadow Fox could not be found.
> And even now people still say, when it is day time, just look at your shadow and make sure it is yours.

George and Gerry finished reading and we in the group conference praised them highly. The story represented tremendous effort and negotiated learning. We told them of the things that we really liked. Writers need to know what works.

But then the questions started: "What do you mean, Shadow Fox could not be found? Where was he? The ending doesn't make sense. Can you explain the ending to me?"

These writers knew what happens when a book is published with elements not clear to readers—the readers keep coming back to the writer to ask the same question, if the writer is available. I had student-made books on my shelf like that, books from other years and from other writers. Most of my students had read the books and would complain to me about how a particular book was written, saying things like, "If only the author had said this, then I would have known what they meant but this way the book doesn't make any sense."

George and Gerry had had this experience too. They were anxious to publish *Shadow Fox* but they were used to listening to their conference-givers and taking their suggestions. They were reluctant to publish a book that made everyone ask the same question. But, the problem was, they really liked the story the way it was—especially the way the ending flowed—and didn't want to change a thing. Writers are like that.

We had a long conference—it lasted for about 35 minutes. They kept explaining that Shadow Fox was a shadow—but, search as we might, we couldn't find that anywhere in the story. It was writer's knowledge inaccessible to the reader.

Ben conferenced with us. When I conference with writers I always ask a student to sit in. One of my goals is to train students to help each other think and sitting in provides an opportunity for me to model questioning and listening. There's always someone "in between" texts who can help by sitting in. Also, I have found that older students listen more to each other's ideas than they do to me. Many times, students have learned better from the language of their friend who was rewording what I was saying. I don't think it's that I talk funny, I think they simply have better lines of communication between each other. And there is power in sharing and accepting someone's idea, social power.

So Ben sat with me and together we conferenced with George and Gerry. We searched the text carefully and made many suggestions. George and Gerry were very discouraged and doodled a lot as we all thought together. Everyone agreed that something was missing in the writing but where to put it in? Ben and I said, "You knew that he was a shadow before you wrote this story but we don't know it."

They went away after a while to work alone. I suggested that they write what another student, Elise, called "a thumbnail sketch" of Shadow Fox so we would know about him. I gave them the paper to do it on. But I knew they wouldn't take this suggestion—I was pretty sure that they would try to come up with their own solution. Writers are sometimes particular people about their process.

In a half hour, they came back all excited. They had written a Foreword. The perfect thing. It looked like this:

FOREWORD

Shadow Fox was created in some dark, evil tunnel beneath the earth a million years ago. He was a shadow. He could change into anything he wanted as long as there was a shadow.

After Shadow Fox was 1,000,000 years old, he had a dream to take over the world so he set off to find armies that would fight with him.

And this was the story of how that battle happened. It was a fine way to resolve the crisis, allowing the writers to preserve the original text and its natural flow, but enabling the reader to share all of the writers' assumptions. But it took a long time to resolve and, as the Soviet psychologist, Lev Vygotsky, had predicted, the learning took place first interactively in a social setting before it was made intrapsychological, before it was internalized and resolved.

When Do We Find Time?

In practical terms, writing time is carved out of the time we used to give to "language arts." During writing time, we cover all the elements we used to cover during that time, such as: working with words as synonyms, antonyms, etc.; vocabulary work; phonetic and word analysis—prefixes, suffixes, etc.; syntax and sentence structure, including using language to talk about language; grammar and usage; conventional speech forms versus slang and dialect; point of view; handwriting and print forms; varieties of genre; letter writing; dictionary work; analysis of book parts and use of indeces; library skills; listening skills; and much more. Writers need many arts of the language and, when working in process, they work with them as they need them. Language arts are infused in context in writing time because they are needed.

We also subsume much of the traditional spelling program during writing time, infusing it into its rightful place as a tool for writing. Writers who write what they are interested in need eventually to work with spelling all kinds of words in context. Did I ever give spelling tests? Yes, sometimes I did, but I might have had as many as ten different spelling groups, which changed from time to time. Students selected the words and definitions they thought they needed to memorize. These words often came from a learning context like students' writing or a content area, and sometimes we drew on a workbook series that had, in my students' phrase, "really hard words" with "lots" of definitions. I found that some of my students' families liked spelling tests. Studying for spelling tests seemed to fulfill a social function in some families and family members succeeded with their spellers. When I had spelling tests in my classrooms, they were occasions for successful performance, and learners had the choice of other options.

I also don't nurse any illusions about the power of learning to spell this way. Many times I—and others—have seen words that were spelled correctly on tests revert to invented spelling in the context of writing. For some writers the processes are not the same and do not inform each other. I think of spelling words as going into "a spelling bucket" which may or may not be open when I need them to write with. I think that reading and writing, lots and lots of reading and writing, is a far better way to improve spelling.

Sometimes we used our spelling words—and other words—to play a Venn circle grammar game. At the upper elementary, and particularly by sixth grade, learners are becoming aware of the language they use. Reflective writers and readers are often curious about words. I felt it was my responsibility to keep this curiosity alive as they began to learn the technical languages of grammar and vocabulary, part of many junior high school curricula—for better or worse—and an item on the spring standardized test given in the elementary school.

In playing the Venn circle game, the main objective was to understand the wonderful flexibility of our language, how each word is dependent on context for meaning and use. Figure 2 shows how the game looked when played with the word "run."

The rules changed each time we played the game, but basically the goal was to get points for defending various uses of the key word. So a player might place the word card in the NOUN circle and give a sentence which used the word as a noun. That would give one point. The next player might do the same thing in the VERB circle for one point and the next would try for the ADJECTIVE circle. After the main parts of speech were used up, the challenge was to come up with multi-meanings. This part fascinated sixth graders who spent long hours at home memorizing multi-meanings to get game points.

For instance, if the first NOUN sentence for "run" had been "I made a

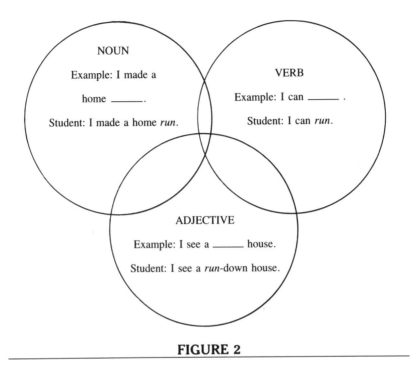

FIGURE 2

home *run*," then a multi-meaning use that would count for a point might be "The dog is tied on a *run*." Another student could get credit for saying "The lady had a *run* in her stocking." Still another for "I took the dog out for a *run*." And so it went. One year we found forty meanings for one word. In the beginning of each year we kept track of the points, but after a while we were all too busy in our dictionaries.

What Writers Know

Giving children writing time for process enabled a great sociological change in classroom interaction and focus. I have worked with children who by fourth grade were already profoundly discouraged, but who nonetheless wanted very much to know that someone cared about the knowledge base which they carried. The scholastic and practical fact is that in traditional educational structures no one is prepared to deal with children's non-academic knowledge, no matter how extensive it is.

These young learners stop me on the street on a Saturday to ask "Will you come to my class on Monday for writing?" Because finally they have a format, a means, a **voice** for telling all the things they have been learning. While we were teaching.

While we were teaching, they learned all about hot rods. And I mean **all** about hot rods. The words flowed out of their minds and into my ears, and I didn't even know what they were talking about. They're willing to tell it any way I ask, even in writing. If I can convince them that it's worth organizing— and I'm willing to hang in there with them till it's done—then they're willing to write it. They're willing to learn to write because it enables them to share their knowledge.

Because of my students' writing I know all about lots of things—Decepticons and Optimus Prime, skateboards, hot rods, and a really fancy bicycle. I learned about how to build a tissue paper house, about the little duck that had no father, and the family that never went to jail in the tough town. I saw my students' hearts on their papers. My questions about their writing were questions about their lives.

People carry with them all kinds of things that we can never know about until we get them to tell us their stories. Their degree of intensity and quality of experience may be difficult to relate in writing and may require patience, time, planning, and preparation. But writers soon see the power of print: the audience available for a vocal rendition may not care, may be distracted, may not understand. The audience who reads your writing **chose you**.

Starting Out in Writing Time With Learners With a History

I would like to offer a few suggestions specific to setting up a writing time at the upper elementary levels, both to explain how I view writing instruction and to highlight a few things which I learned from experience.

Setting up writing time in the upper grades with students who have not experienced it before is hard work. As with adult learners, we are dealing here with learners' histories—and these histories may include negative experiences in writing. Students may have suffered embarrassment or negative response from their early attempts at writing. They may be stubbornly entrenched in the idea that students must only write what they can spell, or punctuate, or that extensive research must always precede writing. They may be unnaturally dependent on writing prompts and assistance before beginning to compose. They may have rejected their own creativity and decided that their stories are not worth telling.

One of our tasks as writing teachers is to help these older learners overcome their own writing histories. We begin by helping them to tell their stories. We ask, "What do you know that I don't—or that three people in here don't know? What are you good at? Where have you been? What have you done that your friend would like to hear about? What did you do last night? What's the best thing that ever happened to you?"

By asking questions like these, we begin the long process of healing for those who have been wounded as writers. We begin to validate the power of their own lives as a source for writing ideas. We begin to redefine for them why people write—not just for the teacher or for evaluation, but because they have something to say. Writers write best what they know. Robert Coles, in his book *The Call of Stories*, writes of "narrative as everyone's rock-bottom capacity, but also as the universal gift, to be shared with others" (p. 30).

When I work with new, older writers, I use questions like these to help them get going. When they get an idea, I ask them "to write it so *they* can read it." I refuse to be a spelling machine, I refuse to scribe for them while they storytell, and I refuse to sit beside them indefinitely as a crutch under their arms. Everyone has to begin alone somewhere, take the first step, if you like. So I work hard to return ownership in the writing process to those who have been disenfranchised by their histories.

I am on constant standby, monitoring those who I know will experience frustration. At the upper levels, we rarely have to transcribe for writers—transcribing is what teachers of very young writers do when they write in script down in the corner of the paper what the writer reads from the invented spelling. We transcribe so that the writer's meaning can be preserved. At all levels, we talk constantly of what writing is: a writer's way of remembering and sharing what they wanted to say.

If writers absolutely can't discover a topic that interests them, after I've helped them by talking and making lists, I tell them that I have a topic for them—I have lots of those "story starter" cards from my old life, mostly in my head. But, I tell them, if they choose this option, then I will decide on the topic and that is what they must write on. Whether with students I know or with students I have just met, I have never had anyone take my topic. Everyone, without fail, under these circumstances, has decided to write their own story. And then I tell them, with a deadpan face, that my topic was "The economic causes of the Civil War." We smile wryly at each other and they go off to work on their own topic. Learners with a history know a lot about teacher ploys and I know they do. So we smile over it. But they know too why I do what I do, that I really want them to try, and I work hard to convince them that I'm there for them, that I'm willing to hang in there until they meet success. By my manner, I try to assure them that I know they will be successful and I will provide the safety net so that it can happen.

Writers who begin to tell their own stories, their personal narratives, often move on to write fiction. As Don Graves observed in his studies of first graders, young children write personal narrative and may do so all year long. I have observed that fiction writing in a classroom often begins as soon as one person in a classroom tries this genre, no matter what the age of the children. Fiction then becomes the dominant mode.

And what do I do while they write? When I can, I write, too, showing them what I can of the opaque process which occurs for the mature writer. I believe it is important for teacher demonstration to be authentic. I used to write on big chart paper on the easel until my sixth graders asked me why would I ever write like that?? I thought it would help them to see what I did when I composed. They knew that what I was doing was only for them and not what real writers do.

Now I write on regular paper during writing time and I talk about my own writing process as much as I can, sharing with my students my growth as a writer. I have become a writer talking to other writers.

During writing time I serve as a publishing house, fulfilling the various roles necessary at any publishing house to develop a book and bring it to publication. During the stage of writing when content is being developed and articulated, the teacher serves as Chief Editor, encouraging, prompting, questioning, and helping the author to draw out the full text. In the classroom, I do what Richard C. Owen and the reviewers from his publishing company have done for me in the writing of this book. In the beginning, they encouraged me, telling me both things that worked and things that were unclear. They helped me to think through what I wanted to say in writing.

The teacher also serves as copy editor, in much the same way that a copy editor serves in real-life publishing houses. Of course, the teacher also takes the opportunity to teach editing skills in the context of the child's writing, but I'll bet if we talked to some copy editors who return a writer's work for "cleaning up," they would say that they must do some teaching, too, teaching of those things the writer is trying to do, but is not doing in a standardized, conventional way.

As copy editor, my first job is assisting the writer to use known editing skills correctly. Usually this is done over time, by developing with each writer a list of "Things I Can Do" or through use of a teacher-made "editing guide" which lists standardizing skills that students at a particular age may be able to use. The list of things added to writing to help it communicate—standardized spelling, punctuation, paragraphing, page numbers—is long and it's not surprising that writers of any age need a written guide to help them remember it all. I have Karen Gordon's *The Well-Tempered Sentence: A Punctuation Handbook for the Innocent, the Eager, and the Doomed* and her companion volume, *The Transitive Vampire: A Handbook of Grammar for the Innocent, the Eager, and the Doomed*, to help my memory.

As copy editor, I also teach. I find in each piece of writing for each writer one skill that the writer is trying to use but is having difficulty with and I teach them the correct usage. Thus, I would not teach quotation marks to students who were not actually using conversation in their writing, but only to those students who were wrestling with the massive problems involved in how writers and readers keep track of who's talking in a conversation. The writer then can go back through the piece of writing and work on that particular skill. Because we keep all writing, finished, unfinished or abandoned, in large folders in a file cabinet, the writer can even go back into old writing and review correct use of a skill by searching it out and correcting it.

Finally, the publishing house guarantees a perfect copy, so as copy editor, I perform any final editing if the piece of writing is going to be published by the students. As much as possible, all books are perfect. Writers have that guarantee. I have it—I know that Richard C. Owen Publishers will do everything possible to make my final writing perfect, even if I don't know how to myself. That's the job of a publishing house. And that's the job of the teacher-as-publisher also.

Generally, from second graders on up, I have found that students prefer to publish their own work—and that means doing all the typing or word processing. If that is the case, then the writer/typist is entitled to work from a perfect draft. I proofread and edit this draft, with the writer sitting beside me, after the writer has done all possible editing and we have worked on one skill.

I do find that in spite of working from a perfect copy, many "errors" go back into the published copy if students do their own typing or word processing. This is because these "errors" are in fact held as rules in the writers' minds (Goodman 1969; Donaldson 1978; Cazden, Cordeiro & Giacobbe 1985; Cordeiro, Giacobbe & Cazden 1983; Weaver 1982 and others). Learners work like little scientists, creating alternative hypotheses, testing them, and revising them in light of new environments for use.

Some of the hypotheses may not match the "rule" we've all accepted as standard. Thus young writers may hypothesize that periods are used between words—as in fact they are—and may initially use them between all words, creating their own alternative hypothesis about the rule for period placement. We as teaching copy editors help them begin to revise that hypothesis by showing them the use of periods in particular environments. And they as learners begin to work on approaching the standardized rule for period use.

This process of hypothesis revision goes on for a lifetime because, as the linguists have taught us, each sentence we create is new on earth and must be internally matched to the models we hold in order to be standardized correctly. We see this best in the adult world as we see mature writers attempting to use apostrophes according to established, standardized use. The earth is strewn with "incorrect" apostrophes and they float like misplaced minnows across the face of many public signs: "Hat's for sale"— "Joe's Used Car's—"Snack's." Many adult writers apparently have created the alternative hypothesis that apostrophes are used in front of the letter s—sometimes.

In the role of dual editor, the teacher also constantly trains other editors, as when Ben sat in on the conference with George and Gerry. When process writing time is going full swing with writers at all stages of composition and publishing, there is no way one teacher can be the sole helper. Nor should the teacher want to be. Training junior editors helps them to be better writers themselves. I've found over and over that the best way to learn something is to teach it.

A classroom is full of people who are quite capable of helping each other, and furthermore, children know which classmates are good at what skills. They know who to go to if they need a drawing, if they need a word spelled, or if they need really good lettering on a cover. We teachers must tap into this motherlode of help and demonstrate for these young teachers how to help and conference in new and improved ways.

During the actual publishing of a book, the teacher and the writer collaborate to prepare a final, perfect copy. I find that in fact I had relatively little to do with publishing. The students at all levels helped each other. I stepped in for troubleshooting, like the time when all the photocopied pages of a collaborative book got mixed up and five copies of the 40-page book were sewed together all wrong. Then they needed me.

And as Don Graves reminded us ten years ago, writers work best when they have ownership of what they write. Writers work hardest on texts that are theirs from start to finish, which express their own ideas, which tell their stories. When students write in a program which focuses on the interactive processes of writing, they are guaranteed ownership of the text which they produce.

During writing time, then, students write and they talk—a lot. Writing times are active, happy times in classrooms where they are successful. During writing time, which in my classroom happened first thing in the morning for about an hour, we all focus on helping writers tell their own stories, whatever they may be. In preserving the integrity of that time, even as the day begins to integrate and content and activities tend to flow into each other, we guarantee writers that there will always be a time during the day when collaborators will be there to help them along in their process.

Working With Writers in Process

Working with experienced student writers is one of the most satisfying times in teaching. By experienced, I mean student writers who have already developed a sense of their own writing processes, who know that writers work in different ways, who know what happens during an instructional time devoted to engaging in the process of writing—students who think of themselves and their classmates as writers.

This can happen very early. Talk to Gretchen, a kindergartener, during writing time, and she will tell you that she's an author. And she will show you her book, a finely illustrated piece of fiction writing, seven pages long, about what happens when someone has to go to the hospital in an emergency. It's called *Calling Dr. River, Calling Dr. O'Neill.* Gretchen is a good writer, and even as a kindergartener, she is not an exception in a process writing time. Many young children now see themselves as authors and perform accordingly.

I had the good fortune for several years to work with upper elementary students who had experienced more than three years of working as writers for part of each school day. In my last two years as a sixth grade teacher, I was gifted with classes who had begun studying the processes of writing as kindergarteners.

In working with these experienced writers, I had the opportunity to work with authors who worked on the same story for weeks at a time. I have had students work diligently, every day, on a story for up to four months. In my years of teaching sixth grade, I worked with writers who had been working on stories for two and three years and were still at it, diligently, every day. It is an astonishing thing to witness in this world of consumable workbooks. Don Holdaway (1989c) has pointed out that "A distinctive feature of the Writing Process movement, and one reason for its power and effectiveness, has been the release of children into self-regulated and approximating strategies. Such emancipation is required for all language learning in schools" (p. 12).

I worked with learners who were used to reflecting on their own processes not only in writing but in all areas. For as I have discovered, writing time became a "way in" to opening up other areas of learning. My first experiences at breaking down the traditional classroom boundaries began when I set up a process writing time. It served to open up the rest of the day.

It's hard to work just for an hour with writers who are peers—because that's what happens when you write and work on process—and for the rest of the day go back to the "guess what the teacher's thinking" type of instruction with everyone sitting in rows but me. I found I didn't want to do it. I liked working side-by-side with my students. I began to enjoy what I was doing.

Stephen Tchudi wrote an article in 1986, called ''The Hidden Agendas in Writing across the Curriculum.'' He was doing consulting workshops for high school teachers who were learning about writing when one of them accused him of having a hidden agenda: ''You're not just asking me to add more writing to my course . . . You're asking me to change my whole style of teaching.'' Tchudi writes he admitted that it was true—he was suggesting a way of working with students which runs counter to traditional, deductive teaching and requires letting students work things out for themselves. Tchudi says:

> When we invite colleagues . . . to teach writing, we are in fact calling for nothing less than a revolution in most of education . . . learning is experiential . . . it requires learners to make connections for themselves . . . (but) teaching still follows the old deductive pattern of instructors presenting concepts and having students show mastery of them. (p. 22)

And so when I worked with experienced writers, we were able to go beyond the normal bounds of sixth-grade writing and into realms of inductive reasoning and critical thinking. I found there were several intersections between the writing process as we were experiencing it and aspects of critical thinking. One of the main aspects was in the world of planning.

Experienced Writers and Their Planning

As writers become better at their craft, they also become better at planning—what to write, how to use their time, how long writing tasks will take to accomplish successfully, how they need to manipulate text in order to accomplish their purpose. In the writing program in my classroom we always had writing plans (*see* Figure 3). These were lists of possible activities during writing time with a place next to each for a checkmark if the writer planned to do that activity. After the first few writing sessions, we extended this activity into ''pre-and post-planning,'' indicating what we planned to do with the writing time and then looking back to see what we had accomplished.

Each writing time we would fill in the planning sheet at the beginning and end of our work period. Before we started, we would fill in the ''pre-planning section'' and after we were all done, we would fill in the ''post-planning section.'' What was of interest to discuss afterwards was whether the two sections matched up, or whether we had wound up doing different things than

WRITING PLAN

	MONDAY		TUESDAY	
	Pre-plan	Post-plan	Pre-plan	Post-plan
Begin a new story				
Add to a story				
Revise a story				
Read to someone				
Listen to someone				
Conference				
Illustrate				
Design a cover				
Make a list				
Word process				
Put together a book				
Research				
Think				

FIGURE 3

we planned to do. We often talked for a while about how our plans had gone. I think this personal knowledge, insight and reflection is the key to growth in learning. Knowing how we operate and being able to control and manipulate it is, to me, a hallmark of a successful learner.

It's important for emergent writers to realize that writing doesn't always go the way it's planned. Things interfere. Sometimes a writer plans to finish a story, but the writer gets stuck, or a friend asks for a conference, or the writer has a really good idea and off the story goes in a new direction.

From time to time I would ask the writers one-by-one to do their pre-planning out loud while I recorded on their chart. That way we shared how we were doing and gave each other new ideas. I often revised the chart. Sometimes I left big spaces for titles. I liked to keep track of which story a writer was working on at any given time. It was also interesting to see that many students worked on two or more stories simultaneously.

At the suggestion of Dr. Bob Swartz, who was observing in my class, I had the students write out their plans informally in narrative form and read them aloud. This planning represented the development of writers' metacognition, the ability to think about their thinking. Extending the planning process would augment this thinking. So, at the beginning of the next writing time, we all took a couple of minutes—me included—and wrote a sentence or two about what we planned to do during the hour ahead of us. And then we all read, in turn, without comment. Louisa wrote and read:

> I plan to tell what happened at the dance and to finish the other story.

The next day, I asked students to be more specific, to tell exactly what had to be written next in order to advance the story. Writers need to develop the ability to control their text.

The students put their stories-in-progress on their desks and sat in thought. Louisa wrote and read:

> Today I hope to finish my old book. And tell what happened at the dance and before the dance when Justine opened the door before Justin could knock.

Her expanded planning demonstrates the deeper level of reflection and writers' knowledge being tapped.

The third time we planned this way, I asked them to tell what had to come next in the writing and then to tell **why** that had to be in the story. Some were at crucial turning points in their fictions and wrote that a particular event had to happen or the story couldn't end the way they wanted it to. Some wrote that a particular character had to be introduced because that was essential to the next part of the story. All demonstrated a clear and deep understanding of story development and writer's control.

Louisa wrote and read:

> Today I plan to write about the dance. I put the dance in the story **because** that's how Justin and Justine fall deeply in love and that's why the story is called my first love on Valentines Day.

Another aspect of metacognition, or thinking about our thinking, that we explored constantly was how writers control readers' expectations in text. We read books and discussed how writers made us expect certain things to happen. We talked a lot about how we tried to do that in our own writing. We constantly thought about whether there was a match between the writer's intentions and the reader's expectations.

We spent about an hour one day looking at this story beginning from two boys in the class:

> It was a long time ago, Sept. 13, 1933, Friday, when the terrible accident happened on that track. The train ran off the track and killed Shawn and Alex's grandparents. Shawn and Alex were not alive when this happened. When their parents thought they were old enough, they told Shawn and Alex. And every Sept. 13, Friday, strange things happen on that same track where the train ran off. . . .

The class discussion was about how skillfully Bob and Henry had manipulated the readers' expectations so that we were led to expect a certain kind of story—scary, exciting, probably supernatural. We substituted other words, playing with how a writer can make a well-written beginning lead to many different expectations.

Ben Grotz wrote wonderful leads, setting the stage for clearly defined readers' expectations, growing as the year progressed, demonstrating the application of literacy across content.

Here is a Ben Grotz lead for social studies:

> Sept. 24, 1985
> One foggy afternoon I was looking in my mail and I found a letter requesting that I would please do some exavations in Middle America.
>
> I immediately booked two discount plane tickets, one for me and of course one for my dear friend and assistant, Neddick Lelong.

For science:

> A Report on Aerodynamics
> Some people think that paper airplanes are dumb and are all the same but not so. Some will fall gently, some won't fly, and others dart quickly

through the sky. Without paper and cardboard models, we probably would not be flying across the world in these high tech jets, which at first were not jets, they were propellor powered and traveled quite slow, but did the job.

And, of course, for fiction:

> Rayson's World
> When Dr. Rayson Weeblox had first discovered a dimension where no time would pass, he started using it for traveling from solar system to solar system.

And, one of my very favorite story openings from, The Frog that Rodney Knew (Later renamed Fearless Froggy):

> Rodney was a nice human, not too smart, but nice. Who would have known that George's cage was . . .

This writer had control of his process. Ben wrote about writing:

> In this class I like the way we write because we get to write what we want to write, without too much criticism, but some. We are also allowed to talk to friends when we need a break, this helps us get fresh ideas and keep our stories interesting, though we are not allowed to talk all the time, because then we would have no time to write.
>
> Our conferences are also good, because they help you to think about what you want to write next, so we can express it on paper.
>
> Another way to get fresh ideas is by making illustrations of what will be next.
>
> I hope that we keep writing this way and other schools catch on because in my view the system is good.

Writing and Problem Solving

Finally, in working with experienced writers, we talk a lot about writing as problem-solving. In a simplified problem solving model (see Figure 1 on page 20), we find that there are components which can cycle back on each other (Rowe 1991). As Figure 4 shows, the writing process has components that match elements of this problem-solving model. In writing process, we solve problems over and over, both at the micro level—small problems with certain wordings—and at the macro level—major problems like how to go about writing something difficult like a research paper.

WRITING AS PROBLEM SOLVING:

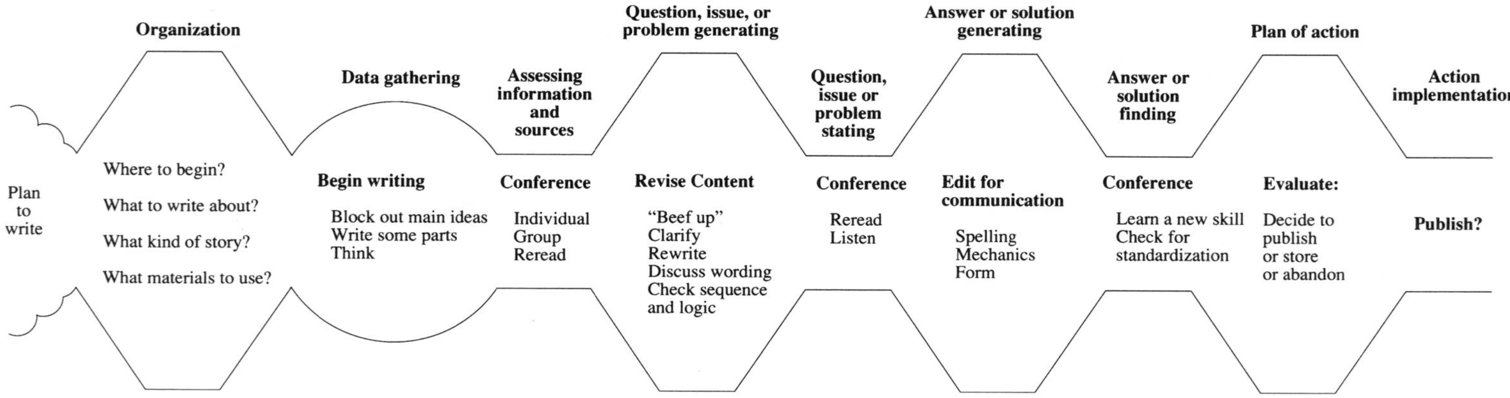

FIGURE 4

© P. Cordeiro 1991

Here is how a novice third-grade writer, who had been working in writing process for only a few months, solved a problem in textual communication. As you'll see, he constantly cycles back through the stages of problem solving as a writer. Jack had been working for about a week on a very exciting story called "Invasion of the Bees." He read it to the class in group conference. After the excitement had died down and the strengths were praised, students began to question the beginning. The story started like this:

> One night on the moon there was an explosion. The explosion sent a creature to earth. It was a giant bee. The giant bee was capturing all the bees in the world.

In conference, students asked, "Why was there a bee on the moon? How did it get giant?" Jack listened to his collaborators and off to work he went, cycling back to the beginning of the model. Jack had reached the stage of Editing for Communication, but the raising of these content problems sent him back into the early stages of the writing process, back to Organization and Data Gathering.

The next time he came to group conference, he read:

> A rocket was sent into space with astronauts and bees. It blew up. The bees got a reaction from the sparks. They stung one of the astronauts. The astronaut got some of the bees' blood. He started to change. The astronaut's eyes grew bigger. He grew a stinger. He was starting to look like a bee. He was ten feet tall. He grew wings. He flew to earth. He landed at a farm. A man came out.

We were very impressed with these changes and said so. But students were concerned about why a rocket was sent up with astronauts and bees, of all things. That seemed strange to them.

Back Jack went into the problem-solving model, back from the Communication stage to the Data Gathering stage, and produced this revised revision:

> A rocket was sent into space with astronauts and bees. The scientists thought that the bees could live in space. The spaceship started to slow down. It blew up.

Don Graves was right: writers who understand their own processes and have ownership of their writing care about the texts they create and are willing to work on them long and hard. Robert Ennis (1987) defined critical thinking as "reasonable reflexive thinking that is focused on deciding what to believe or do." I can think of no better definition for the process that informed writers of any age undergo as they produce text than Ennis' definition with a slight modification: "reasonable reflexive thinking which is focused on deciding what to write."

The Things They Write

To work with experienced student writers is to work with professionals. For example: Crista and her 84-page book entitled "Home is Where the Heart Is," (*see* Figure 5) beautifully bound, complete with chapters and table of contents, and on the back, comments from reviewers and a summary; Harry, agreeing his fiction is too violent for a school bookshelf, where children of all ages come to read, finished the full volume at home with friends and published an abridged version for the classroom; Alice and her wonderful book, "Hospital Life" where "the doctors lose their patients," pun intended, and it's hard to learn to be a nurse (*see* Figure 6); Anny and "To Provincetown with Braces" (*see* Figure 7) about adjusting to having a mouth full of metal; Roberta's "Horses I Have Known and Loved and Not Forgotten; and Mike's "Story of My Life" dedicated to "my father for all the good times he gave me."

In my office at work I have a shelf full of these books, full of the humor, care and concerns of these upper elementary lives. In these books, they cemented friendships, worked out problems, dreamed grown-up dreams: "To Luci, for reading this book so many times"; "I'm 11 and this is my first book this year. I've loved horses all my life"; "I dedicate this book to my good friend, Anny, for helping me sort out my dream and put it into a story."

And then there was Mike and his book about trucks. After many hours of work in fourth grade, the book was finally finished and on the shelf. And there it resided with so many others as the years went by and Mike grew up. It got read by new students from both sixth grades along with the other books—I often found students lingering by these books, reading stories written by people now in high school. The books were the artifacts of literacy.

When Mike was in seventh grade, and over in the high school building, he was one of the students chosen to come back to sixth grade at the end of the year and tell the outgoing sixth graders what they might expect. I was teaching sixth grade by that time and I was at the panel discussion the afternoon Mike and the others came to talk and answer questions. It was very successful and the students were rightfully impressed.

As Mike was leaving, his friend from sixth grade, Charlie, spoke to him. "I read your book about trucks," Charlie said, "It was terrific." It made my years of work worthwhile.

Table of Contents

1 This is Where it All Started....7
2 The Explosion..................17
3 Where are the Children?........27
4 Where Will We Live?............47
5 The Search....................53
6 Walking Bubba.................61
7 The Reunion...................73

FIGURE 5

To work with writers like these is to be able to explore realms I'm only getting around to thinking about myself. To work with these dedicated professionals is to break the bonds of the classroom and to dwell in a world where making meaning matters.

Books to Help

This chapter is not intended as a complete guide to setting up a process writing classroom. There are many fine guides available for those who are starting from scratch. I would especially recommend these:

Don Graves. *Writing: Teachers and Children at Work.* Portsmouth, NH: Heinemann, 1983.

The original handbook for us all, *Writing* continues to inform teachers setting up a new writing classroom. All process writing classrooms which I set up and advise are patterned after the ideas in this book.

When you go to the hospital
you see doctors and nurses
and you may find   patient
too.But you will not   see
dogs or cats.In the hospital
they have rules and one of
the rules are no smoking.
They are careful with you.

They don't scream   at you
but they do raise there voice
some times.But not a lot.So
don't be scared when you haftoo
go there.You can see some one
else. That has been.

FIGURE 6A

FIGURE 6B

Don Graves. *The Reading/Writing Teacher's Companion Series: Investigate
Nonfiction.* Portsmouth NH: Heinemann, 1989. *Experiment with Fiction.*
Portsmouth NH: Heinemann, 1989. *Discover Your Own Literacy.* Portsmouth
NH: Heinemann, 1990. *Build a Literate Classroom.* Portsmouth NH: Heine-
mann, 1991. *Explore Poetry.* Portsmouth NH: Heinemann, forthcoming.

The books in this recent series by Don "stress learning within a literate
community," as he puts it. Intended to help teachers explore their own literacy
both for personal satisfaction and as a model for subsequent teaching, these
books provide concrete, hands-on, guided activities, "Actions" as Don calls
them. These books will not provide the concrete "where to put things" advice
of *Writing* but can be kept nearby as helpers once the writing environment is
established.

Nancie Atwell. *In the Middle: Writing, Reading, and Learning with Adolescents.* Portsmouth, NH: Boynton/Cook, 1987.

Nancie was a junior high school teacher when she wrote this book but I
have recommended it to teachers from kindergarten through graduate school.
In it, Nancie describes her process of change and her development of class-

The doctor can be man or a
woman.He took a kids blood
 pressure and takes a sample of
your blood and he takes a rubber hammer and taps your
knee.it doesn't hurt when
he taps your knee.

FIGURE 6C

I was scared at first but the
nurse told me there was nothing
to be scared of. But the
doctors lose their patients.
And she said I would like it there
but I do not know how to nurse.
She said, "You'll learn." I
said, "I hope so." Then the next
morning I went there.

FIGURE 6D

room writing and reading workshops. She gives many helpful suggestions on organizing the classroom space, time, and activities. But it is her description of herself as a teacher-in-transition that is most valuable to other teachers on the brink of risk taking.

Lucy Calkins. *The Art of Teaching Writing*. Portsmouth, NH: Heinemann, 1986.

Many teachers I have talked to have used Lucy's book as a handbook when they were starting out. It is especially valuable for its description of Lucy's concept of ''mini-lessons,'' times when teachers teach about writing, briefly, giving a strategy which students can use, after observing what they know and what they seem ready to learn. These are what Lucy calls ''a time for teacher-input.'' Lucy also has sections on writing across the curriculum, report writing, and poetry.

Harste, J., K. Short & C. Burke. *Creating Classrooms for Authors: The Reading-Writing Connection*. Portsmouth NH: Heinemann Educational Books, 1988.

This useful book has many, many practical suggestions well described for setting up what the authors call ''an authoring cycle.'' They see this book as

So the next day was Saturday, and Paula had to go to the dentist s office!

That afternoomwent by quickly.Dr. Ross had put on the braces on Paula and she didn't even notice they were on!

FIGURE 7A

FIGURE 7B

"a conceptual starter kit" and encourage teachers to go beyond the suggestions, which include such ideas as Authors' Chair, Readers' Theatre, Learning Logs, and Poetry in Motion.

Parry, J. & D. Hornsby. *Write on: A Conference Approach to Writing.* Portsmouth NH: Heinemann Educational Books, 1985.

This very handy book, originally written for Australian teachers, is designed to take teachers new to writing process through the development of a workable program. The authors begin with a section to help teachers evaluate what they know and believe about writing instruction. The book is designed to assist teachers to enter change slowly, in an organized, reflective fashion.

These books are the ones I find most useful as of 1991. Books being published more recently extend writing process across genre and curriculum.

Integrated Learning: Social Studies in Context

Remembering Social Studies

Like me, most people I talk to only seem to remember one or two activities from their past times in social studies. No one reports fond memories of tests and reading the textbook—even though that's what we mostly did.

As I think back, my first memorable social studies event was in eighth grade when we had a classroom debate about whether or not Communist China should be allowed to join the United Nations. We took sides and did research and after about a month we dressed up and held a debate. I represented Czechoslovakia—a country I knew nothing about—and was in favor of inviting them in—a losing position in the climate of the times. We lost. I got a B. But I did come away with an appreciation for debate and a certain fondness for Czechoslovakia.

Before that I have few memories. Two incidents stand out. One was making a salt map—that impressed me. I don't remember when it was or even what my part in it was. But I remember that huge map—I was small, it was huge—

probably made on plywood with all the mountains and a river carved into the salt mixture. We painted it, I remember.

But what specific geography it showed or what we were supposed to be learning is lost for me. I didn't develop a sense of the topography of the earth—that came much later in my life when I was hiking with my husband and learned the true meaning of hills and valleys.

I also remember refusing to memorize the capitals of the states. It was a private decision, made in my room at home as I struggled to commit all 48 of them to memory. That was the year I developed a sense of how big this country is because I realized how many capitals there were. I was probably in fifth or sixth grade—that's when that kind of activity was done in those days. I was a good student, which means partly that I was a compliant student and I usually did what I was told. But when it came to memorizing the capitals, I remember thinking, I'm just going to fail this because I'm never going to be able to learn them and it's never going to do me any good.

My memory for decontextualized information, names and dates on a list, is not good. I need a lot of firm connections before I can store and retrieve such information. I am much better at making links—especially between ideas and concepts. And so when it came time to go home over the weekend and come back to a Monday morning test on the capitals, I refused to learn them. I don't think I ever told anyone at the time about this decision—it seemed momentous to me. The funny thing is, nothing ever happened. I didn't do my homework and it didn't matter. I failed the test but I passed the grade. My parents weren't called in and the whole thing disappeared out of my life.

I have never been sorry that I don't know the capitals. Even when my mom and I drove across the country, I didn't need to know the capitals. When I need to know one, I ask my husband who has a good memory for details, or I look it up. I think that's what disturbed me in fifth or sixth grade—this was information that could readily be found. I was good at looking things up and all the information was right there—why would anyone want to go through all the agony of rote memory of something that didn't even rhyme and take up a whole part of their brain with something like the capitals?

Sometimes, I get teased because I don't know my capitals—even as a grown-up—and I lose at the television game shows on the capitals questions. But other than that, I've never missed them. How many other things do we ask students to do in social studies that they will never miss if they don't have them in their heads—things that can't even be justified under the current "basics" banner, "it's good for them as citizens." I think I'm a good citizen—I just don't know the capitals.

Problem-Based Thematic Simulations

The social studies program that I took part in as a teacher at the upper elementary grades was specifically designed to help students learn reliable information about important topics in a contextualized, relevant, and authentic way. It was also taught to them as a model for how similar learning might take place. In working with a topic, students worked beyond it into the process of learning they were going through, so that they could master that process and use it to learn more.

As a teacher, I worked within a teacher-designed, social studies curriculum based on infused critical thinking and problem solving. That meant that as we worked on social studies topics, and the whole school did four topics a year together, we highlighted aspects of critical thinking and problem solving so that students would have those as tools for learning. For instance, as we did research on a topic like "Egypt," we discussed how we might decide if a source was reliable, what criteria we should use, and whether the criteria were always the same, not just for the source we were working on but for any source. And as we went about determining and solving a problem, we talked about what stage we were at in the problem-solving process, how we were improving as problem-solvers, and how what we were learning in this problem could help us solve other problems.

The practical aspect of working within a curriculum like this, globally organized, was that it was logical for me to use social studies as the central theme of an integrated and blended curriculum. We always had a topic to refer to and we were always in the middle of a big investigation in social studies.

I usually framed these broad themes—themes like "Portugal," "Pre-Revolutionary America," and "Egypt, Past and Present"—as simulations, as role-playing, as literate involvements that extended over several weeks. I have called these "problem-based thematic instruction" and have published an article with that title in *Language Arts* (January 1990).

In problem-based thematic work, students focus over a long period of time on a theme. Within that theme, they are asked to solve a broad problem. For instance, in studying the Westward Emigration in America, students were asked to act as "emigrants" and solve the problem of how to travel across America in 1850, a simulation that lasted for about a month and a half.

In this chapter, I will share the development of three problem-based themes. The first, on the Westward Emigration, was based on a simulation called, "Pioneers: A simulation of decision-making on a wagon train," written by John Wesley, published by Interact Company. This simulation taught me how to put together a good simulation, providing the model for the other two. The second and third I developed myself—far more fun. The second was on ancient and modern Egypt and the third was on a study of pre-Revolutionary America. The "letters" I gave the students to organize these last two simulations are in the Appendix of this book.

It's important to know that there are different kinds of simulations, especially among those which are purchased as ready-made. Some are designed to permit a lot of teacher input, student involvement with literacy, and generative activity. "Pioneers" is such a simulation. There is no end to what can be added to the activities which are blocked out in the teacher's manual and student booklet. And the time frame is flexible enough so that the simulation can be contained in about two weeks, or can be extended over a long period of time.

Simulations like "Pioneers" are are also designed to promote cooperation among participants, an important factor for me. There is much in elementary school to promote competition, grades and sports, for instance. There is less structured opportunity for students to develop cooperative skills. Simulations work very well when cooperation is structured into the overall design. In "Pioneers," students function in "wagon trains," cooperative, decision-making groups that often help one another while "on the trail."

Some simulations, however, are competitive, "trivia," board games. I have purchased, sight unseen, simulations which were complicated to set up, difficult to interpret in their directions, and boring to play. They required students to memorize, often as the game proceeded, specific factual information so that they could proceed around a board with a marker. Some set the students up to compete in teams with no crossover between teams to enable cooperation.

The primary goal of these simulations seems to be to give students something they can do without the teacher, the old "learning center" way of teaching. But this is not how I approach social studies learning. I expect to be actively involved during the time the students are in the classroom. I expect to have fun and enjoy the topic, too.

These trivia board games are not simulations, to my way of thinking. Simulations should help students to solve problems by looking at them from an enlarged point of view, by temporarily becoming someone else. Simulations, when framed as problem-based thematic instruction, fulfill Dorothy Heathcote's (1975) definition of what a "role" is, as in roleplaying: "an emotional reaction and the state of being trapped, a state from which one can only escape by working through the situation" (p. 91).

Dorothy feels strongly about the power of tapping into people's ability to become someone else for a while, to walk in someone else's shoes:

> The material of drama then consists of, first, our ability to make 'another room' for ourselves, in order to examine something . . . It becomes a no-penalty area in which the two parts of people can have equal status. The spectator part, which allows us to stand back and see what it is that we are experiencing at any moment, and the participant part, which has to deal with the event in a practical manner. (1980, p. 129)

Dorothy Heathcote would have us use drama and simulation to "release the energies of our children" (1975, p. 89) so that we can help to "bring about a change, a widening of perspective, in the life of the real person, as well as to offer systems of learning and knowing" (1980, p. 106). In this the teacher is the "journey-maker" (1983, p. 699) and essential to the journey is the concept of authenticity, the very component most often lacking in my old way of teaching upper elementary social studies. Heathcote gives a central position to the power of authenticity, "the tenuous thread which links all the previous gleanings" (1984, p. 174) and believes this can be accomplished through:

> . . . the pressure, or the authenticity, of that dramatic moment that creates the new knowledge, that makes new connections, and that suddenly brings connections that have been dormant in my previous knowledge into active use in making sense of new information I encounter. (1983, p. 695)

For when we ask students to cooperatively solve problems within a theme, we not only ask them to walk in someone else's shoes, we also give them the chance to do what Dorothy Heathcote calls "walking in the time of the event" (1983, p. 695.) Not only is a process of learning revealed and information acquired in a successful simulation, but students are given the opportunity to be "human beings confronted by situations which change them because of what they must face in dealing with those challenges" (p. 48).

The Westward Migration

We had a great time one year with the "Pioneers" simulation, the first one I had ever done. The sixth grade students prepared for the day's work by reading the previous night's "diary entries" to other members of their wagon train (*See* Figure 8). As travelers together on the Westward emigration, they had a community interest in each other's lives and troubles. They shared each other's happinesses and sadnesses.

> *1844 April*
> *Well, we've made the big decision.*
> *We're gonna move to Oregon. It's*
> *gonna be hard for the kids but*
> *for that matter it's gonna be hard*
> *for John and I as well. Granmat*
> *Granpa are going with us (I have my*
> *doubts about them goin'; they might not*
> *make the trip).*
>
> *We have all the item's we expect*
> *we'll need on our trip. In the way*
> *of livestock we're bringing a pair*
> *of oxen, 2 goats, 3 cows, and 2 mules.*
>
> *Thank the lord that John is a*
> *farmer 'cause that'll be a good*
> *livin' in Oregon.*

FIGURE 8

When children are placed communally in authentic situations, learning becomes a shared process. We all felt bad when "Mrs. Roger Ellery" read her entry:

> I felt a lump arise in my throat as we were driving away. I looked back and felt a warm gentle tear roll down the side of my face. The children asked why I was crying. I said, "I'm just a little bit sad." Later that night, my husband repeated the question. I said, "I feel like I am dying." I miss my beautiful clapboard house, the general store, and all my friends. Oh, it's just so hard, Roger."

We cheered her on when she read,

> Then Roger promised me he would build me a new house with all the trimmings and a plentiful crop right beside it and of course very plump animals. I think that dream is what drove us on. The next day I felt better.

At that moment we all could sympathize with what "Mrs. Ellery" was going through because we all were in the act of sharing her experience. In the midst of authentic learning, acting like adults, classmates had a common experience and shared a "flexible reality."

Time was spent in communal groups, "doing math," helping each other calculate the total weight of selected items. Each wagonmaster knew approximately what each imaginary wagon could hold. As a class, we had done some real digging into available facts on what the real "prairie schooners" did carry on the Westward crossing.

There was much problem-solving and decision-making going on in each group as I circulated around, "kidwatching" (Goodman 1985). The class previously had spent a long time discussing what had actually happened to wagons that were too heavily loaded to complete the trip. We had read several authentic accounts. Prospective travelers had researched the geography, terrain and seasonal weather patterns for the routes they selected.

"Wagonmasters" had been chosen for their levelheadedness and their ability to work with their classmates. The wagonmasters were especially aware of the responsibility which had been taken on by real wagonmasters on the Westward journey. They knew it was their responsibility to help "Jenna Mingo" when she lamented: "This house is very beautiful. We have a lot of old stuff that I don't want to get rid of but I guess I have to." Her wagonmaster knew that the success of the wagontrain depended on the good decisions of each member.

As the "camp meetings" continued, some students finished a draft of their packing list and checked their calculations by consensus. Comparing results with others, students were able to verify their own results and make any corrections before turning in the list.

Getting the list right required a lot of communication and sharing. Many students, for instance, tried to talk one student out of taking four guitars in his wagon, saying that they were a waste of space and weighed too much. But "Joe Moffatt" argued that he made his living with guitars, making music, so he would need them. Calculating their weight, however, took several students quite a while.

On other days, some students went off in twos and threes to rehearse. Since each "family" would be making a presentation to all the wagon trains, telling about themselves and their past history, some students tried out their speeches on their friends. In natural learning, learners do best when they are given an opportunity to practice before they are asked to perform.

Often, students met with me to select books to take back to their camp meetings. These books were ones we had chosen from the library, ones which we all thought might help each family decide on what to take on the trip West. We had some primary sources, some accounts with special sections marked by me which might be useful for sixth graders, some materials from students in past sixth grades. We knew from our research that travelers on the real wagon trains had used lots of guide books to help them make similar decisions.

I brought resources to the simulation, to fill the gaps I felt were left open.

This was my first simulation and I was feeling my way along, taking advantage of my own creativity in ways I had never done before in teaching. I owned and brought in several accounts of women's diaries of the westward movement, like Lillian Schlissel's *Women's Diaries of the Westward Journey*. I also brought in reproductions of original accounts. One was written in "the winter of 1818–19" by J. Wright and was called *Letters from the West: or a Caution to Emigrants: Being Facts and Observations Respecting the States of Ohio, Indiana, Illinois and Some Parts of New York, Pennsylvania and Kentucky*. This is available from Readex Microprint Corporation and I got it through a bookseller in Connecticut who sent me his flyer.

Another favorite source was a reproduction of an authentic guidebook by a Captain Marcy and was called *The Prairie Traveler*. Although it was written late in the emigration years, 1859, it was valuable to us not only as an artifact of the times but also as a guidebook. By the time we used it, we were all deep in character and deeply in need of guidance on how to go West, even though we knew that it might not be accurate and might paint a too-rosy picture of a difficult trip. This particular guidebook is part of a Time-Life series called "Classics of the Old West," and is available now as a remaindered book.

A book that we found useful—but hard to read—in that series was *Life on the Plains and at the Diggings; Being Scenes and Adventures of an Overland Journey to California: with Particular Incidents of the Route, Mistakes and Sufferings of the Emigrants, the Indian Tribes, the Present and the Future of the Great West* by A. Delano, 1854.

Another book in that series that we read parts of was *Captivity of the Oatman Girls: Being an Interesting Narrative of the Life among the Apache and Mohave Indians. Containing an Interesting Account of the Massacre of the Oatman family, by the Apache Indians, in 1851; the Narrow Escape of Lorenzo D. Oatman; the Capture of Olive A. and Mary A. Oatman; the Death, by Starvation of the Latter; the Five Years' Suffering, and Captivity of Olive A. Oatman; Also, her Singular Recapture in 1856; as Given by Lorenzo D. and Olive A. Oatman, the only Surviving Members of the Family, to the Author*, by R. B. Stratton, 1857.

This book led us to fill in with literature a gap in the original simulation: the native American perspective. We read parts of *Bury My Heart at Wounded Knee: An Indian History of the American West*, the tribe-by-tribe account of the decimation of the original inhabitants of this continent that we were "emigrating across." For a while, we focused on the chapter on the Navahos because they were betrayed by Kit Carson, a name well-known to sixth graders. Later we read about the Ghost Dance and the Long March.

I brought in my book of E.S. Curtis' photographs of native Americans, taken in the late 1800s. We knew, and talked over, how even then, the native cultures died quickly. When Curtis came to photograph them, these peoples had to recreate many of the old scenes that Curtis is well-known for. The old life had already died out.

In the women's diaries, which some of the girls in the class were working with, we read accounts of how native Americans helped the settlers. In her book, *Pioneer Women: Voices from the Kansas Frontier,* Joanna Stratton tells of Christina Campbell, newly married and removed to the new town of Salina, who said that ''if it had not been for the friendship of the squaws she did not know how she would have survived those first years of loneliness in the little new town on the Smoky'' (1981 p. 116).

We tried to evolve a balanced view of the time period. We looked at the emigration for what it taught us about cross-cultural experiences. Outside the simulation, but inspired by it, we looked at parallels between what happened in 19th century America and what is currently going on in the jungles of Brazil as the culture of native, aboriginal Brazilians conflicts with the in-rushing culture of the gold-seekers in the Amazon valley. We viewed a video about the problems of the region and the decimation of the tribal peoples of the forests.

When we read the books, we worked hard together. These sources were all written for adults, some in an older style of language than even I was used to reading, and they were all hard to read. I helped the interested students to work through them. We all thought the effort worth it because they were original sources and I found the extra work rewarding because I learned much about the westward emigration that I had never known before. Often, I transliterated the material, reading it beforehand, and then alternately reading and talking it through out loud to the students. I didn't find that students minded this. They knew that the alternative was a watered-down version written with a readability formula, if the material was even available. And I got better at doing this kind of reading-talking. Working with original sources made it all worthwhile.

We worked roughly within the bounds of the purchased simulation but we did a lot of the writing and reading as homework and we added many activities to increase the opportunity for individual expression.

One of the most inspired students was Ben Grotz, also known as ''Mr. John Adams,'' emigrant farmer. Ben—and other students—took to the simulation—expressed by moving a small, cutout wagon across the bulletin board—with an intensity only seen that year in the writing program. They were sixth graders and capable of much literacy.

One of the early assignments added to the simulation reflected the students' understanding of preliminary map work which enabled them to grasp how and why America's frontier line changed before the period of westward expansion.

Figure 9 shows a typed report that Ben submitted after working with maps. In this homework assignment to write a travel plan to his wagon master, Ben demonstrates what he has learned from researching how some emigrants went west. With other students, and me for support, Ben had read a firsthand account of a man who began his trip west traveling by boat down through the Great Lakes to the Mississippi River to St. Joseph, Missouri, a "jumping off place" for emigrants. Ben then wrote his own version:

Traveling West (MY WAY)

Like the other man, I will start in Buffalo, and go on a boat on the Great Lakes, but unlike him I will not travel as an employee, though I will go back and forth several times, and earn money to buy a wagon and join the wagon train, and go along the Oregon Trail. Along with me I will bring a family, charging them 50$ for the whole trip, though I will not go the whole way on the Oregon Trail, me and the family that is coming along will turn off with me, the turn will be at the conjunction of the Mahoon Trail, and keep going on along the California Trail.

Once in California I will become a merchant, (starting my business with the 50 dollars from the family).

Ben fell completely into character when, at home, he wrote a letter to his wagon master, explaining why he wanted to make the trip,

Me and my wife knoed each other since childhood bein that we live so close togethar. another thing we knoed is that we would someday be wed. though one thing that weren't planed is both of our homesteads bein' raided . . .

"I wrote it like that on purpose," he said to me. He wanted it to sound like a real emigrant farmer had written it. Who could ask for more?

But Ben and his classmates did produce more. Ben was responsible for our extension of the simulation past literacy and into projects. In the setup of the purchased simulations, "emigrants" got points for doing assignments and making decisions together; with those points they moved their wagons across the map. Because the simulation was well-written, there was enough flexibility to allow for the addition of ideas generated by the theme.

So at Ben's suggestion, "emigrants" could also get credit for special projects. Within a few days, Ben brought in the first, a miniature wagon that he and his father had made, stained brown, with a cloth covering. Inside the wagon were tiny tables and benches, small artifacts of the emigration. Ben wrote descriptions for the items and a label to explain the project's role in the simulation. His team's wagons moved forward.

After that, other projects appeared from Ben and other students, small wagons, a diorama in a shoebox, maps and small models of things of the period. All advanced the cause of their respective emigrants. Ben had re-

                    The Movement West
when setlers first arrived in what was to be the U.S.
People were few and land was plentiful, but as time went
by,, and every couple had six children,. things got pretty
croudedfor the next generation.
          So by 1800 people had altready begun to venture
beead the Appalacian Mountains, from then on the movement west was pretty much stop go, stop go.
          The next obsticle (jin1821)) was the Ohio river
leading into the Mississippi river. The reason for
this is obvious, noone was prepared   there were no rafts,
wagons cant float, ● eventual (in 1840)   and
          After that river was all cressed the settlers
hit the rest of the Mississippi though they were prepared
for oneriver people couldn't cross both , and so time
went by and the population grew but had no place to go,
so the young generation made the move to cross over onto
the other side of the river.
          The fourth and final map has no reason for its
frontier line accept that that'sas far as they went..

                    THE END

FIGURE 9

___

minded me of the necessity for providing for many student strengths and for
the power of enabling homework to become a family project.

   This simulation allowed for inventiveness, for creatively drawing on our
prior knowledge. Other students brought much knowledge, insight and inven-
tive thinking to the simulation as well. Some girls, aware that women alone or
women with children would have a hard time, wrote for ''illiterate husbands,''
something not uncommon in that time, or reported the premature death of
their husbands at the start of the journey, leaving them to go on alone, also a
common happening in the actual diaries of the time. ''Mrs. Christina Wright''
records this in her letter in the simulation:

   We were going to move sooner but the death of my husband, James,
stopped us. It's been a month now and I've decided to go on with it. After
all, that is what James would want.
   We need more farming land, and more room for my 2 oxen, 2 cows, and
3 chickens and from what I've heard, there's a lot of land, and plenty of
room in Oregon.

As in the real life of the times, emigrants traveled in all sorts of conditions and with many concerns and fears. "Mrs. Colloni" wrote this letter:

> I have three sons and I'm having a baby in four months. My youngest is six. His name is Thomas and he puts a little laughter into our family's serious talks. He doesn't understand why we have to move . . . Work was pretty good back home. I wonder if it is any better in Oregon.
>
> Now I'm looking forward to going. I'm ready for anything that will happen along the way. My family is ready for the long, hard trip West.

As Figure 10 shows, emigrants came with various skills and backgrounds, all reflecting the students' independent research into the life of the times:

> (Figure 10 transcription)
>
> When we first moved to Ft. Independence we didn't like it. Until we met Mr. and Mrs. John Butler, a nice, big, happy family. They're from Missouri. The week after we met them we found our perfect wagon train to go west. Our wagon train has five wagons.
>
> My last job was a seamstress at home. I hope to do some more loom and sewing work on the new homestead in Oregon.

And there were ongoing diary entries:

> July 3
>
> Today is our anniversary. My husband says I am brave and very smart. I guess I am. And he also says he's kindhearted. The children were talking about Indians. I pray we will make it safe without any trouble.

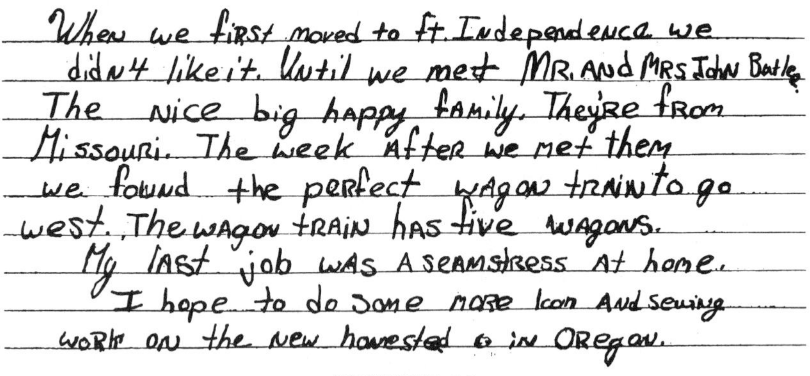

When we first moved to Ft. Independence we
didn4 like it. Until we met MR. AND MRS John Butle
The nice big happy family. They're from
Missouri. The week After we met them
we found the perfect wagon train to go
west. The wagon train has five wagons.
My last job was A seamstress At home.
I hope to do some more loom And sewing
work on the new homested in Oregon.

FIGURE 10

From using the purchased "Pioneers" simulation, I learned how to structure events to accomplish my long-range goals. In this simulation, the goal was to learn both geographic and historical information about the westward emigration and to develop an understanding of the reasons why Americans made such moves at the time they did.

From my students I learned to develop flexible simulations, with lots of space in them, to allow for innovations along the way. I learned not to overplan but to listen, watch, and wait. I learned that when students are engaged and immersed in such a journey, learning happens naturally and arises from the needs and interests of the learners.

The Royal Archeological Institute of Cairo

While "Pioneers" was a fine simulation to use, well-designed and clearly written, I would always now design my own. For me, that is the exciting part. That is what lets me in on the fun that the students have as they roleplay and experience the social studies we are trying to learn. Creating simulations was one of the first times I was really excited about material I was teaching.

When I first began to conceptualize "the Royal Archeological Institute of Cairo," I drew on my experience with Pioneers. I thought that I would plan a scheduled "route" or sequence that we would undergo, have such things as "fate cards," which were random happenings built into the "Pioneers" simulation that affected the ongoing activities, and design some sort of a map that would be the bulletin board, visual component. I thought that I would need to design some sort of point system to show progress. At first those things seemed the most significant learnings that I had acquired from working with the purchased, "tried-and-true" simulation.

In fact, we did none of those things. I put up maps of the U.S. and Egypt and had students indicate their points of origins in the States with colored pins, but once we got underway, that activity was dropped, and we used the map when we needed it, the way real travelers do.

Once we got going, I never did get to the "fate cards," or some similar planned intervention. We were much too busy. And as for the scheduled sequence, the real joy of that was its evolution over the course of the two months that the simulation continued. We tried keeping track of points, but we all commented that it felt like I was only doing it so I could grade the participants. It didn't feel authentic so we dropped it.

During the course of the Pioneers simulation, I had abandoned the built-in pre-and post-tests. We took the pre-test but never took the post-test. What we had learned was evident and was not in need of testing. In fact, the built-in tests didn't begin to cover the depth of knowledge used by the students on a day-to-simulation-day basis.

Topically, in this unit, we were to cover aspects of ancient and modern Egypt. In conceptualizing how the simulation would evolve, it seemed logical to me that we would investigate ancient Egypt as "Fellows at the Royal Archeological Institute of Cairo," experts in a variety of researchable fields relevant to ancient Egypt.

The exploration of aspects of modern Egypt would then logically occur as Fellows prepared to travel to Egypt on an archeological dig. To facilitate this, I became the "Director of the RAI." That was the general framework. This particular social studies topic would conclude with a written research report for each of the "experts" and I would write a description of how we went about doing our research. All classes in the school would be putting together a similar piece of research writing from students and teachers as a "culminating activity" to this school-wide social studies topic, one of four for the year.

The details of how this simulation would happen were the exciting part and they evolved as the simulation grew. For as we began to work our way through this problem-based theme, solving the overall problem—what would real expert Fellows at an Institute do to investigate ancient and modern Egypt?— we became involved in solving the immediate problems that naturally resulted: How can we find appropriate research on relevant topics? What should those topics be? What do Americans have to do these days to travel to Egypt? What do experts do on an archeological dig?

Answering those questions as we encountered them became the stuff of the day-to-day life of the simulation, and those became the problems I framed in the "letters to the Fellows from the Royal Archeological Institute of Cairo." Those letters are in the Appendix of this book, not as an intact simulation, but as a model for how one might develop a simulation that suited the needs of the participants. Throughout the study the Fellows and the Institute communicated primarily in writing, by letter and report. For although the content is primarily social studies, my agenda is always literacy. We did, however, have a "social hour" to "meet and introduce each other" and we had a "formal meeting" at the end to present oral reports on each other's research.

When I actually began the unit, I authenticated the learning by "inviting" the students by letter "to become Fellows at the Royal Archeological Institute—the RAI—of Cairo Egypt." The RAI, it turned out, was beginning a dig and needed experts to contribute to the final Institute project, a written report on Egypt. The invitation asked for "letters of introduction, resumés, letters of recommendation"—all invented, as homework assignments—from each of the Fellows.

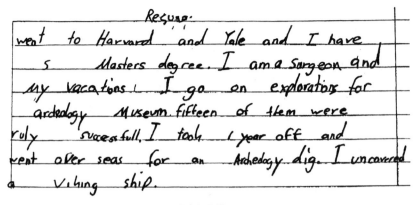

FIGURE 11

I made up letterhead from the RAI, complete with an official seal and I ran off blank copies on the school Xerox machine, typed up my letters of invitation to the prospective Fellows, (*see* Appendix) distributed them, and we were off and running.

But there were many sidetrips. We had to make up a list of things we would need to take for time in the desert, we had to get passports and identification, we had to have money. Usually, we communicated by letter, writing to each other at home, but sometimes I put up notices on the classroom easel about events that would be occurring that day—meetings, and so forth. I tried to have something each day to keep the simulation going.

Some days we focused for most of the day on RAI activities. Some days, there was only an exchange of letters. Always, I listened to the students and their interests to find direction for the next day's activities. Developing curriculum like this is a very creative, satisfying activity.

I received detailed letters in return, (*see* Figures 11 and 12) representing some research on students' parts into how this process was done, what resumés looked like, and what would be good credentials for someone chosen to join such an institute.

> My name is Tracey Lynn Myer. I am thirty-one years old. At my home in Astrulia, I lived with my family. At eighteen, I moved to Oakland California, then went to Harvard Medical School for five years. Took a year to get things together, found a new apartment in the same California town.
>
> I worked as an intern for Oakland County Hospital. A group of archeologists asked me to come to Egypt to serve as a doctor if an accident should occur. It was a one year trip. I agreed and went alone. Soon after leaving, I became interested in archeology . . .

```
                                    I wanT
To Be in your Group. I have Been an
archeoLogist For 15 years.
              I have Found a mummy's
Tomb,  dinosaurs Bones,  A Ancient
cup,  People Bones, and different Kinds oF
Rocks,  Diamonds,  Gold, Rubies,
Bird Bones, Monkey Bones,  Money,
   Treasure at The BoTTom oF sea,
  ShipwRecks,  I Found The Titanic,
      I am  25 years old...
      My Name is  Bud LighT.
```

FIGURE 12

(Figure 12 transcription)

I want to be in your group. I have been an archeologist for 15 years. I have found a mummy's tomb, dinosaur bones, an ancient cup, people's bones, and different kinds of rocks, diamonds, gold, rubies, bird bones, monkey bones, money, treasure at the bottom of the sea, shipwrecks, I found the Titanic. I am 25 years old . . . My name is Bud Light.

Fellows were accepted and research began. We had a social hour advertised by a sign on the classroom easel. It read:

> The Royal Archeological Institute of Cairo
> cordially invites you to a presentation
> and social hour.
> Please be prepared to make a short presentation
> about your area of expertise.
> Wear a name tag.
>
> Looking forward to meeting you!

One speech went like this: "Hi—I am very glad to be here today. I just recently graduated from Harvard. I've already begun to study archeology . . ."

Time and research activities went by. Students picked expert topics, everything from tropical medicine to the influence of the Nile River to family life in ancient and modern Egypt to foods of Egypt to architecture in the pyramids.

[Figure 13: handwritten letter]

Included in this
letter are my driver's license,
my social-security card,
and a page from my recent
checking-account book to show
you I have $2,000 in to the
bank. You have also received
my essay on "The Life on the
Nile." I hope my forms of
identification are good enough.
(Included are also 2 of my credit cards.)
Sincerely Yours,
Aurelia Pashenova.

FIGURE 13

The simulation proceeded in part by Fellows pairing up by topic and working
in the classroom and in the library.

The next major event in the interaction between the Institute and the Fellows—between my "letters from the Director" and their responses—was to
solve the problem of what procedures Americans must go through when they
decide to leave the country for a short period of time.

They filled out passport applications—which I had obtained at the local
post office—and complied with U.S. immigration laws and fees—primarily
with Monopoly game money.

Fellows were asked by letter to produce a driver's license and other identification and to show that they had $2000 credit in this country. We decided
that grownups would probably not go abroad without some form of security
here in this country. The class thought that such an institute would probably
not be responsible for so many grownups who were old enough to take care
of themselves. Some showed their security by demonstrating a "line of credit"
on a "credit card statement" and some reproduced "bankbooks" that showed
transactions resulting in a balance of $2000. Figures 13–15 show the documentation one fellow presented to the Institute.

(Figure 13 transcription)
    Included in this letter are my driver's license, my social security card
and a page from my recent checking account book to show that I have

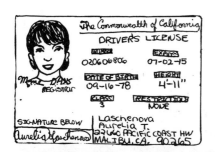

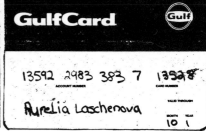

FIGURE 14

NUMBER	DATE	DESCRIPTION OF TRANSACTION	DEBIT	√	FEE	DEPOSIT	BALANCE $4000.00
278	12/1	Telephone Co.	75—				$75.00 / $3,925.00
279	12/2	Gas Company	50—				$50.00 / $3875.00
280	12/13	Filene's Store	200—				$200.00 / $3675.00
~	12/16	Deposit				35—	$35.00 / $3,710.00
281	12/17	Groceries	95—				$95.00 / $3,615.00
282	12/17	Pay for Insurance (Health?)	140—				$140.00 / $3,475.00
283	12/19	Xmas Shopping	250—				$250.00 / $3,225.00
284	12/30	New T.V. set	600.00				$600.00 / $3,625.00
285	1/5	Telephone Bill	120—				$120.00 / $2505.00
286	1/7	Husband's B-day	250—				$250.00 / $2,255.00
287	1/9	Gas Bill	55.00				$55.00 / $2200.00
~	1/10	Deposit				650.00	$650.00 / $2,850.00

(This is a copy of my account-book)

Aurelia T. Laschenova.

FIGURE 15

$2000 in the bank. You have also received my essay on "The Life on the Nile." I hope my forms of identification are good enough. (Included are also 2 of my credit cards.)

Spontaneous unsolicited letters sometimes arrived at the Institute:

January 8, 2009

Dear Mrs. Dr. Cordeiro,
    Sorry, since I have not notified you of my recent move. I have moved to a closer location next to where I work at the Pepperdine University. I still live in Malibu, California, though . . .

    . . . I appreciate you accepting me in your trip to Cairo to learn and experience the history and past of mankind. I have been waiting for this kind of trip and expedition throughout my career. Thank you for accepting me to your scientific research group and I hope I live up to the standards and the goals you have set for us.

Sincerely Yours,
Dr. Aurelia T. Laschenova

P.S.—(pronounced La-shin-o-va)

Fellows were notified that they needed to present a list of items they would be taking for their two week stay in the desert at the site of the dig. They were notified that there were occasionally formal dinners in Cairo but that otherwise things were quite primitive. Each traveler was limited to 40 pounds of luggage. Every list was rare and unique and showed great thought and concern (*see* Figures 16–18). An assignment like this showed me what they were learning about the geography and climate of the region we were studying.

As the simulation proceeded, I felt I needed to focus more on the geography of the region. Most of the expert topics were socially and historically oriented. So the "Director of the Institute" wrote a letter to the "Fellows" notifying them that during the time they were in Egypt, they would have five days off and funding for travel. They needed to submit an itinary of where they would go and why (*see* Figures 19 and 20).

Finally, our reports were finished and we typed them into the computer and printed them into a book entitled "Final Reports 1989–1990, Royal Archeological Institute of Cairo, 1111 Pharoahs Boulevard, Cairo, Egypt," (*see* Figures 21–23) complete with hieroglyphics from our expert in the field.

The Institute posted a notice on the classroom easel that read as follows:

The Royal Archeological Institute of Cairo
Cordially invites you to a
Pre-Publication Report Sharing

Institute Fellows will present summaries of each others' work.

FIGURE 16

Egypt Trip!
2 to 3 weeks

1) 17 blouses (Long sleeved)
2) 19 pairs of pants
3) 20 pairs of socks
4) 2 pairs of sandles 1 pair tennis shoes 1 pair Leather hiking boot
5) tooth brush
6) tooth paste
7) Scope mouthwash
8) 6 towels, 2 hand towels, 3 Faceclothes
9) 4 bars of Dove soap
10) Advil
11) Sinus medicine
12) cough drops
13) 3 dresses light spring dresses long sleeved ankle length
14) make up bag with my toiletries Lipstick, blush
15) Panty hose 2 pairs
16) Gum (Big Red)
17) Sunblock 25 2 bottles
18) hairbrush
19) Hair spray
20) Hair clips, Elastics, baretts
21) 1 bottle shampoo 1 bottle condition
22) Skin Lotion
23) 5 sweaters a few light few heavy

FIGURE 16

FIGURE 17

Samantha Brown My list
1) toothbrush
2) tooth Paste 2 tubes
3) hiking Boots
4) 2 blouses /2 skirts
5) 5 T-shirts
6) 7 pair of shorts
8) My Medication
9) Bandaids /Aa Bandage
11) Sunglasses
12) gum
13) Pens / Paper
14) All info. that I have on
Family Life –
        Samantha Brown
18 Sunflower Ln. Hollywood Calif. 11987

FIGURE 17

FIGURE 18

Dr. Lascheveua   January 16, 2009
2-3 wks. in Cairo   Tuesday

Packing List:

    2 bottles of Sun-tan Lotion
        camera
    6 rolls of film
can Bug-spray
    Money (2000 in traveller's checks)
1 pr. sneakers
1 pr. sandals
    Light-jacket
1 pr. hiking-boots
    water-canteen
(Lots!) chapstick
            Clothing –
4 pairs of blouses
4 pairs of light (Khaki) pants
4 pairs of sox & underwear
3 Bathing-suits
    9 prs nightgowns

FIGURE 18

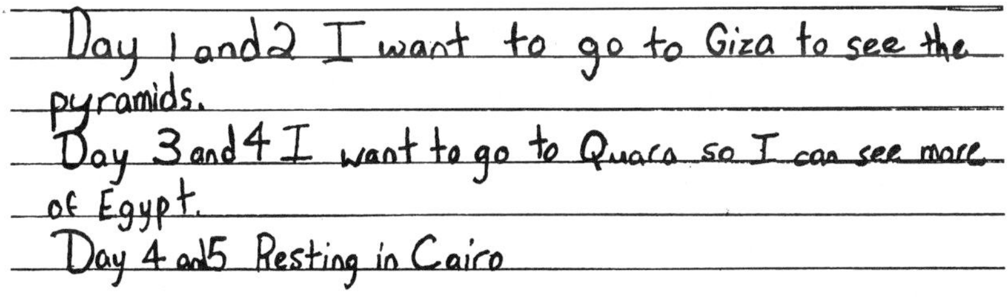

Day 1 and 2 I want to go to Giza to see the pyramids.

Day 3 and 4 I want to go to Quara so I can see more of Egypt.

Day 4 and 5 Resting in Cairo

FIGURE 19

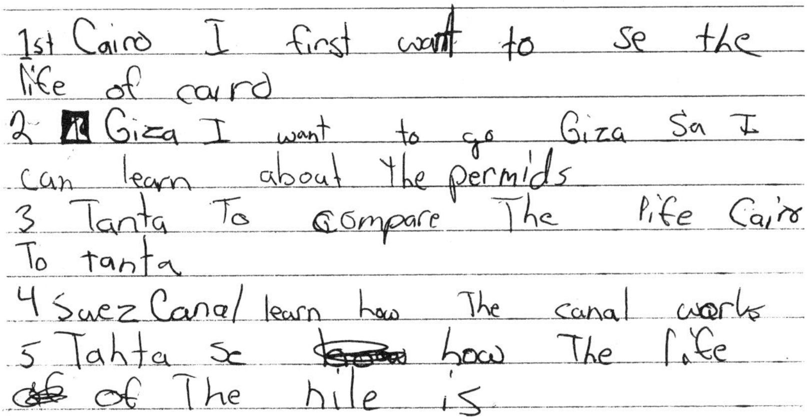

1st Cairo I first want to se the life of caird

2 ⬛ Giza I want to go Giza Sa I can learn about the permids

3 Tanta To compare The life Cairo To tanta

4 Suez Canal learn how The canal works

5 Tahta se ~~known~~ how The life ~~of~~ of The hile is

FIGURE 20

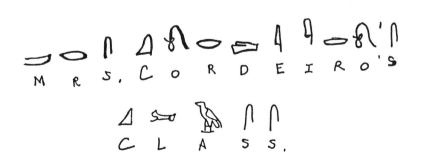

MR S. CORDEIRO'S

CLASS.

FIGURE 21

"DON'T BE SICK
ON YOUR TRAVEL IN THE TROPICS"
The tropical disease guide
by
Dr. _____

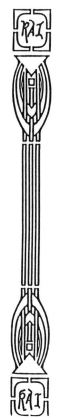

TABLE OF CONTENTS

INTRODUCTION....II

INTESTINAL OBSTRUCTION....III

AFRICAN SLEEPING SICKNESS....IV

AMEBIASIS....V

ONCHOCERCEASIS....VI

THINGS TO REMEMBER....VII

CONCLUSION....VIII

BIBLIOGRAPHY....IX

II. Introduction

This guide will warn you of some of the illnesses in Egypt
or other tropical places.

This guide will include a Table of Contents, a Bibliography,
footnotes, diseases, the symptons, if it's serious, and what
to do if you catch it.

So if you are planning a vacation to the tropics, read this
manual first so an illness won't be the downfall for your
vacation ang remember, make your vacation a safe vacation.

III. INTESTIONAL OBSTRUCTION
(Medical Encyclopedia, Vol. 4, pp. 1327-1328)

WHAT IS IT?

Intestional Obstruction is sort of like a clog in your
intestines. This is a serious illness if it's not treated
right.

FIGURE 22

And that's just what we did. We met in the classroom after recess, with
cookies and juice and made speeches about each other's research. Everyone
had read someone else's report and gave a summary to the other visiting
Fellows. The pre-publication party was a great success.

We did actually "go to Egypt." We took the schoolbus to the Fine Arts
Museum in Boston as a final activity for the Fellows and toured the Egyptian
exhibit. Many of the students had not been there and we had a lot to talk
about. That day, the simulation came to life.

ARCHEOLOGY

An archeologist is like a detective. What an archeologist
does is to try to figure out how the Ancient people lived. We
can learn things like what they ate, what tools they had,
pottery, wall ofundations, and who the.;r enemies were.

But an archeologist can't do everything. They need
climatologists to figure out what the weather was. Still an
archeologist can't do everything. They need botanists to know
what plants existed. Zoologists figured what animal existed
and which were domesticated. Here are some of the things I
learned.

On pages 14 and 15 in a book called "Ancient Egypt," they
talk about how they talk about how they made tombs along time
ago. The first pyramid ever built was for a royal dude. The
most unusual thing I found was the first tomb ever built was a
rectangle.

The next thing they talk about is the Great Pyramid. It
was 275 square yards and stood 479 feet high. The Great
Pyramid was built by 5,000 workers. They would work on the
pyramid every day for twenty years until they finished.

In the article "Yankee Cruises the storied Nile", I
learned about the great Pyramid in Giza. In a picture a guide
stands on top of the Great Pyramid. It was raised 4,5000 years
ago as a tomb for a pharoah named Cheops (Khafu.) A woman
named Mrs. Gilbert climbed the Great Pyramid sat 479 feet high.

In the"Science-Hobby Book of Archeology", I learned that
in Egypt there is a tomb near the Aswan Dam. The water is
raised more every year and it would have covered up the tomb.
So they cut up the tomb like a jigsaw puzzle and moved it 200
feet away from the water level.

The next thing they talk about is King Tut's tomb. In 1923
Howar Carter a student of the famed Egyptologist found King
Tut's tomb. They say when they went to the tomb there was a lot
of traps. They found all kinds of jewelry, spears, gold, silver
and all kinds of other things

T-H-E
E-N-D

-1-Fortimer J. Virginia, The Science-Hobby book of Archeology.
Minneoapolis, Minnesota. 1971 Copywright Pg. 33 to 35. These
pages are about seven Tumes and the Aswam dam.

-2-Hart George, Exploring The Past Ancient Egypt. 1988 C
Galliver books, San Diego, New york, London pg.14 15. It tells
about the early tombs to the late.

-3-Johnson,Irving Electra. "Yankee Cruises the Storied Nile."
In National Geographic, 1965, pages 583-635. This article is
about the tombs of Egypt along time ago.

FIGURE 23

Everyday Life in Early America

This theme, pre-Revolutionary Days, was a difficult one for me at first because I felt it was a period that I knew little about. I was helped by *Early Life in Colonial Times*, a book for grownups about that time period. I did read some of it to the sixth graders who shared the simulation with me, but primarily it served to give me background about the time period.

The problem used to frame this thematic instruction was how English people went about immigrating to the colonies. I had a hard time finding information to help me frame out the possible sequence of activities. This sequence would be controlled by the "letters" that I would write to the "immigrants," and would result from confronting the problems that were encountered by colonial immigrants. Finding out what those problems might have been was very hard and I relied a great deal on logical deduction from my knowledge of the times, coupled with problems that had gone before in simulations.

Because I had such a hard time finding accurate, reliable information on problems of immigrating in the colonial period, this simulation primarily evolved out of issues that occurred once we were underway. Students shared in this creative process; they made suggestions about what real immigrants in the early 1700s might have encountered and what procedures and concerns would have affected them at that time.

There was a lot of fun in this simulation, one which resulted in a schoolwide outdoor "fair" with activities typical of the time period. For us in the sixth grade, the simulation involved lots of reading and writing back and forth, some research, map work, the development of expertise in an area relevant to the problem and the time period, the writing of letters and speeches, and public speaking in character at "town meetings."

This was also the first simulation in which parents, by writing in character, got actively involved in the spirit of the roleplaying. This was a thrilling development for me and opened up all kinds of possibilities I had never considered. I had always worked towards having students involved in the topic and simulation, in character 24-hours-a-day if I could manage it, the way we saw with Ben in the Westward Migration simulation. But the thought of having parents roleplaying too, the thought that a school simulation could become a family activity, was beyond my wildest dreams.

I have since done parts of this simulation with undergraduate and graduate students and had wonderful results. With the graduate students, we had a "board meeting of the Royal Trading and Exploration Company" at which prospective immigrants interviewed each other and reported on plans for immigration to the colonies. Many older students had never done anything like this before. One, a history buff, became the local authority and posted a warrant for the ''arrest'' of the entire Royal Trading and Exploration Company and the immigrants for seditious and treasonous acts. He then proceeded to develop a log for the journey which took a very long time as the immigrants escaped in the night. It was lots of fun.

In the sixth-grade classroom, we communicated in writing in the beginning. As ''Sir Johnathan Hyphen-Smythe, Esquire, Director of the Royal Trading and Exploration Company, 1600 Trevarney Square, London, England, British Empire,'' my first letter was to notify the prospective ''immigrants'' that they had won a lottery for immigration and needed to provide the usual introductory information to the ''Company'' which would be supporting them and making their arrangements (*see* Figure 24).

''Sir Johnathan'' stressed during classtime that the Royal Trading and Exploration Company could never encourage colonists to emigrate if they were unable to support themselves, so an immediate research problem became to acquaint ourselves with possible means of employment of the times. Students paired off and worked in teams to inquire about areas of expertise of interest to them. The immigrants then wrote their introductory letters (*see* Figure 25).

> Hello, my name is Lady Victoria Elizabeth-Smith-Lite. I am writing this letter to tell you that my family and I have gotten your message and we are very pleased and excited about going . . . I am from a wealthy family . . . My husband on the other hand, came from a family of servants loyal to the King and Queen of England. His parents died of disease when he was 11 . . . With some of my money we built an estate which we named Berkshire Hall. That was the beginning of our farm . . .

Students showed great inventiveness. ''Christopher Augustone'' confided in me—in character—that he would share his secret with me but not with anyone else. His secret related to why he wanted to emigrate to the colonies: his Grandfather had buried a treasure there. He wrote to the Royal Trading and Exploration Company:

> Colony For My Emigration—Mass.
> Many years ago in the year 1621 at the age of 21, my Grandfather went to Massachusetts Bay Colony and learned many ways to fish, hunt, plant seeds, etc.
> The Pilgrims told my Grandfather the correct ways to plant seeds and where to plant seeds and how to identify these places. The Pilgrims then told my Grandfather how to set traps and the best way and places to fish.
> When I was ten, my Grandfather was very old. He told me of his———.

Royal Trading Exploration Company

1600 Trevarney Square
London, England
British Empire

Britain Sailing under the Protection of
Her Royal Highnesss Queen Mary II,

Queen of England, Scotland, Ireland, protector of thr Faith;

21 May 1691   and, His Royal Highness William III,
King of England, Stadholder of Holland

To Loyal English Citizens applying for Emigration to the Colonies:-

·Your name has been selected from the Lottery for those loyal English
Citizens applying for Emigration to the Colonies. In order to Qualify
for this long and arduous Journey, please provide the Royal Trading and
Exploration Company with information as follows, :-

   -Letter of Introduction:- Please inform the Royal Trading and
   Information about you and your Family, your present
   Address, Ages, State of Health, & etc.

   -Chosen Destination:- Please inform the Royal Trading and

   Exploration Company as to which Colony you prefer for your
   Emigration. Include Information that proves that you know
   enough about this Colony to make it your Home.

   -Trade or Profession:- Please make Clear what Trade or
   Profession you will Pursue when you are settled in your
   Chosen Colony.   State your background and qualifications
   for this Trade or Profession.   If you were an Apprentice
   give the Name of Your Master. If he is still living, have
   him write a Letter testifying to your Good Performance as
   an Apprentice.

   The Royal Trading and Exploration Company cannot allow any
   Citizens to Emigrate if they are unable to support
   Themselves and their Families.

The Sailing Ship, Her Majesty's Sailing Ship "Henry VIII," will be
sailing on the Tide before May 30, when Wind, Tide and Weather permit.
Therefore, do not Delay to Notify us of this Information.

We remind you that Their Gracious Majesties, Queen Mary II and King
William III, support this Voyage. Therefore, Passage for you and your
Family is Paid in Advance.   Please respond without delay.
God Bless Their Royal Majesties, Queen Mary II and William III, and
Preserve the Royal Empire,

Your Faithful Servant,

Sir Johnathan Hyphen-Smythe, Esquire
Director, Royal Trading and Exploration Company

FIGURE 24

Here, in the text, was a big, blank space. As he read to me, "Christopher
Augustone" whispered when he reached the blank space: "secret treasure."

He said he never told anyone of his————. On the next two days, he
told me of his————, he told me what the Pilgrims told him.
   Two days after he told me of his————, he died. I'm the only one who
knows of my Grandfather's————.

Lady Alexandria Tramaine 22 May 1691

<u>Personal Background</u>

Name - Lady Alexandria Tramaine

Address - 14 Tramaine St.

Age - 27

Health status - good

Kids' names & ages - Mary - 7 and Joshua Adam Jr. - 3

Husband's name - Lord Joshua Adam Tramaine

my occupation - Secratary for my sister Lady Victoria Tramaine

Husbands occupation - a Taylor with his brother

age of husband - 29

<u>Our Destination</u>

We picked, Concord, New Hampshire. The reasons for moving here are, and some things we know are;

    1) It was founded in 1629

    2) There are many Mts.

    3) I have family there

<u>My Profession</u>

    I plan to work with my sister, Lady Victoria Tramaine as her secratary. My husband is working with his brother as a taylor which was inherited by there Grandfather in 1686. They both enjoy doing that job. My husband's brother's name is, Lord Jonathan Tramaine

FIGURE 25A

I hope you will send me to Mass. Bay Colony to have the same experiences that my Grandfather had and because I think it will be challenging and fun.

Some immigrants' letters were tongue-in-cheek and just plain fun.

Dear Royal Trading and Exploration Company,
I am a retired Viking. I've gone straight. My name is James Thorvalson.
I'm from Norway . . .

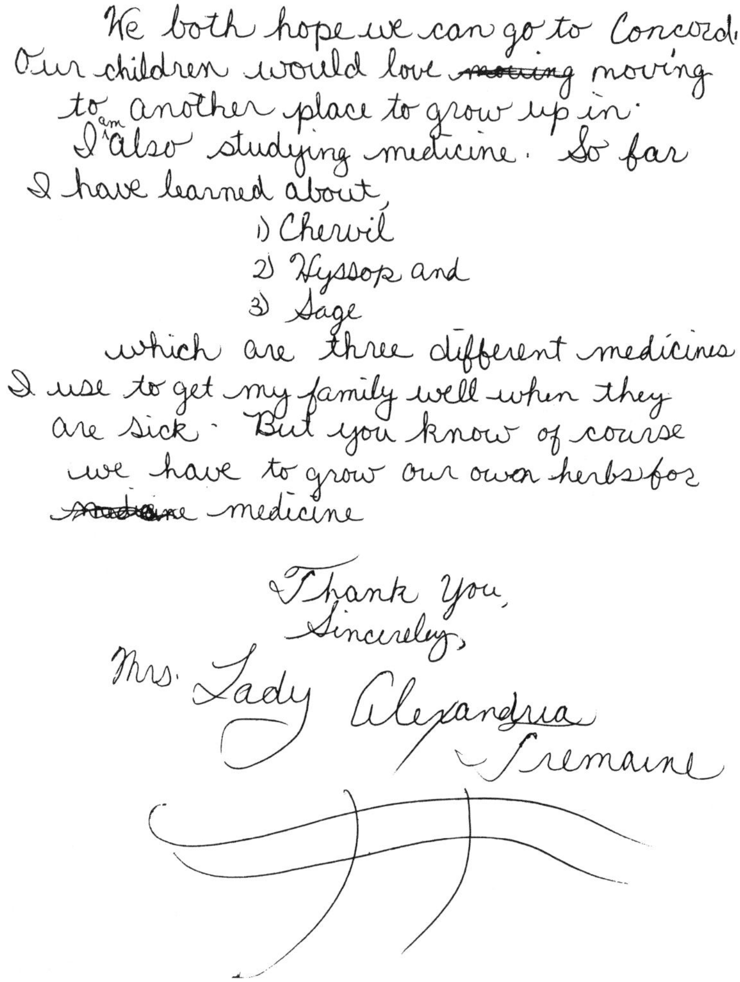

We both hope we can go to Concord. Our children would love ~~moving~~ moving to another place to grow up in. I'am also studying medicine. So far I have learned about,

1) Chervil
2) Hyssop and
3) Sage

which are three different medicines I use to get my family well when they are sick. But you know of course we have to grow our own herbs for ~~medicine~~ medicine

Thank you,
Sincerely,
Mrs. Lady Alexandria Tremaine

FIGURE 25B

The letter continues, giving details of family membership, ages, states of health, and concludes:

I have a wife, Dian. I also have six children, 4 boys and 2 girls. I am 27 years of age. I am in great health.

I wish to go to Williamsburg, Virginia. I visited there once on an accidental voyage to the New World. It is a great climate for growing tobacco and since it's stationed so close to the ocean, I could work on a boat carrying supplies and barter to the other colonies.

I have many qualifications on a boat because of my experience as a

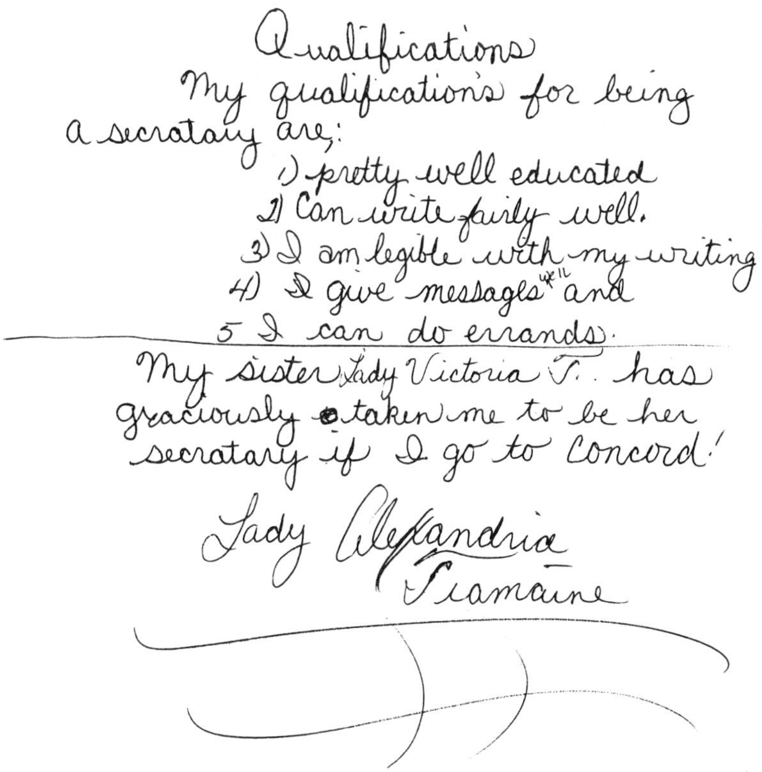

Qualifications
My qualifications for being a secratary are;
1) pretty well educated
2) Can write fairly well.
3) I am legible with my writing
4) I give messages*" and
5 I can do errands.
My sister Lady Victoria T. has graciously taken me to be her secratary if I go to Concord!

Lady Alexandria Tiamaine

FIGURE 25C

Viking. Unfortunately I have no qualifications in the line of growing to-bacco. I hope to learn and give myself a future.

I would like to thank you for this opportunity.

Sincerely, James Thorvalson

It's hard, being a retired Viking—not much call for the job skills. Not much opportunity in many classrooms to actually speculate—as this student has done so successfully—about how a person solves a problem like the development of new job skills in a changing world.

As they wrote at home, some students thought a lot about how literacy has changed since the time of this simulation. "Christopher Augustone" was fascinated with the information that in 1691, elements of composition such as regular spelling and punctuation had not been standardized. Multiple punctuations were common, as evidenced by the writing in the Declaration of Independence and the American Constitution. Figure 26 shows an example

Hear are the things my Grandfather
told me about the New World::-

The best way to plant Seeds is to
dig the hole and tilt the Seeds
before you bury the Seeds.::•|-,

He told me that the best
place to put the traps is under
the trees that the animal eats
from.::•!-.

He also told me the laws
Suchas-It is against the law
to go out Side at night and
that it is against the law to
laugh or Play on Sunday/Lord's day.

It is good he told me
these #Laws so I wan't get fined
or Put in goal :-!-: On the Grant of land
I hope you give me I will Plant tabbacco
and Set up a silver smith Shop
to use my trade.

FIGURE 26

---

of "Mr. Augustone's" Colonial writing. Note how carefully he has reproduced an invented mark more than once. He also has done substantial research
on his self-designated topic. His information is accurate and he has noted and
used the colonial spelling of "jail" as "gaol."

As part of the correspondence back and forth, immigrants wrote a last will
and testament, (*see* Figures 27–29) a warning of the seriousness of the voyage
they were about to undertake. Everyone grasped the essential elements of
writing a document like this. Some were brief: "All my worldly possessions

LAST WILL AND TESTAMENT
of
James Braut Thorvlson

I, James Braut Thorvlson

First: I direct that all my just debts and funeral expenses be paid as soon after my death as may conve·ent.

Second: All my furnishings and personal belonging shall go to my brother Eric John—Thorlson.

Thrird: ~~My estate~~ Seven(7)gold pieces to be donated to the Calvary Church.

Fourth: Ten(10)gold peices ~~to gibe to be~~ devided evenly between Ryan F. Joans and David J. Andrews.

Fith: My ship and 15 gold pieces shall be divided evenly between my two cousins Marc N. Orssaud and Eric F. Orssaud.

Sixth: My summer home shall be given to my brother Eric J. Thorvlson.

Seventh: My estate and all my wealth shall be given to my wife Dian L. Thorvlson and be passed down to my children.

Jim Gohm

Severly sworn to before this 25th day of June, 1691

FIGURE 27

My Will and Testament

If I pass away, on my trip to the New world, I would leave my things with my husband's mother and father. Because mine have died. If we should die and my children are still alive I want my kids to go with my sister, "Lady Victoria Tramaine." But there is still my mother's (valuble) jewelery box which I would like to buried in. Plus all of my Jewelery goes to "Lady Victoria Tramaine.

America
yeah!

Bank Of England

		Money in at the time	
3 sept. 1690 –	$	40.00	ammunition
4 sept. 1690 –	$	10.72	Food, Material
5 sept. 1690 –	$	5.19	Food, 2 pans
25 Dec. 1690 –	$	2.58	x-mas Presents
27 Dec. 1690 –	$	1.19	late x-mas gifts
29 Dec. 1690	$	5.77	Food and bullets (6)
1 Feb. 1691	$	4.12	seeds, leather, bread
24 May, 1691	$	3.97	B-day gifts, seeds, a little food
26 May 1691 – Emm. for trip.	$11.02	Total – 84.56	

then jumped to may

Sig – Lady Alexandria Tramaine

total – 84.56 / even
total – 96.66 / hundred

Mrs. Cordeiro,
I don't know how to put English money into pounds!

$44.33 goes to my sister
$40.33 goes to my husbands Mother and father.

my bank account figures so you know how much money I will split up between my sister and paternal mom & Dad.

is
the money from my will.

$44.33 – Lady Victoria and Husband Lord Jonathan Tramaine

$40.33 – Goes to My husbands mother and father.

FIGURE 28

Last Will and Testament,

Be it Remembered that We,

Sir JONATHAN and Madam CORINNE WELLINGTON

Of London, England, the British Empire,

Being of sound mind and memory, but knowing the uncertainty of our lives, do make This our Last Will and Testament, hereby revoking all former wills by us at any time heretofore made.

After the payment of our just debts and funeral charges, I bequeath and devise as follows:

FIRST: WE GIVE, DEVISE, AND BEQUEATH all of our Estate including all property We may acquire or become entitled to after the execution of this Will, to be divided equally among our Five Beloved Children: Jonathan, Steven, Charlotte, Christopher and Clara, whoever of them shall remain alive and shall not have predecease us at the time of the execution of This Testament.

SECOND: In the event that Our Five children, whosoever of them shall not have predeceased their parents herein named, shall not have attained the ages of 21 years at the time of our deaths, We hereby direct that Madam Corinne's Beloved Mother, VICTORIA FOXWORTH, shall be the sole Guardian of our Beloved Children and the Executrix of Our Estate, and She shall execute the Terms of This Will for the Beneficial INterests of Our Children only and shall not use said Estate or monies thereof for any personal usage.

THIRD: Let it be Known that MADAM CORINNE's Jewelry shall be separate from such said Estate and that She doth Bequeath all of her Jewels to be divided Equally among her daughters, Charlotte and Clara,

FIGURE 29A

We do so direct the Executor of This Will to also
bequeath the Jewelry belonging to Sir Jonathan to
be divided Equally among his sons, Jonathan, Steven and
Christopher.

FOURTH: All Heirlooms from our ancestors shall
be bequeathed herein and divided Equally among our
Five Beloved children whosoever shall remain alive
and shall not have predeceased us.

FIFTH: In the event that I, CORINNE WELLINGTON,
shall die First, Sir Jonathan Wellington, my Beloved
Husband shall be inheritor of this Estate and Executor
of this Testament, and If He shall die First, than I
Corinne Wellington shall be the INheritor and Executrix
of this Testament. Each Inheritor and Executor shall
abide by the Terms of this Will as stated Herein.

SIXTH: WE expressly leave to the discretion of our
Executor during the administration of Our Estate the
retention, continuance, sale, liquidation or other
disposition of any business interest We may have at
said time of our deaths, and if the same shall become
part of my Trust Estate Herein created, I give my Trustee a
like discretion over any such business interest.

SEVENTH: We authorize and empower our Executor to pay,
compromise and settle any Taxes at any time, whether upon
present or future interests, and any compromise
o f such taxes shall be final and binding upon all persons
interested in Our Estate.

EIGHTH: In accordance witht the Laws of Their
Gracious Majesties We hereby request that our Executor
fulfill the Terms of our Last Will and Testament as
stated Herein.

God Bless Their Gracious Majesties, Queen Mary II,
Queen of England, Scotland, Ireland, and Protector of
the Faith, and His Royal Highness William III, King of
England, stadholder of Holland.

FIGURE 29B

In Testimony wherof WE hereunto set our hand and
in the presence of two witnesses declare this to be our
last will this   Twenty-Fifth   day of   May
in the year one thousand six hundred and ninety-one.

Madam Corinne Wellington
Madam Corinne Wellington

Sir Jonathan Wellington
Sir Jonathan Wellington

On this   Twenty-Fifth   day of   May
in the year one thousand sic hundred and ninety-one,
Sir Jonathan and Madam Corinne Wellington of London,
England, British Empire, did sign the foregoing
instrument in our presence, declaring it to be Their
last will; and thereafter as witnesses thereof we two
at Their request and in Their presence, and in the
presence of each othe, hereto subscribe our names.

Lynne Tudor
Lynne Tudor

Abigail Foxworth
Abigail Foxworth

SUBSCRIBED AND SWORN TO BEFORE ME BY SAID TESTATOR AND
SAID WITNESSES THIS   Twenty-Fifth   DAY OF   May
AD 1691.

Samuel Killingly
Notary Public, whose

commission expires: 12/30/1695

Samuel Killingly

FIGURE 29C

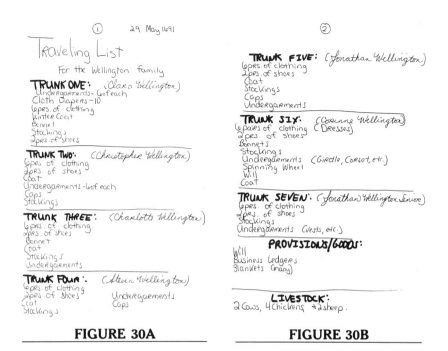

FIGURE 30A   FIGURE 30B

will go to my wife who will hopefully divide evenly between my children in her will. If we all die at sea, give all my stuff to my uncle in Worcester, England.'' Some were quite detailed. All included witnesses. One included a reproduction of recent transactions at ''the Bank of England'' to document how much money was being divided between surviving family members. One was three pages long, typed, and was an accurate adaptation of a real-life model.

All reflected a clear understanding of what kind of things people in 1691 would be willing to survivors: ''my jewelry . . . my paintings . . . my horses, cows, chickens, pigs, . . . and my clothing and all my kitchen utensils.'' In fact, wills of the time were often a detailed listing of limited household goods, right down to the last pair of stockings.

''The Royal Trading and Exploration Company'' also required a detailed listing of items to be transported and specified the amount of space available. As Figure 30 shows, the lists were very detailed and reflected students' in-depth understanding of the times and their thoughtful concern for their ''families.''

Some immigrants decided to hire an indentured servant, responding to the colonial equivalent of junk mail from ''Killingly, Johosophat & Snydely, Brokers-at-Large.

The "contracts" drawn up by the immigrants specified the term of service, the responsibilities, fees and payment for services (*see* Figure 31).

Some immigrants provided "letters of recommendation" testifying to their good character and ability to work. This was where parents got involved on their own, often writing as "Masters" under whom the immigrant had served an apprenticeship. One wrote: ". . . he hath been over the nine years of service the most honorable and delight of workers . . . He has shown . . . great talent and gift in his trade and no doubt will do so for you . . ."

Most of this simulation was carried on by correspondence. Often the immigrants would simply leave their responses in the "mailboxes"—individual manila folders for each student—and receive their next letter as homework. I found that I did not have to go to great lengths to get them involved. They were involved on their own. I often heard pairs of students when they were on their own talking in character, using their roleplaying names. In some ways, the simulation almost happened without me.

Some days, just to keep us all on track, I would post a notice from the Royal Trading and Exploration Company on the classroom easel. Sometimes it simply asked immigrants to sign the "ship's log" or to register to send a letter home by "mail packet."

> Dear Christopher,
> Sorry I haven't written in so long. Just so much has been happening.
> My wife has not been feeling well for at least a week now. I have been trying herbs but nothing seems to work. Do you have any suggestions of what could be wrong and what I should try?
> Aside from that, everything's been good. I made friends; the house is finished; we have great tasting oranges in our backyard and now I'm working on an addition for my house.
> I have a few questions for you: is the business good? How's the climate? Do you have any sprouts from your plants? How's the family?

This simulation happened at the end of a busy year. A few days before the end of school, we all decided to finish things up "in the colonies." I posted a notice from the Royal Trading and Exploration Company that a year had gone by, everyone was settled in the colonies, and all should request a "license or a grant of land." This would require that they go before a town meeting and make a speech. All colonists were required to sign up and indicate the kind of license or land grant they were requesting (*see* Figure 32).

Everyone wrote and rehearsed speeches and for two afternoons we had small mock town meetings. No one objected to the fact that they had all settled in different colonies but all were appearing before the same town meeting. In games, rules are flexible and no one knows this better than elementary school students.

```
              Sir and Madam Jonathan and Corinne
                         WELLINGTON

              ABIDING AT      23 Cobblestone Lane
                             London, England

                             British Empire
   24 May 1591


   TO:   Killingly, Johosophat & Snydely, Esq.
             Brokers-at-Large

       Upon having received your letter questioning whether
   we shall sponsor an Indentured Servant to come to the
   Colonies, I am responding as Follows:

              My Family and I do Hereby sponsor an
              Indentured Servant to travel to the Colonies, and
              whose terms of service shall be:

              1.    My Family and I shall be responsible for paying
              One-Half of the Servant's Passage to the Colonies,
              which shall include all Fees and Taxes.

              2.    We shall provide board and room for said
              Servant in the Colonies for the term of Seven Years.

              3.    After the term of Seven Years, we will pay
              the sum of Five Pounds so as this Indentured Servant
              may be assisted to have his own home.

              4.    For a Period of Seven Years, the Indentured Servant
              will perform agreed-on services for myself and
              Family as according to a signed and Sworn Contract
              drawn up by the Bonded and Licensed Brokerage House
              listed herein.

   Having been a believer in and understanding of the Quest
   for Freedom, I do Hereby solemmly pledge my sponsorship
   of one INdentured Servant.

   God Bless Their Royal Majesties, Queen Mary II, and King
   William III, and Preserve the Royal Empire.

                              Yours Faithfully,
```

Sir & Madam Jonathan Wellington III

              Sir and Madam Jonathan Wellington III

FIGURE 31

February 17, 1692

For those petitioning for a license:
Please sign your name and indicate
what kind of Licence or Grant you will require:

Name	License or Grant
Marylyn E. Taylor	Teaching License
Sir Raybern Andrews II	Land Grant
Lady Victoria Tramaine	Job license + land grant
Gabriella Maples	land grant
Madam (Corinne) Wellington II	Land Grant/License for tobacco store
James Thorvalson	Land Grant (½ acre)
Eric Williams II	Land Grant & license for Blacksmith shop
Sonia A. Jones	Land Grant & Job License
Lady Alexandria Tramaine	Land grant for tailors shop
James Feildmore III	Gunsmithing license
Lady Victoria Lite	Land Grant
Christopher Augustone	land grant & license
Fred Swarchanegga II	Land Grant

FIGURE 32

The meetings were a great success. I left the speaking arrangements up to individuals. That is, I did not give classes on public speaking. Many systems for making a good speech were tried out, from sentences on 3 × 5 cards to elaborately revised written documents. One "colonist" rehearsed her speech in private and then wrote on the top of the paper she was speaking from, "Look up—Slowly—Speak clearly" and at the bottom of the page she patted herself on the back.

> Look up
> Slowly
> Speak clearly
> Hello, My name is Marilyn Elizabeth Taylor. I have a daughter of eight, Carol Anne.
> First of all, I'd like to tell you a little about my background. I grew up in London, England and was schooled there. I married John Taylor and two years later, we had Carol Anne. Just four years ago John passed away. I stayed with a friend until I got my feet on the ground again. I met Johnathan Colbert and became his assistant. I plan to move to Jamestown, Virginia where I'll be staying with friends until I've enough money to support my child and I.
> Thank you.
> Bow, come up slowly, look at audience. Good Job.

Colonists at the town meeting were allowed to ask three questions of the speaker. The questions reflected a concern with the speaker's ability to make use of the license or the land grant and also a knowledge of issues of the times. One speaker who was requesting a license was asked to defend his qualifications as a gunsmith. He drew himself up to his full colonial height and replied with great dignity, "I never comment on my work."

Working Within Simulations

Blending and integrating is easiest to accomplish when it is framed in the context of a simulation, or imaginary role-playing within a scenario. Here, students fulfill academic tasks for a created authentic purpose in the service of performing a larger job. "Wagonmasters" calculate the weight of household goods in a wagon, "settlers" measure and design land grant settlements, and Fellows at the Institute lay out squared grids for archeological work.

Looking in from the outside, the taking on of a character—the playing of a role—and the element of pretend may appear artificial, but for the participant it has a powerful and authentic effect. I have done mini-simulations with adults and found, even there, the same wholehearted entrance into the realm of the simulation that I have observed with elementary school students. Together, participants enter a negotiated world and share their knowledge and interests.

The power of pretend and people's own flexible reality elevates learning to a higher plane, blurring the walls of the classroom and the established relationships. Participants in such a "play" can be anything they like and their learning takes on new dimensions.

When I work with students in this condition of literate immersion in a simulation topic, I try to blend in as much as I can throughout the day, using reading, writing, speaking and listening as threads. But two considerations are limiting factors: when the blending and integrating becomes "stretched" and inauthentic, and when blending and integrating becomes an end in itself, obscuring my goal.

In the first case, when blending and integrating becomes inauthentic or artificial, I realize I am verging on the "bears' birthday party," described earlier in this book, a situation where I'm working so hard to integrate everything that I'm creating odd links. For instance, if the Fellows at the Institute of Cairo were suddenly asked to take an intelligence test or some such thing so that I could work the memorizing of division facts into the simulation, that would feel like an artificial linkage and would create a very inauthentic situation. As a class, we might even laugh about it, and something of the reality of the world we had jointly created would be lost in the process. Professional archeologists would not suddenly be asked to take an intelligence test in the middle of the desert. My students would know this and so would I.

In the second instance, when the blending and integrating becomes an end in itself, the simulation would be in danger of collapsing under its own weight. For instance, if I were to make students stay in character, we might get so snarled up in trying to do some small routine bits of work that we would never get past it. Staying in character is the business of those who hold the character and I have found that my proper role is to stay out of it, except within the lines of the simulation. I never, for example, talk to my students in character unless we are working on the simulation. I never speak as the "Director" unless I am distributing letters or posting a notice or unless I am clearly working within the bounds of the "game."

Now it may be that some students go around in character all the time. They don't tell me of course, and maybe they don't tell anyone. But I have heard my sixth graders talking to each other as "Institute Fellows" when they were in the halls, calling each other by their invented names, discussing Institute business. I call that a bonus.

In either case cited, we maintain the integrity of the simulation by simply forgetting it sometimes and going about our daily business. Blending and integrating works best when everyone is involved and enthusiastic.

I don't have books to recommend for help in integrating social studies. The books and articles written by Dorothy Heathcote that I have cited in this section are the only ones I used to help me. Some chapters in Nancie Atwell's edited collection, *Coming to Know*, are helpful and are directed at social studies work. Several social studies strategies in *Whole Language Strategies for Secondary Students* could serve as jumping off places for broader work with simulations.

"The Mantle of the Expert"

Dorothy Heathcote and Phyl Herbert speak of the power of role-reversal in working with children, in which the child assumes the "mantle of the expert." In this learning experience, "the teacher assumes a fictional role which places the students in the position of being 'the one who knows' or the expert in a particular branch of knowledge" (1985, p. 175).

In simulations like these, the traditional teaching situation is altered so that "communication is invested with the group" (p. 174). In the last simulation described, I stepped aside. My role was truly that of "journey-maker," in Dorothy Heathcote's words. I was not the primary knowledge base. Rather, participants drew their knowledge from a multitude of sources.

Why do I enjoy this teaching situation so much? It is because I am engaged, too. I am an enabler, "placed with the group" (p. 174). When my students are lost in the roleplaying, so am I. It is an exciting experience when "a class becomes engaged with the teacher in the task of developing understanding" (p. 171).

The real excitement in working in social studies through such simulation activities is best expressed by Dorothy Heathcote & Phyl Herbert:

> Encouraging students to assume the mantle of the expert and to play out their respective roles in projects . . . enables drama to fulfill its primary function—namely, the exploration of the affairs of humankind. (p. 180)

Integrated Learning:
Science Lab

Remembering Science

When I was in school I never could figure out what science was. We had our science book, of course, and we read about a lot of different things and memorized words like *lever* and *fulcrum, oxygen* and *amphibian*. We looked at a lot of pictures—sometimes by ourselves in our textbooks and sometimes all together when the pictures were on big charts. Then they were usually of the inside of a volcano, the inside of somebody's body, how a plant looked if you could see under the ground, or the earth in between the sun and the moon.

But I never could get it all together in my mind, this world of science. My dad once brought home a bat in a shoebox, a live bat from the aircraft engine plant where he worked. We kept it overnight looking at it, and then he let it go. That seemed like science, too.

He brought home other things, too—a micrometer so we could each measure one of our hairs, live butterflies and moths to look at and then release, plants and flowers and things that had caught his interest. The bat was the best.

He used to take us outside to look up at the sky, to study the stars, to watch for satellites, to see an eclipse of the moon. He loved airplanes and we would watch them fly overhead and talk about what the jet trails were and why the sound barrier could be broken. It all seemed like science—but it didn't seem to have much to do with what I read about in school.

Even when we did an experiment with beans in sixth grade, growing some in a dark closet and some on the window ledge, it didn't connect to science in my mind. The ones in the closet didn't do too well, in spite of all our care—and we learned a new meaning for the word *chlorophyll*, which was just beginning to come into common, childhood use, as something nice in chewing gum. But I still had no sense of science, of its role, or purpose in education and in life, or in how one went about it.

From my dad and mom, I learned to look and investigate. And in the long run, that has taught me more science than I learned in my textbooks. John Passmore (1980) writes about seeing: "In general, to learn is to be better prepared to learn by observation" (p. 63). The teacher's role, the mentor's role, the parent's role is to arouse interest and provide information. My sister and I agreed, one of the most valuable gifts our parents gave us was their deep love of the world around them, their ongoing interest in it, and their sharing of observations.

So in science, as in the rest of the subjects, I looked back and found that I didn't want to teach the way I was taught. While I wanted to lay down a foundation of basic science knowledge for my students, I also wanted to sustain their natural curiosity, to give them the gift of seeing, and help them to gain insight into what scientists do and why they do it.

From my life with textbooks, I did not gain a "foundation of basic science knowledge" or a way of seeing, or even the ability to perform the scientific method. I have spent the last three years, idly in the back of my mind, trying to remember what the four basic machines are. I know it was in those books. Now it is an idle curiosity.

Whole Learning and Science

Most of my present foundation of basic science information has come from television, probably over the last ten years. I—like some children and a lot of grown-ups I know—have learned a lot from what is commonly known as "public television broadcasting," those stations which broadcast programs with names like "Nature" and "Miracle Planet" and "Wild America."

With students I tried to draw on the visual, real world. We did some work in science from books, but very little. Usually when we used books in science in my upper elementary classroom, they were either very good picture storybooks with strong science content, like Joanna Cole's *Magic Schoolbus* series or Joanne Ryder's *The Snail's Spell* or her *Catching the Wind*, or publications like *National Geographic*. We didn't do much science work from "dense print."

Once in a while, I would transliterate a difficult book for sixth graders as I read it out loud to them. I did that one year with David Bodanis' *The Secret House: 24 Hours in the Strange and Unexpected World in Which We Spend our Nights and Days*, a book about the microscopic world around us. It was hard to read, but once we got into it, we loved it. Especially the microphotography of things like bedbugs and dust mites and the funny-looking things that live on dishtowels. The dust mites were our favorites. I sat inside the semicircle of desks and before I began reading, all the students would stand up and lean over their desks and shake their arms on the rug, feeding the dust mites because we had read that they lived on "tiny rafts of human skin. . . . these mites only have to wait, mouth up, for this perpetual haze of skin flakes to rain down on them" (pp. 15–16). The book was full of the wonders of the microscopic world around us. They usually asked me to read it right before lunch.

In fourth, fifth and sixth grade, we did a lot of activities. In sixth grade, one ongoing activity centered around a comprehensive, multi-media, purchased science kit known as "The Voyage of the Mimi." This program comes in two "expeditions" and each has a video tape series, student workbooks, teacher editions, activity kits, computer programs and computer hardware. This kit is available through Bank Street Educational Services in New York.

Many of the activities we did in the sixth grade related to our work with the "Mimi" project, activities related to the ocean, to environmental and ecological concerns. Most of the activities were ongoing and drew on data from the real world around us.

Sometimes, at my suggestion, we would all go home to do observations at the end of the day. We might, for example, try to determine by looking whether birds walk or hop when they are on the ground. Some walk, like pigeons, some hop, like blue jays and sparrows, and there are some that walk and hop, like crows. We tried to closely observe whether birds jump before they fly. Or do they just sort of fall off the branch?

We kept track of weather, we read the newspaper and discussed new scientific findings—I read and interpreted sometimes. We went outside to look up at the sky a lot during the day, and we talked about things we observed. We did experiments individually, often at home.

In this chapter, I'll be describing some of the activities we did in my upper elementary classrooms as we tried to get a sense of science, as we tried to "do what scientists do." As in all other learning in my classroom, the focus was always first on the process we were going through and then on the content we were learning. In science this is most important, for in elementary school, students are beginning to grasp the processes involved in the scientific method. And so, as we do science, we observe, classify, hypothesize, experiment, test, and revise our hypotheses. We search for patterns, disjunctions, connections and disconnections. We find meaningful ways to interpret and communicate our findings. We relate what we are learning and how we are learning it to other things in science that we might like to learn. That's the process of learning in science.

Charting and Graphing

One of the continuing activities that I did with students in fourth, fifth, and sixth grade involved making charts and graphs. I have found that students coming up through the primary grades have quite a bit of experience with reading and interpreting graphs—it is part of standardized testing and so is in all kinds of workbooks and activity sheets. Students are generally quite good at receiving information from pictographs, bar graphs, line graphs and sometimes even pie graphs.

But standardized tests cannot accommodate the construction of charts, so this tends to be downplayed in most educational materials. And creating charts involves a whole different set of skills and problems than reading and interpreting charts.

The first thing that surprised students in my classrooms as they began to construct their own graphs is the amount of decision-making involved. There are many, many choices to be made by any graphmaker. Some of the choices are contingent on the type of information to be graphed, some of them are practical matters, some are aesthetic: Should I graph the dates down the side or along the bottom of the graph? Should I go by hours or half-hours? Should I use big or small squared graph paper? How will I know till I make a graph and use it for a few days?

And that usually was what happened when we began to develop charts and graphs. Students—with my help and experience—constructed a graph, tried it out for a few days, and then often decided that they needed to make changes. Sometimes there is no way to know how to make good decisions until you have worked with the data a little. The lessons are invaluable, for they teach not only about charting and graphing, but also about the data. Students who graph data must learn a lot about what they are tracking. There is as much to be learned about the data from the construction of a good graph as there is from the interpretation of it.

And what did we graph? We began by working with the almanac in the local newspaper. There is a tremendous amount of information in such an almanac and students graphed the following:

the daily temperature

the daily highest temperature in the U.S. and where it was

the daily lowest temperature in the U.S. and where it was

the time of sunrise

the time of sunset

daily length of the day

daily height of one high tide

daily time of one high tide

daily height of one low tide

daily time of one low tide

Some students used a ''farmer's almanac,'' the kind you can buy in the fall in the supermarket, and expanded the range of available information for graphing to include:

the time of moonrise

the time of moonset

daily length of time the moon is overhead

To accommodate this study of graphing data, I made available different kinds of graph paper, different both in the overall size, some 9″ × 12″, some 12″ × 18″, and in the grid available, anywhere from ¼″ to 1″ square. Some kinds of graphs require big grids. Some require small. Some people have preferences for the scale on which they work.

The biggest and most pressing decisions a graphmaker faces when first confronted with the task of designing a graph is what elements will actually be on the graph, what will be on each axis, and what increments will be used for each. Students making graphs quickly learned words like ''axis'' and ''increment'' because they needed them to talk to each other. That is why people learn a technical vocabulary—not simply for the sake of learning it, but because it is just too hard to work together without it.

In deciding what would actually be graphed, some students needed help and others didn't. In creating the graph, some forgot that dates need to be one of the graphing categories if they are keeping a daily record of something. Some needed help in reading the information from the almanac and sorting out which information they needed.

Once the two graphing categories were established, students had to decide which axis to use for each category. This matters because graphs are commonly read from left to right, which means that the specific information being graphed must be indicated along the vertical axis, up the left side of graph, while the dates—if dates are needed—must be written along the bottom, on the horizontal axis.

Once this was learned, students had to decide if they would make a line graph or a bar graph. This had to be decided first, I have discovered, because it impacts on whether the dates—and the intervals of information—are written on the line or in the space. If the graph is to be a line graph, then the increments need to be written on the lines, so that there are clear intersections for the points that get connected to make the line. If the graph is to be a bar graph, then the increments need to be written in the spaces, so that the bar can be filled in. This was very hard to grasp in the beginning.

Most students agreed that bar graphs look nicer but they take longer. However, bar graphs were the delight of some students' hearts. I had students who began to develop affinities for bar graphs in fourth grade, working with me, and were experts by the time they reached sixth grade, where the work continued as I taught them again. But in spite of these colorful, careful models, most students opted for line graphs.

I had one student who did a line graph of the daily lowest temperature in the United States. Next to each entry, she wrote the name of the city which had recorded the lowest for that day. Beside the line graph, on the bulletin board, she did a scattergram with colored pins on a map of the United States to show the cities which were recording the lowest temperatures. The data display was very effective.

A big problem for many students was deciding on what increment to use. If students were charting sunrise, for example, then they had to use one-minute intervals, usually from about 5:00 A.M. to about 7:00 A.M., on the time axis because sunrise changes from day to day by only one to three minutes. The boundaries of the time axis must be determined by how long in the year the students are keeping the charts. We usually kept our charts every day all year so that we established a good database to study.

However, if students were charting moonrise or moonset, they had to use half-hour intervals on a 24-hour basis, since the moon comes and goes over a 24-hour period. This makes a very big chart if the student uses a large grid. One such chart covered the back of the door, with graph paper taped together.

I encouraged students to be creative in the design of their charts. I have a

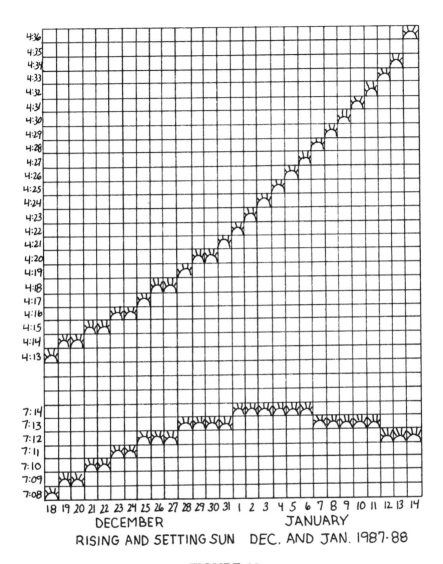

RISING AND SETTING SUN   DEC. AND JAN. 1987-88

FIGURE 33

friend, Whitney Powell, who is a graphic artist, and she has made me aware of the power of graphs that incorporate their content into their design. *Time* magazine is particularly good at this. For instance, if the line graph is about changing hemlines, the line itself would be drawn to resemble lace, rather than just a line, so a viewer immediately begins to think about the content as the chart is analyzed.

The most successful, student-developed graph like this was from a fourth grader. She decided to graph the daily sunrise and sunset on the same chart

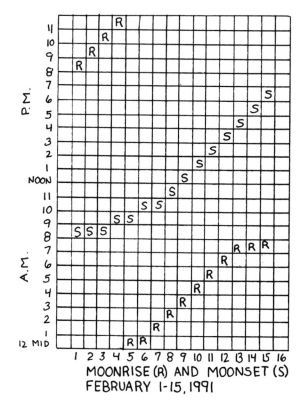

MOONRISE (R) AND MOONSET (S)
FEBRUARY 1-15, 1991

FIGURE 34

and used inch-square graph paper, many pieces taped together. We hung the chart in the hallway, and eventually it stretched all the way down the hall to the lobby. She constructed a line graph, but used little cut-out half-circles that looked like rising and setting suns, yellow for the rising suns and orange for the setting (*see* Figure 33). She glued each into the proper square and each touched the one next to it, constructing the lines of the graph.

It was a beautiful chart and the converging lines showed the sun rising later and setting earlier each day in the fall until the winter solstice. At the solstice, the lines made by the little yellow and orange suns began to diverge, as the sun rose earlier and set later with the advent of spring and summer. The resulting picture looked from a distance like an hourglass on its side. At the end of the year she rolled up this huge chart and took it home.

One student did a huge chart of the moonrise and moonset times, showing the changing length of the "moonday" in between the marks for the times (*see* Figure 34). It was the first time I really had a chance to think about how variable the habits of the moon are and how hard it is to see the patterns.

We saved the newspaper almanacs throughout the year, so that students who fell behind could get caught up, or students who decided to track a different set of information could do that. Some students kept two graphs.

During the year, we charted other things. We collected original data, temperatures, rainfall, and made graphs of those. We made graphs of the highlights of our own lives. And all the time, we kept graphing the information in the almanac.

At intervals in the year, we wrote about the patterns we saw developing on each others' charts. Once clear patterns began to emerge, we made predictions about what might happen to the patterns as the year went on. We wrote descriptions of what the graphs in the classroom—or the graphs that lined the halls nearby—were about so that visitors would know what they were looking at. We wrote titles for the graphs and made legends and keys for any special symbols on them.

Every so often, we spent the better part of the day working on our charts, especially when we were setting them up. It takes a surprisingly long time to do this well. And part of my personal agenda was to stimulate pride in product in my students so I needed to give them the time it took to do the careful measuring, writing, labeling and coloring that they did so willingly. I found care and concern for graphs from most of my students no matter what their age.

Special Projects

Each year, in sixth grade, we engaged in two special projects in science. There were other projects that happened from year to year, making ecosystems in terrariums, creating dioramas to show different environments, playing computer simulations that taught us about survival and how ecology works. But there were two projects that we worked on over a long term, usually with the other sixth grade. These projects could have been done at any of the upper elementary grades. They were the Moldy Bread Contest and the Egg Drop Contest.

Neither one was really a contest, even though we called them that. Sometimes we talked about what kind of prize might be awarded for winning a "moldy bread contest"—what could it be? A book on molds? A moldy piece of fruit? A new loaf of bread? And what on earth would a person get for winning an "egg drop contest?" In that contest, it was a reward enough not to lose.

Sometimes there were little prizes—stickers, pencils, a book—but mostly, we did the projects for the fun of it. The winning was in succeeding at either of the projects.

The Moldy Bread Contest was just that. Students were asked to grow a piece of moldy bread at home. Usually, in the beginning, they had two weeks to do it, but as the contest wore on, time spread out, and it often took as long as a month for students to get a good entry.

I always offered to explain the project to their parents, just in case there were any problems with such an odd assignment, but no one ever seemed to have a problem once they explained it clearly. I always reminded them that some people are highly allergic to molds, that they should not be inhaled, and that they should be kept in a private place away from human population.

Most students grew their entries in a closet or in a drawer. It was not unusual to have a parent help and then the moldy bread was cultivated in the kitchen. We also had other moldy entries as the contest evolved. Moldy vegetables, particularly squash, were quite popular in one class.

Once the challenge went out—"Create a piece of moldy bread within two weeks and bring it to school"—the discussion began: How on earth does bread—or anything—get moldy? What is mold, anyway? In the beginning of the project, I did not provide information. Part of my goal in the assignment was to encourage the students to seek out sources for themselves, to do research on the topic. One year a girl told me with great glee, about two days into the project, that she had found it all in the school library, in an encyclopedia—complete instructions on how to grow moldy bread. She didn't tell anybody else.

I did make sure that sources were available in the school library—although the encyclopedia was a surprise—but I was also interested in stimulating two other sources of data collection: experience through experiment, and interviews with experts; there are a lot of grown-ups who know how mold grows.

The standards for "winning" were established at the beginning of the project. The more colorful and larger the molds, the better. Also, the molds had to be alive, that is they had to be submitted for inspection while they were still moist and soft, not after they were dried out and powdery.

And so the two weeks went by each year. After the first few days, reports would come in: "My mold has started to grow," "I had a mold growing but it died—it got all dried out and powdery." After a few more days, some students would report the development of colors in some of their mold experiments.

By this time, there was much talk of sure-fire ways to get good moldy bread, how to "feed it," what "foods" were best, what base was best, degrees of dampness, what kinds of conditions molds like best. After the first week, each year, everyone came to agree that bread from the bakery, bread without preservatives, grew the best bread mold. That got us started thinking about the role of preservatives in food.

Some students didn't have much luck—a couple of experiments were accidentally thrown out by moms in the act of cleaning, somebody's dog ate the experiment which was behind the bed. Those students started over and were given time extensions. Some students discovered moldy "finds"—a food with mold that was already started—and they set about to learn how to keep it growing.

Each year we did some writing about how the experiment had gone, how we had set it up, and what our theories were. Before growing began, I asked the students to write out what they knew about molds from their own experience (*see* Figure 35 and 36).

(Figure 35 transcription)
Mold is a fungus. It needs a warm, dry climate to grow well. Mold usually starts growing on some sort of old food. It starts growing in about a week after some mold spores hit the old food. After about two weeks, the mold dies. When it dies, the spores from it spread elsewhere.

(Figure 36 transcription)
"What I know about molds"
I don't know anything for a fact but I think some stuff that may or may not be true. Mold grows on foods when they are old. I think moisture helps things get moldy. I don't know how to grow mold or anything like that. So I guess I have a lot to learn.

After about two weeks, some students brought in their entries. We kept them on the counter near the radiator where it was warm, but not too near. Some students were very protective of the molds they had grown and knew that too much heat was as bad as too little for such fragile experiments. Some of the molds had names on tags, like "Charlie." Some students kept their molds covered, others theorized that open air was better. Some students were given permission to keep growing them at home. Nobody wanted to bring in a mold until it was ready.

Theories abounded as the products were brought in each year. I gave no positive, "this is the only way" statement. We looked at the molds through magnifying glasses and sometimes students went back several times during the day to check and compare the entries.

Mold

Mold is a fungus. It needs a warm, dry, climate to grow well. Mold useally starts growing on some sort of old food. It starts growing in about a week after some mold spores hit the old food. After about two weekes the mold dies. When it dies the spores frome it spread elswere.

FIGURE 35

"What I know about Mold"

I don't know anything for pact but I think some stuff that may or may not be true. Mold grows on foods when they are old. I think mosture helps things get moldy. I dont know how to grow mold or anything like that. So I guess I have alot to learn.

FIGURE 36

My mold paper
Here are the steps I took
① I took a piece of bread & put it in a ziplock bag. I kept checking on it but for some reason it didn't grow.
② I decided to blow air in to it for moisture and it still didn't grow.
③ My mom found mold in a tomato paste can so I spread it on the bread, put it in the bag, blew air into it & put it on the top of the refridgirator.
Now it is still trying to grow.

FIGURE 37

My mold

My mold process is going okay. I
put it ~~into the~~ in a baggy and
put it in the back of my bread drawer.
You can see a couple of dark
dots but not a lot. I am watching it
every day to see how it is progressing.
I am growing it on another
piece of bread to but nothing is
happening really.

FIGURE 38

We did on-site observations once the entries came in. In their writing, students combined some of the theory they had learned through research and the observations they had made as they experimented.

Students in process learning classrooms are skilled at describing the process they have gone through. So in this science project, they were asked to describe in detail, to write an informal "lab report," (*see* Figures 37 and 38) about how they went about growing moldy bread at home.

After a reasonable length of time, the contest would end. The entries stayed with us for a long time and every so often students would check them. Gradually the interest in keeping them alive was replaced with an interest in growing spring flowers. Sometimes we talked about the similarities between the two processes.

The "Egg Drop Contest," first described by Al Renner at Cal Tech (Renner, 1977), was developed for our use in the form I'm describing by the other sixth grade teacher, Helen Motto, and both sixth grades engaged in it every April. In this contest, the object was to build a system that would prevent a raw egg from breaking when dropped from near the classroom ceiling to the floor, a height of about eight feet. During the actual "contest"—again, we usually had no prizes—the entrants would stand carefully on the counter, reach toward the ceiling and drop their eggs onto the plastic covered area on the floor. Most eggs broke.

Students worked at home to prepare their entries. There was much talk about how it was going, but not much sharing of sure-to-be-perfect systems. It became a challenge to preserve the egg.

Over the years, there were many ingenious systems. Many encased their eggs in styrofoam, cotton, cloth, or foam rubber. Some built boxes that held the egg rigid in the center of a padded box. Some suspended their eggs in Jello, and one put hers in a water balloon. Some altered the outside of the egg itself with fixatives and filming solutions.

All these things were "legal." We had no restrictions on the size of the "saving" device or on the materials used. The only hard and fast rule was that the egg could not be hard-boiled. Winning entries were officially cracked open by the teachers with great ceremony to demonstrate that they were indeed legal entries.

It got messy, but we had a lot of fun. We learned after a year or two not to let the preparation for the contest go on too long. One year a losing entry broke. The contestant had carefully packed it into its capsule two or three weeks before and kept it—unrefrigerated—on the bureau in the bedroom. When it broke, we all had to leave the room for quite a while.

In both of these projects, the students developed a sense of experimentation and exploration to such a degree that any notion of "contest" was forgotten as the project got interesting. Accomplishing the project became the goal, and even though good-spirited competition continued, no one seemed to worry about winning. That's what scientists do, too—they work hard to be the first to do something, to explore something successfully, and succeeding is the reward.

Moonwatching

One of the major ongoing science projects in my upper elementary classrooms was called "moonwatching." Moonwatching is just what it sounds like: we watched the moon, recorded sightings, and tried to understand its habits. Eleanor Duckworth, professor at Harvard's Graduate School of Education, started me on moonwatching in her graduate class entitled "Teaching and Learning." Moonwatching enables a teacher-in-coursework to become an active learner again, and what generally results is a reconstruction of prior knowledge. Eleanor writes:

> As a student of Piaget, I was convinced that people must construct their own knowledge and must assimilate new experiences in ways that make

sense to them. I knew that, more often than not, simply telling students what we want them to know leaves them cold. (1987, p. 122)

We all hold knowledge we have learned about the moon, its habits, and its role in the near universe. The near universe is a term that I use to characterize that part of the universe closest to us here on earth—the moon, the sun— parts we can see, track, and consider firsthand. For many of us, the knowledge we hold about the near universe is, in Lev Vygotsky's (1962) term, scientific, learned in an abstract way, usually in school, from a book. When I was young, everything I knew about the relative movements of the near universe was analyzed "scientifically," in terms of schoolbook learning.

What happened to me in Eleanor's class was that my school-acquired, scientific learnings collapsed when they collided with my firsthand observations, or, in Vygotsky's terms, spontaneous learnings. What I saw and recorded as data in my journal did not coincide with what my book learning led me to predict.

The theories about the near universe which I had held since I was a child were only founded on knowledge acquired abstractly from books and lectures and not from actual personal experience. Strange, since it's so easy to go outside and look up. But I have found in doing moonwatching with teachers that it is not uncommon for us to teach an entire unit on the universe without ever going outside to look at it.

I believe that it is essential that we help children to lay down a foundation of concrete understanding based on direct observation and data collection and organization of the near universe before we teach about the far universe— Pluto, "black holes," and the like. Our understanding of the workings of the near universe—which we can see—becomes a model for understanding the far universe—which some of us may never see.

And so we began at upper elementary with the habits of the moon. The habits of the sun are fairly easy to grasp, but the moon is quite another matter. Some adults have spent many years tracking the habits of the moon and still report not feeling confident in their ability to predict patterns. There is a certain arbitrariness in the moon's habits.

I have reported on how to begin moonwatching with fourth graders in an article in *Language Arts*, February 1986. Here, I will outline some of the main activities and understandings we strove toward in a year of thinking about the moon and its relationship to the near universe.

The first thing I want moonwatchers to be aware of is that the moon can regularly be seen during the daytime. This appearance is predictable and occurs for about one-half of the month. A trip to the *Old Farmer's 1991*

Almanac reveals this pattern of moon rising and setting for the first half of the month of February 1991:

	Rising Times	Setting Times
Feb. 1	8:11 PM	8:01 AM
2	9:20 PM	8:24 AM
3	10:27 PM	8:48 AM
4	11:33 PM	9:12 AM
5	------	9:38 AM
6	12:38 AM	10:09 AM
7	1:40 AM	10:45 AM
8	2:39 AM	11:27 AM
9	3:33 AM	12:16 PM
10	4:20 AM	1:12 PM
11	5:01 AM	2:13 PM
12	5:35 AM	3:16 PM
13	6:04 AM	4:22 PM
14	6:30 AM	5:28 PM
15	6:53 AM	6:34 PM

For the first half of the month, the moon becomes visible later and later during the night and is overhead—within our horizons—through most of the day. Sometimes it can't be seen because the sun's light is too bright, sometimes it is cloudy, but it can be seen a lot more than some people realize.

Many people don't seem to know this. I have worked with teachers who told me that seeing the moon in the day was ''an accident,'' ''random.'' Once someone told me that there were two moons, the nighttime one and the daytime one. I trusted the person was speaking metaphorically.

We hold all sorts of misconceptions about when it is possible to see the moon. Our understanding of the habits of the sun are so strong that we tend to use that as a model for the moon, when in fact, they behave quite differently.

Most of the literature—and I speak as one who has bought a lot of these books—does not tell anyone that the moon can be seen during the daytime. I have many good science books on my shelf, some written for children, some for adults, that do not give the slightest clue that it is just as possible to see a daytime moon as a nighttime one. Many begin their section on the moon with, ''Go outside tonight and . . .'' Notable exceptions are the fine and accurate works of Seymour Simon, and Terence Dickinson's *Exploring the Sky by Day* and *Exploring the Night Sky*.

As for children's picture storybooks, the situation is even worse. I have found only one picture storybook that gives accurate information about the habits of the moon, that says it is possible to see the moon in the daytime, and that is Anna Hines' *Sky All Around*.

Most other books imply or state outright that it is not possible to see the moon in the daytime, or that the moon must be seen at night. On my shelf I have children's picture storybooks that teach children through words or pictures that the moon comes up every evening in a different phase when in fact, certain phases can only be seen in the day, in particular some days of the quarter-moon phases. Some picture storybooks imply that the full moon "rises" every night at sunset—in fact, it "rises" full only once a month—rarely twice—at or just after sunset. One book even shows the moon "setting" in the east over the "rising" sun when in fact, the moon appears to "rise" in the east and "set" in the west just as the sun does.

We might argue that these are just children's books, we might call it "poetic license." But I believe that we owe it to children to present accurate information in books like these. Authors like Joanna Cole and Joanne Ryder have taught us that children's picture storybooks are learning tools, too. As for poetic license, my friend, Candice Reffe, the poet, tells me that at Columbia University in the Master's program in poetry, the first thing she was taught was that information, even in poems, had to be accurate. We can play with the feelings, we can even play with the characterizations, but we cannot play with the facts.

My sixth graders listened to some of these children's picture storybooks as we worked on moonwatching. They were good critical listeners and many of them had younger brothers and sisters. They were very concerned with the reliability of sources. They said, of the inaccurate books, "What if that was the only book little kids ever read about the moon? They would have it all wrong."

And that, in fact, is what happens, I think. We have grown accustomed to looking down, to learning about the world outside from the books inside. We are like the cartoon I once saw of the scientist sitting next to the world's biggest telescope and watching a show called "Star Trip."

And so in my classrooms, we went outside. We waited for times when the three elements in the near universe, the sun, the moon and the earth, were visible to us all at once during the day. We watched for the moon in the daytime and we charted it on a large calendar, noting the time we observed it and the shape it showed. We put a small landmark, like the flagpole out front, in our small drawings so that others could get an idea of where the moon was in the sky when we saw it. If we didn't see it, we noted that. As the drawings accumulated, we looked for patterns in the data.

At the same time as this was going on, some people were making charts from data taken from the *Farmer's Almanac*. These charts showed the moon's "rising" and "setting" times, and some showed the length of the moon day. As can be seen from the moon's "rising" and "setting" times previously shown, the "moonday," the length of time the moon is overhead, varies a great deal. On the days shown, February 1 to 15, the length of the "moonday" varies from about seven hours to about twelve hours. We all studied those charts and looked for patterns. As the year wore on, students who did the firsthand moon observations used students' developing moon charts from the Almanac to help them determine if they were likely to see the moon in the daytime. We got to know after a while each year which phases were most common in the daytime and where to look on different days.

We read books about the moon, from picture storybooks to science books, assessing the quality of the information given in terms of the observations we were making. Did the books give an accurate portrayal of the habits of the moon, as we were observing them? That was the question that kept coming up. If such-and-such a book was the only one students read, would they have an accurate notion of the habits of the moon?

We did not build models or walk around in circles in the classroom with flashlights. We did not spend time trying to make sense of that commonly used, and misleading picture of the sun, the moon, and the earth, which shows the earth in the middle, the sun on one side, and the moon on the opposite side (*see* Figure 39). The picture is usually labeled "how a full moon happens." It's a drawing in most science textbooks and to me, to this day, it is an accurate drawing of how a full moon *can't* possibly happen. The earth is clearly in the way and the positioning—as drawn in the diagram—should result in a total eclipse of the moon since the sun's light is blocked by the earth. Of course, what is missing from this two-dimensional drawing is the third dimension. And that is a powerful weakness for me.

I am quite good at going from two-dimensional representation to two-dimensions—I am a good copier on paper. I am not good at working with the dimension shift, at going from two-dimensional representations to three-dimensional reality and back again. And I don't think that I am an uncommon case. I think it is very difficult for children to transfer conceptual information between dimensions in their heads and that is what diagrams like this ask them to do—envision the workings of a three-dimensional, near universe from this inaccurate and limited two-dimensional drawing.

A better way is to go outside and "become" the diagram. I have had students do this with me and I still do it myself when I can see the moon and the sun. Standing here on the earth, I raise one arm to point toward the sun and the other to point toward the moon (*see* Figure 40). If I imagine a line being drawn between my right and left hand, a line that would stretch from the sun to the moon, I form a triangle with my arms and the imaginary line. This triangle and the angles inside it give me a concrete feeling of the positioning of the three bodies in the near universe, the earth, the sun, and the moon.

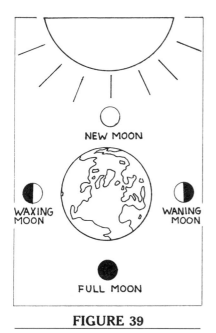

FIGURE 39

FIGURE 40

With this concrete experience, I begin to "get a feel" for how the angles and the triangle will be for different phases of the moon.

For a quarter moon, I make a small angle between my arms at my body, because the sun and the moon are not far apart and as I stand with my arms raised, pointing to each, the angle at my body is about 45 degrees. That feels right, given that I am looking at a quarter moon. When the moon is full, the sun's light is falling fully on it and I am standing with my arms outstretched, almost at 180 degrees.

Here, out in the real world, making a diagram with my body, I can see how the sunlight falls fully on the moon, unlike the translation I was unable to make from the diagram in the science book. The earth I am standing on is clearly out of the way because we live in three dimensions and that is as plain as my outstretched arms.

Through making myself into a diagram whenever I see the moon, I have gradually begun to evolve a sense of how I will need to stand with arms outstretched when I see a particular phase of the moon. I am beginning to be able to predict how to position my arms just from seeing the phase of the moon. And I know in advance how the moon will look, what phase it will be in, just from the position of my arms and the angles I am forming as I triangulate the near universe.

And that ability to predict begins to inform me about how the sun's light creates phases of the moon. It is not just that the sun's light only falls on part of the moon, it is also that it is reflected to us. We are the third part of the triangulation process.

In working with students, this kinesthetic sense, so often ignored in education, is a key piece of understanding. To feel the workings of the near universe in one's own body, to predict by becoming a living diagram is a powerful learning tool. And it all happens when the moon is out during the day, the only time when we can actually see the sun illuminating the moon.

We also used to think about the phases of the moon by letting the sun's light fall on a soccer ball. We often noticed the moon when we were coming in from recess at about 1:00 PM. Then, the sun was beginning to sink to the west and the moon was up fairly high in the east. We discovered one day as we lined up to come in that if we held the soccer ball up with the moon behind it, we could see the sun's light shining on it in relation to us just the way it was shining on the moon. And the lighted section of the soccer ball looked just like the shape of the moon. We were able to recreate the phase right on the soccer ball. It is a much more effective and instructive activity than having students with flashlights walk around students with oranges.

These were our main activities. We talked a lot, theorized all the time, read little tidbits about the moon when we could find them, and began predicting and hypothesizing about implications for the far universe. Eleanor Duckworth (1987) says, "Much of the learning is in the explaining" (p. 130). Some students took wonderful pictures of the moon during the day. We looked at Ansel Adams photos of the moon in the daytime, his "Moonrise, Hernandez, New Mexico, 1941" and his "Moon and Half Dome, Yosemite National Park, California, 1940."

My students and I speculated about things I am still trying to grasp, like why we have the phenomenon commonly called "the new moon holding the old moon," which happens because of earthshine. The new moon is reflecting the light of the sun but the old moon is reflecting light from the earth. It's going to take me awhile to get that one settled into my conceptual framework. For now, like my students, I just keep going outside and looking at it when it occurs, trying to grasp the three-dimensional implications, trying to understand the workings of the near universe.

Doing What Scientists Do

Throughout all of these activities we talked, read, and wrote about what we were doing, how we did what we did, how we learned new things, how our theories were developing. For that is what scientists do.

Some of the projects arose spontaneously. All took a long time. We learned and questioned together, what Eleanor Duckworth (1986) calls "the collective creation of knowledge" (p. 1). I tried to help students strengthen those attributes I thought would serve them best, their curiosity, their powers of observation, and their ability to communicate their findings.

Books to Help

One of the most interesting books in science that I have seen lately is Carol Butzow and John Butzow's *Science through Children's Literature*. This 1989 book is available from Teachers Ideas Press in Englewood, Colorado and provides us all with jumping off points in science for such old favorites as *Make Way for Ducklings*.

There are several publications from Little, Brown and Company that are good science activity resources, *Blood and Guts: A Working Guide to Your own Insides, The Reason for Seasons*, and *Gee Whiz*!

For a book to give a teacher a good perspective on science and inquiry, I would recommend Eleanor Duckworth's collection of essays, *The Having of Wonderful Ideas and Other Essays on Teaching and Learning*.

And, finally, Heinemann Educational Books has recently published a book by Ellen Doris called, *Doing What Scientists Do: Children Learn to Investigate their World*.

Mathematics Lab

Remembering Mathematics

My earliest memory of mathematics in action must be from when I was about six. It was then that I started to play the license plate game, which I still play to this day. The game started after I began to learn the basic facts of computation, adding and subtracting, and deepened when I learned my multiplication and division tables. The game is played by searching for perfect license plates, ones in which all the numbers are accounted for by use of basic facts. It's best if the answer is in the plate number, too. So a perfect plate would be 459734 because $4 + 5 = 9$ and $7 - 3 = 4$. Or 236842 because $2 \times 3 = 6$ and $8 \div 4 = 2$. Of course, a more interesting plate would be 237156. This one takes some work. But with a little juggling—perfectly acceptable in this game—we can account for all the numbers with none left over: $2 + 3 = 5$ and $7 - 1 = 6$.

As I started to master the facts and tables, the game became an obsession. To this day, I can't see a number without working it out to see if it balances. My teachers never knew that I actually was using my school learning in a practical way to solve the problems of the world, like all those uncalculated license plates.

We never know the uses that mathematics in the classroom will have to serve once they see the light of day in the outside world. But we do know the uses that never occur for some of us. I can't remember the last time I had to multiply $\frac{11}{14} \times \frac{17}{29}$, or the last time I needed to write a number in its expanded notation—like $367 = 300 + 60 + 7$—or when I **ever** needed to find a lowest common denominator for tenths, seventeenths and twenty-thirds (It's 170×23—not a commonly used number). I have never converted from metric to English measuring systems and back again, except for the time I measured something with the wrong side of the yardstick where the centimeters were marked off and had to convert it on another yardstick when I got to the hardware store.

But in elementary school I had to learn to do all these things—and I have taught students to do them all. Our ancient mathematics curriculum rattles along in spite of mounting evidence that these kinds of learnings—so hard for me and others—are not what the stuff of daily life is all about.

I'm glad I learned the basic operations and I've needed a familiarity with some fractional and decimal operations and concepts. But there was a lot of mathematics, especially in the realm of operations with fractions and decimals that I have never been called on to use, not since my last standardized test.

I **have** had to do a lot of problem posing, figuring out what the problem was to start with and then trying all kinds of little tricks, including asking my husband, to figure out what operations and numbers I would need to use. Problems in the real world, even in mathematics, always start out, as Jane Rowe (1991) says, with a "situation." Problems in the real world don't even start out as problems.

For instance, a recent "fuzzy situation" for me was: is it cheaper for me to use regular gas in my car than super, given that I get more miles per gallon with super but it costs more? That's a real fuzzy situation for me and it took me a long time to settle onto what exactly the mathematical problem was and then figure out how to go about solving it. My husband, by the way, solved it a completely different way by creating a different problem as the basis for calculations. I compared extra miles traveled with super to the extra gallon I needed to buy of regular. He compared the number of trips with each type of gas before I got a free trip. Same situation, different problems, same solution: for my car, it's the same either way.

But nothing in our mathematical backgrounds was of much use. In school we were never asked to pose problems based on real situations, arising from real needs. Here in real life, we had to think the situation through from the beginning and then use some very basic calculation which would have been better done on a calculator, leaving our minds free to concentrate on the practical implications.

Mathematics in school for me was mostly calculation and measurement, all on paper. If we actually measured anything it was the paper itself or pencil marks on the paper. We all got pretty good at measuring little things. Not so good at measuring walls and pictures and couches.

Mathematics in school never tapped into my innate ability to judge size and shape, often within fractions of an inch. I have always been very good at spotting the board that will exactly fill the empty space. I would be really good at finding the exact rock that would fit the funny-shaped space in the stone wall. Things in my office at home, living room, bedroom, fit together as if they had all been built to specifications. But, in fact, they fit together because when I saw them, I knew they would exactly fill the available space. To the inch. My mother is very good at this too.

But school learning in mathematics never knew that this existed in me, this ability to "measure by eye." Sometimes I wonder what an inborn skill like this could lead to if it was recognized and trained, the way school is supposed to amplify individual strengths.

It might, for instance, have been used to strengthen my incredible weakness with estimation of volume. Here "my eye" fails me and I could no more tell whether dinner leftovers will fit in this bowl or that one than fly to the moon. Many, many times I have poured leftovers from one container to the next, trying to find one that is the right volume. And as I do it, and wash all the dirty ones afterwards, I silently send mathematical curses to those who made me memorize those useless conversion tables of quart to liter, and pint to cups, volume conversions that left me permanently disabled in the real world of converting from one size and shape to another.

We all have things like this, games we play with numbers, inborn facilities with space, shape, time and quantity, and disabilities in the real world of measurement, calculation, and problem posing. What I have done at the fourth, fifth, and sixth grade level is to try to set up a learning situation which promotes discovery and amplification of innate abilities, which allows learners to strengthen areas of weaknesses, and which provides opportunities to explore together concepts in higher order mathematical thinking, the "big ideas" of math.

As long as standardized testing reigns supreme in public education—and it shows no dwindling of power—we will continue to teach about $11 \div 14$ and how to divide mixed numbers by decimal numbers and make children do problems in expanded notation. We will persist in what Mary Lindquist in the National Council of Teachers of Mathematics 1989 Yearbook calls "the preoccupation on computation" (p. 5).

This chapter will not be a guide for revising mathematics curriculum. The publications of the National Council of Teachers of Mathematics are the best source of information on the 1989 Standards and recommendations. In this chapter, I will discuss some of the activities and strategies that I use to enlarge the scope of my students' mathematical experiences, to enhance the learning process in the field of mathematics, and to promote an environment of trust and love of learning in mathematics.

Computation in a Concrete Way

One of the most valuable mathematical lessons that I learned over my 18 years of teaching, was that taught originally by Piaget, that learning must take place first in a concrete way before it can be made representational and abstract. This was the message of my early teaching of the division algorithm—I found it very hard to teach. And that was because I had only learned it algorithmically—I had memorized a procedure without knowing what I was doing, why it worked, or how it related to the real world.

When I began working with young children and the primary computations, adding and subtracting, we always worked with mathematics manipulatives first, rods and beans and charts, that helped us to understand what was happening when we performed operations on numbers. We set up problems with the manipulatives first and then solved them representationally on paper. Only then did we begin to try to internalize the process and memorize the algorithms we all use routinely as adults.

This philosophy of working from concrete to representational to abstract is important to sustain when doing computation with older children, too. We teachers at grades four, five, and six need to continue to have available the mathematics manipulatives and charts, the visual, tactile support systems that help learners to see and touch what they are trying to learn abstractly. There are many fine guides, manuals, and materials available through educational publishers to assist upper-level teachers who have not approached mathematics instruction this way.

The purchased math manipulative I found most useful at the upper grades was a set of wooden blocks known as base ten blocks. These relatively sized blocks have as the smallest unit square centicubes, one centimeter in each direction. In terms of place value in our number system, these can be looked on as "ones." The next relative sized blocks in the set are "strips," ten-centimeter long strips, one centimeter thick, and scored to show each centimeter of length. These are taken to be "tens." Next come the "flats," flat squares, ten centimeters long, ten centimeters wide and one centimeter deep, scored to show one hundred interior units. These can be called "hundreds." And finally in the set are large, cubic blocks, scored to show one hundred centimeters on each side, for an interior volume of one thousand centicubes. These are "thousands." There are many blocks of each size in the kits.

At the upper levels, students are beginning to evolve a sense of the concept of place value, that a 2 is not always a 2, sometimes it is a 20, depending on how and where we write it. They are beginning to be literate in mathematics, developing an understanding of the abstract, symbolic code which is the writing of numbers. Base ten blocks are a great help for strengthening the mental image of place value and giving a tactile understanding of the concept.

We learn a great deal through the tactile intelligence in our hands. I find that my inborn ability to find just the right size and shape to fill the empty space has something to do with handling it and looking at it. I don't measure in traditional terms. It is all a matter of kinesthetics and visualization. Our tactile intelligence, coupled with our visual intelligence, together contribute to the overall learning as our cognition, our mental understanding, grasps and encodes mathematical learning.

Base ten blocks are useful also in helping upper elementary students develop an understanding of parts of numbers, the world of decimal and fractional numbers, a major learning at grades four, five, and six. In these grades, students lay down the foundation for work with fractional and decimal numbers, those notations which represent parts of one whole unit. In using base ten blocks to think visually and tactilely about fractional parts of one unit, we take the "thousands" block to be "one," one whole unit. Then the flat "hundreds" block becomes "tenths" because it takes ten of them stacked up to make the big block. The "tens" strips become "hundredths" because it takes one hundred of them to fill the big block. And the small centicubes become "thousandths" because it takes one thousand of them to fill the big "one" block. This is especially effective if it is charted out on the floor, on a mat divided into the decimal places.

The development of fractional and decimal number concepts also presents the first major collision for learners between mathematical "laws" taught in the primary grades, and the realities of fractional and decimal numbers. In primary grades students learn that addition and multiplication are operations that make quantities bigger while subtraction and division serve to make quantities smaller. In fact, this is not always so when we deal with fractional and decimal numbers. Multiplying by a fraction or a decimal can actually make a quantity smaller. It takes upper elementary students quite a while to sort out disjunctions like this.

Indeed, when we reach the upper elementary and begin to deal in concepts we find that even simple addition is not always true. As Pat Davidson of the Mathematics Department at the University of Massachusetts at Boston, points out, $1 + 1 = 2$ except when we are talking about a problem involving raindrops, where $1 + 1 = 1$, for as two raindrops come together, only one is formed. Some of the heuristics, memorized tricks of the trade, and slogans found useful for primary teachers in teaching small children become "partially adequate strategies" (Brown & Day 1983, p.13) which have to be undone before more advanced learning can take place.

In working with upper elementary students, I talked about these things. We also discussed why we learn some things. If we were learning something like writing expanded notation so that we could do well on a standardized test, I said so. Writing numbers out, expanding them, may help some students to learn place value concepts, but I don't think it is the best way for all. Learning standardized notation will, however, help them to succeed in an important environment, that of standardized testing. And one of my constant goals is to enable my students to succeed in many settings, not just with me.

A Climate of Trust

One of the essential ingredients in my classroom was a climate of trust. In this climate I told students why we needed to learn a particular item, and that knowledge promoted more involved engagement because students trusted that the program was designed to help them succeed.

We did what I call "consensus correcting." I never owned any teachers' editions or answer keys. Back in the days when I corrected everything myself I usually borrowed one or worked out the problems on a calculator. When students began correcting their own papers nearly all the time, we did correcting by consensus. The first two students who were finished put away the pencils they worked with and took out a pen for correcting. They compared answers. For any answers which did not agree, they checked with the third person who finished, who was able to use their agreed-on answers to correct from. They were on their way to developing an answer sheet. As more and more students finished, the consensus grew. Students compared and located discrepancies which they checked in ever-widening circles.

"Don't the students ever cheat?" someone once asked me when I described this process. I try very hard to set up a classroom situation in which there is no advantage in cheating. The way I try to accomplish that is by establishing the learning of the process as the most important thing—not the accumulation of correct answers. We all try to get the answers right, not to compete with each other for grades, but to show that we have successfully understood the process we are trying to learn.

Also, we all help each other. It is pretty rare to have a situation in which students collaborate to mark wrong answers right, to collaborate against the teacher, in effect. If that situation occurs, then I look at the situation I have established. I'm not supposed to be the enemy. "Tricking me" about what they know should be self-defeating for students interested in learning. If I found myself in that situation, it was usually early in the year when I was the recipient of old attitudes developed during students' past histories or when someone new entered the classroom during the year and brought with them baggage from another classroom.

Because the whole point for learners is to learn. I'm there to work with them to help them learn—not to trick them into making mistakes. Early in the year, I explained this philosophy to students. I told them that I see the classroom as a place where people come who want to learn and succeed, so everything that we do aims toward this goal. We would try to work together in "cooperative competition" so that everyone might win.

Also, working together seems to promote honesty among students. I wrote an article for *Teaching Pre K–8* which described how to set up the first day in a sixth grade whole language classroom. In it I said, "I've found that students who correct by consensus don't want to cheat, perhaps because the peer relationship fosters honesty" (p. 85). In traditional classrooms, students try to "cheat the teacher." In the situation I work to create, the only person one could cheat is one's self or a collaborator.

Following correcting by consensus, I would ask students to do an error analysis. In this, they wrote a little note next to any incorrect calculation about why it was wrong: "I divided wrong," "I copied the problem wrong," "I added 2 and 2 and got three," "I made a silly mistake." This helped learners to begin to sort out what the quality of their errors was and this is key to beginning to grow in mathematics. It also gave me a chance to see if students were all making the same kind of error or if one student consistently made the same type of error.

Margaret Donaldson (1963) in her interesting *Study of Children's Thinking*, focused on mathematical thinking and proposed three categories of error: structural, arbitrary, and executive. In structural errors, children fail to grasp essential elements in the problem or fail to note an essential principle.

Arbitrary errors "have as their outstanding feature a lack of loyalty to the given" (p. 183). Children making arbitrary errors may interpret a problem using outside information drawn from real-life—as when children solve a word problem about dogs in terms of their own pets rather than in terms of the information in the problem—they "appeared simply to decide 'it is so' " (p. 184). In making arbitrary errors, children either added to or ignored information in the problem.

Executive errors are the result of "some failure in the actual carrying out of the manipulations involved" (p. 184) and not from a failure to understand the problem. The usual immediate cause of failure in these errors is, according to Donaldson, "loss of hold on reasoning" (p. 184).

Donaldson found developmental implications in this study and recommended further error analysis studies. She also found evidence "suggestive of widespread conceptual difficulty" (p. 220) in children's mathematical thinking. In pursuing error analysis in the classroom with students, teachers can pursue "a better appreciation . . . of what things are the most important signs of how a child's thinking has progressed and is likely to continue to progress" (p. 221). Thus we may be able to make better predictions of developmental trends in that thinking and learn "how to guide it with a more enlightened understanding" (p. 221).

Problem Posing

One of the goals of my mathematics curriculum was to develop in my students a love of learning mathematics and problem solving, in spite of the Educational Testing Service's astute observation in the June 18, 1963 *Time* magazine that "Future teachers pass through the elementary schools learning to detest mathematics . . . They return to the elementary school to teach a new generation to detest it." That certainly applied to me in the first half of my teaching career. I have tried in the second half to "do unto others as was not done to me," to use my understanding of my own education as a means for developing a reflective practice which promotes success and love of learning.

Consequently, one avenue my classes have pursued in studying mathematics is the area of problem posing. As I pointed out earlier in this chapter, my experience in the world has reinforced the idea that mathematical problems never present themselves as such in the world, rather, mathematical problem posing and problem solving arise from need, from a "fuzzy situation" that needs to be solved.

So some of the mathematics that we did in my classroom arose from need, usually from the simulations that the students were involved in as a part of social studies. Some problems were clean and obvious: "Pioneers" on the move West had to calculate the weight of the items they were taking with them in their wagon from charts of average weights. "Fellows" at the Royal Archeological Institute of Cairo had to estimate the volume of two suitcases, 40 pounds total weight, in creating their packing list for the trip to the archeological dig in Egypt.

Some were not so neat: How much suntan lotion would a fair-skinned archeologist from the Royal Archeological Institute of Cairo need for two weeks on a desert dig? A problem of volume versus usage. How much cargo including animals could an immigrant to the colonies fit in a shipboard living space 6 feet x 6 feet x 6 feet, not including space for a small cooking fire?

We also did worksheets based on simulations, as when Fellows to the archeological dig were asked to draw a diagram of a dig site divided into tenths and indicate the location of wells, foundations, stone walls, patios, and so on.

On some worksheets the problems fell into the realm of "fuzzy situations" with the problems to be isolated, posed, and solved. All Fellows received a letter from the Royal Archeological Institute of Cairo asking, among other things that the Fellows show "proof that you have $2000 credit or $2000 in a bank account before you plan on making this trip." Most Fellows posed this problem: How do you show that you have money in a savings account? They decided to produce a "copy" of an imaginary bank book with a variety of transactions and calculations resulting in a balance of $2000.

This was a homework assignment, so the problem posing fell onto the students and their own resources. I found that in simulations I often got better results when much of the work was done outside the classroom with students on their own, and on the telephone. Stephen Brown and Marion Walter (1983) in *The Art of Problem Posing* point out that:

> Problem posing . . . can create a totally new orientation towards the issue of who is in charge and what has to be learned. Given a situation in which one is asked to generate problems or ask questions . . . there is no **right** question to ask at all. (p. 5)

Assignments like this began informally in class as I heard students discussing how they would go about solving them, as they isolated what the actual problem to be solved was. And I knew from talking to them that collaboration went on outside of school as they brainstormed ways to problem solve effectively. One of my hidden agendas is to strengthen personal resources and develop independence and interaction in problem solving.

G. Polya (1945) in his classic *How to Solve It* observes:

> The teacher should help, but not too much and not too little, so that the student shall have a reasonable share of the work. . . . The best is, however, to help the student naturally. The teacher should put himself in the student's place . . . and ask a question or indicate a step that **could have occurred to the student himself**. (p. 3)

So I try to offer help that is necessary in problem posing and problem solving and otherwise, stay out of the way. I try to "understand what is going on in the student's mind" (p. 3) as Polya suggests. I also heed his observation that people learn to solve problems by posing them and solving them, we learn to do by doing, and it helps students to see adults in the act of problem posing and solving. Polya says: "when the teacher solves a problem before the class, he should dramatize his ideas a little and he should put to himself the same questions he uses when helping the students'' (p. 5). Following this advice, I show my students how the teacher teaches herself.

Writing in Mathematics

Throughout this development of Whole Learning we have emphasized the integration of literacy across the content areas, so here in mathematics we continue the work. There are three main areas of writing that I did in mathematics. The first involves problem posing, the second, writing understandings of processes in math, and the third involves writing to learn big ideas and concepts.

In working with problem posing, students were asked to write word problems based on number facts. This is something students have always done, but I have added a few new wrinkles. Here is the basic problem writing:

> $18 + 14 = ?$ There are 18 hamsters in the petshop. The petshop got 14 more. How many are there now?

To this we can add *two-step problem solving*. In two-step problem solving, the numbers needed to solve the problem are not directly in the problem itself. Rather, the solver must perform an extra operation to get the actual numbers needed. While this kind of math problem is common on standardized testing, we rarely give students the opportunity to reverse the process, to discover how that extra step can be written into a problem and to construct one for themselves.

There are two ways that problems can have an extra step added in. The first requires the solver to perform some other operation to derive the needed numbers:

> $18 + 14 = ?$ There are 20 hamsters at the petshop. 2 went home with Sally. The petshop got 14 more. How many are there now?
> $20 - 2 = 18 + 14 = 32$

In the second kind of two-step operation in problem solving, the solver must possess extra information in order to solve the problem:

> $18 + 14 = ?$ There are a dozen and a half hamsters in the petshop. The petshop got 14 more. How many are there now?

Finally, we can have students write problems with irrelevant information in them. These kinds of problems are very common on standardized testing but rarely do we show students how to insert irrelevant information to see how it can be identified. A student might write:

18 + 14 = ?   There were 18 hamsters in the petshop. They got 14 more and I bought them all. One had a baby. How many did I buy?

In the last problem, the major debate becomes when the hamster had the baby.

A second avenue of writing in mathematics is in writing the process one goes through, the thinking behind the calculation. For most students, the first time they are asked to do this kind of writing is when they take geometry in high school, often as a sophomore. There, they are asked to write out the process and the thinking behind the stages of calculation. That writing is called a *proof*. This is very difficult for students who have had no experience in moving from numbers to words in mathematics, who have never been asked to concisely write what they are doing in a mathematical process.

So I start early, sometimes asking students to do what is known as a *double entry* in writing in which the paper is divided down the middle by a line. On the left is the computation and on the right is a place for words. I ask students in upper elementary to begin the calculation on the left. When they get stuck, when they no longer know what to do, they are to switch to the right-hand column, switch from writing numbers to writing words, and record their confusion.

Here's an example of how this works. I was visiting in a seventh-grade mathematics classroom and as the students worked, I flipped through the math textbook and came to this problem:

A certain corporate bond opened on Monday at 71 points. During Monday the bond changed in value by − 2 points, Tuesday by + 1 point, and on Wednesday by − 3 points. What was the bond's closing value on Wednesday?

My thoughts as I read this problem were in confusion. Even if I somehow arrived at the correct answer, it would be by default, and someone correcting my work should know what I'm thinking about. Here is my double entry work:

71−2	This can't be so simple! I must be doing something wrong. It can't be so simple as subtract 2, add 1, subtract 3—this is the seventh grade. I don't know anything about economics!

I asked students earlier in their careers to write out their thinking and their understanding of the mathematical processes they were working with. I got results like these (*see* Figures 41–43):

(Figure 41 transcription)
Multiplication: Do the problem. Count how many numerals are to the right of the decimals in the upper numbers. Count from left to right on the answer, the number you counted before. Put the decimal to the left of the number you are on.

(Figure 42 transcription)
Divide: move the decimal in the divisor to the end of number(s) now you move the decimal in the dividend as many spaces as you did in the the the divisor (see picture), then bring the decimal in the dividend up into the answer box. Now you can divide.

(Figure 43 transcription)
On subtraction, you do the same thing as adding but you have to put zeros down so the number will have the exact number as the other number has.

The third option for mathematical writing is to help develop concepts in higher order thinking in mathematics. Here are students explaining what they have learned in a long-term study of infinity:

It never ends, it goes on forever like space. It brings questions like what's on the other side of a black hole—is it a bunch of infinite space or an infinite planet? It goes on forever.

Infinity is something that never ends. It is a big number and other things. People are not infinity because they are alive and then they die. It is a space, distance, period of time or quality.

Never ending, Infinity, for as an example, numbers are infinity because they never end. Infinity is something that never stops and keeps on going. I wonder how anyone ever thought of infinity? Who knows!!

Exploring Big Ideas in Mathematics

One of the most exciting areas of study I have engaged in with students has been the exploration of big ideas, concepts in higher order thinking in mathematics. The original rationale for these explorations came from examining my own limited experience.

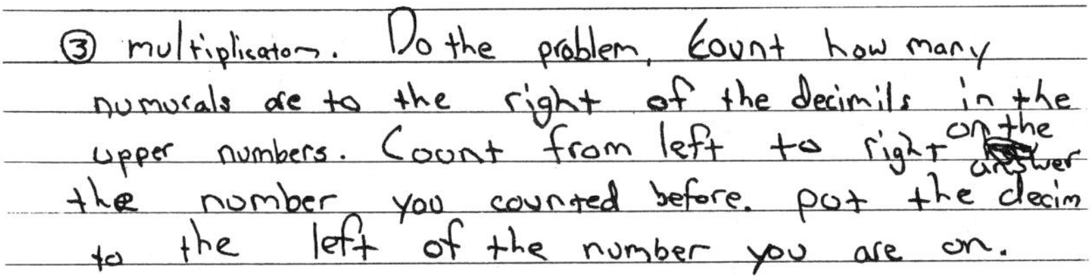

③ multiplication. Do the problem, count how many numerals are to the right of the decimils in the upper numbers. Count from left to right on the answer the number you counted before. put the decim to the left of the number you are on.

FIGURE 41

I was tracked into computational mathematics and I ended my studies in high school. I never explored some of the mathematical ideas I knew were floating around, like infinity and topology and why algebra is a good symbol system for thinking in other realms like physics. I read about them, I thought about Einstein's mind, and when books like Gleick's *Chaos* and the works of Robert Penrose were published, I read those.

The educational programs I was in left me bogged down in the "dirty work" of mathematics, the ditch of computation, and never led me to the heights of higher thinking. It wasn't until I took a course in the Critical and Creative Thinking Graduate Program at the University of Massachusetts at Boston, a course taught by Dr. Patricia Davidson and called "Higher Order Thinking in Mathematics," that I realized how much I had missed.

So I became concerned for students in upper elementary school, students who were very interested in issues like infinity and topology, patterns and chaos. I was afraid that they might never have the classroom opportunity to explore some of the big ideas of mathematics, that they might, like me, be tracked into programs that focused only on computation.

Each year I engaged my students in a month-long unit on the implications of infinity. This study dwelt on the border of math and science and involved reading and writing. But primarily it was interactive. And it was generative. Although there were certain activities and learnings that I hoped to promote, there was a lot of room for innovation and new activities.

I wrote this study up at length in an article for the October 1988 issue of *Language Arts*, the journal of the National Council of Teachers of English. I will summarize some of the activities here.

In order to begin this study of the big idea of infinity, I usually reread parts of Gamow's (1947) *One, Two, Three . . . Infinity*, just enough to get me into the swing of things. In the early stages of thinking about infinity we did things like creating circles with our bodies and then tried to decide where they began. We explored the computer LOGO possibility where students typed in "repeat 9999" and then discussed when the design would stop and is that infinity? We made Moebius strips, those wonderful constructions of twisted, joined circles that have no end and only one side.

Devide = move the decimal in the divisor to the end of the numbers
now you move the decimal in the dividend as many spaces as you did in the
<u>answer box</u>
7.63.|32.79   divisor (see picture), then bring the decimal in the dividend
up in to the answer box. Now you can devide

FIGURE 42

We then studied some of the drawings of M.C. Escher, looking for things that had no ending, which circled back on themselves, infinitely. We began to talk at this point about linear infinity that "goes on in a straight line into infinity" and the concept of infinite regression.

We explored the mathematical idea that the set of even numbers is as large as the set of counting numbers, even though the counting set seems like it should be twice as big. But when a one-to-one matching is done into infinity, the two sets will always match, they are the same size—infinite, like this:

Counting numbers: 1 2 3 4 5 6 7 8 9 10 11 12 13. . .
↓ ↓ ↓ ↓ ↓ ↓ ↓ ↓ ↓ ↓ ↓ ↓
Even numbers: 2 4 6 8 10 12 14 16 18 20 22 24 26. . .

This led us to Gamow's problem of the Infinity Hotel: what if all the rooms at the Infinity Hotel were occupied and another mathematician arrived, looking for a room? To make the problem more interesting, we considered the problem this creates for poor Walter, the desk clerk at the Infinity Hotel. Mathematically, he solves the problem by asking all the inhabitants to move over one room, since in the world of infinity there is always a "plus 1" and, of course, that frees up Room 1 and the mathematician can check in.

There are other mathematical problems that can be considered for the Infinity Hotel, but my students came up with some original ones: How did the mathematicians get there? What kind of a vehicle runs to the Infinity Hotel? What does the hotel look like? One year we spent several days building models of the Infinity Hotel and the vehicles available for getting there, including the "infinity sneaker."

Part of the study of infinity involves understanding the difference between infinity and a big number. So to facilitate that understanding, students took the class on "a tour of a million." "Touring a million" meant that students had to locate something in the real world—usually something like tiles on the ceiling or bricks on a building—and show us what a million of those items would look like. Students were allowed to ask us to picture ten of whatever they designated, thus reducing the number they had to show us of any given

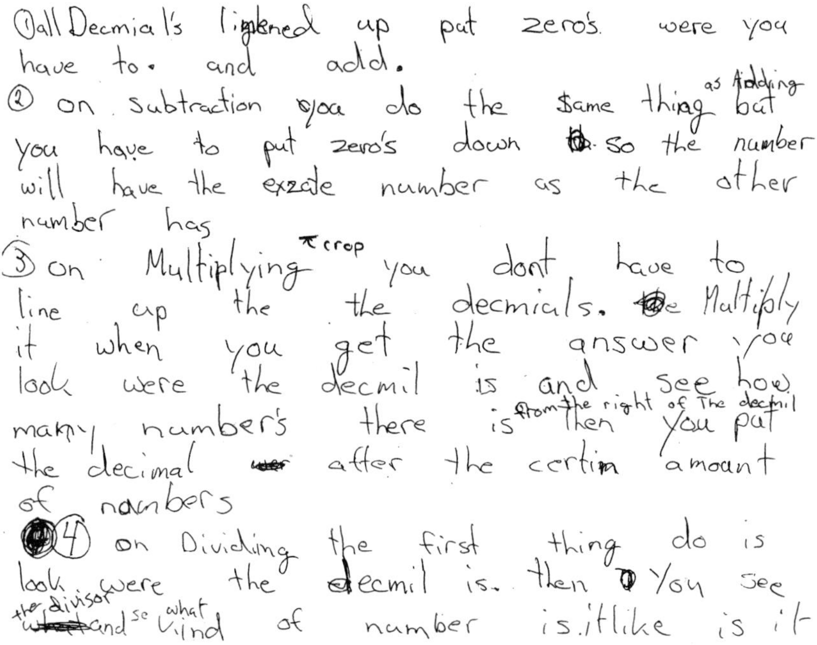

① all Decmials lightened up put zero's. were you have to. and add.

② on Subtraction you do the same thing as Adding but you have to put zero's down so. So the number will have the exzate number as the other number has

③ on Multiplying ⟵ crop you dont have to line up the the decmials. Be Multiply it when you get the answer you look were the decmil is and see how many numbers there is from the right of The decmil Then you put the decimal after the certin amount of numbers

④ on Dividing the first thing do is look were the decmil is. then You See the divisor and so what kind of number is.it like is it

FIGURE 43

item to 100,000. The day the copy paper supplies for the year came in and were stacked in the hallways was a big day for the millions tours. We all stood out in the hall, looking at the stacks of paper, while the "tour guides" explained how we were seeing a million pieces of paper.

Figures 44 and 45 show students explaining in writing the processes they went through, or as one put it, "How I Made My First Million."

In sixth grade we worked hard to comprehend parts of numbers too, so students took the class on "a millionths tour," usually done in the form of a diagram, with increasing magnification. On a millionth tour, students had to show the class what a millionth of something looks like.

As the study went on, the word *infinity* fell into common currency, the scientific concept and the spontaneous experience met, and concept development resulted. The study took a long time and gave us a lot of opportunity to "play" with the notions.

I have pursued other "big idea" studies. This past year we spent about a month and half studying aspects of group theory in mathematics. Group theory is an abstract mathematical concept governed by certain postulates. Sets which fall under group theory obey these postulates. My study with students of group theory is written up and available through the Critical and Creative Thinking Program at the University of Massachusetts in Boston, and in a chapter

3/26/1990—

Essay: How I made my first million.
I used the squares on the
white (small) graph paper in our room.
First I calculated the width times
the height ~ 44×34, which equaled 1496
squares, per graph paper.
I then divided 1496 into a
million, which totaled 668.44919.
So I would need about 668
(and almost a ½) pieces of graph
paper.
668 times 1496 gave me 999,328,
so that would be too less. 668.5
(668 and a ½) times 1496 gave me
1,000,076, which is about as close as I
can come to a million.
I would 668 ½ pieces of
graph paper to equal 1,000,076.

The End

FIGURE 44

entitled, "Vygotsky in the Classroom: An Interactionist Literacy Framework in Mathematics," in a forthcoming book edited by V. John-Steiner, C. Panofsky & L. Smith, entitled, *Interactionist Approaches to Language and Literacy*, published by Cambridge University Press.

In the study of group theory, we initially drew on Marion Walter's *Boxes, Squares and Other Things: A Teacher's Guide for a Unit in Informal Geometry*. In this guide, Walter leads learners through an exploration of pentominoes, shapes made by joining five same-size squares in different configurations. This study falls into the realm of the abstract concept called group theory because the created sets conform to the postulates of the abstract theory.

Our study carried us also into the world of modular mathematics, the "clockface mathematics" of finite sets. This work was guided by Stanley Bezuska, Margaret Kenney and Linda Silvey's *Designs from Mathematical*

My Million
First we found out there are 484 dots
on each square 22×22=484. We also found
out there are 748 squares on a ceiling not
including the indent or the cut off squares.
We multiplied them together 784 × 484 = 362032.
We multiplied 362038 by 3 rooms Carl's room Mrs Motto's
room & Mrs. Cordeiro's room & ended up with 1,086,096.
We had extra so we had to take away 86,096.
It equaled 5 rows of squares. If you have all the
dots in 3 rooms not including the indents the squares
that are cut plus taking away 5 rows in one of
the rooms you will have 1,000,000 exactly.

FIGURE 45

Patterns. We created modular designs and transformed them into wonderfully colored patterns, creating a large bulletin board which grouped the designs into factor groups—we grouped the designs with a factor of 2 together, those with a factor of 3 together and those with a factor of 5 together. And then we searched for recurring patterns. What we found were areas of "chaos" (Gleick 1987) where, in the middle of apparent disorganization, small patterns appeared. We were fascinated and that took us off in yet another direction. But all of our directions were governed by a common bond, conformity to principles of group theory.

I'm not "good" at math, but I am a good reader and I'm willing to explore new realms with students. In a climate which encourages learning by all, which allows learners to immerse themselves in active engagement, in which social interaction is seen as the key element in learning, delving deeply into big ideas is possible. I'm always amazed at how far and how deep we go.

As David Hawkins (1972) points out, one of the most important factors is the attitude of the teacher: "His mathematical domain must be ample enough, or amplifiable enough, to match the range of a child's wonder and curiosity, his operational skills, his unexpected way of gaining insight" (p. 112). This is what we should be good at, letting children lead us through our topics.

Hawkins calls such a teacher, "an elementary mathematician, one who can at least sometimes sense when a child's interests and proposals—what I have called his trajectory—are taking him near to mathematically sacred ground" (p. 113). And I find that I am best able to do this when the idea we begin with is big enough and rich enough to promote lots and lots of thinking, when the climate is interactive and engaging, and when time is given to learn.

Mathematics as Whole Learning

All of these devices, attitudes, and philosophies are designed to assist the classroom participants to immerse themselves in learning mathematical concepts. I try to set up a situation, even when we buckle down to work on straight computation, which promotes optimal learning conditions by assuring that learners know why they are learning certain things, that materials are appropriate and available, and that there is an atmosphere of positive expectation, cooperation, and trust.

I want to produce a mathematics program in my classroom that allows, in Lev Vygotsky's (1962) thinking, scientific concepts which develop as a result of "a face-to-face meeting with a concrete situation" (p. 108). We engage in much interaction so that concepts can be learned and internalized. And I try to support my students so that they can work on the edge of their ability, in their zone of proximal development (Vygotsky 1978), the "construction zone" (Newman, Griffin and Cole, 1989) where new learning takes place in a socially supported way.

David Hawkins (1972) in his essay "Nature, Man and Mathematics," says that the teacher is both a diagnostician and a user of the diagnosis:

> As a diagnostician the teacher is trying to map into his own the momentary state and trajectory of another mind and then, as provisioner, to enhance (not to replace) the resources of that mind from his own store of knowledge and skill. (p. 112)

What I have had to do is to take leave of my mathematical history and explore. My students and I found last year that the most fascinating thing in mathematics was talking about what went on in the minds of great mathematicians. We talked endlessly about how they thought of things we read about and experimented with. Imagine, students wanting to talk about mathematicians' minds.

Books to Help

I would use *any* book authored by Pat Davidson. Also useful are books by Marilyn Burns, particularly *A Collection of Math Lessons From Grades 3–6*.

There are several books put out by Heinemann Educational Publishers which will help and inspire in mathematics and Whole Learning. Here are some of the more recent titles:

How Big is the Moon? by Dave Baker, Cheryl Semple and Tony Stead

Books You Can Count On: Linking Mathematics and Literature by Rachel Griffiths & Margaret Clyne

Maths in the Mind: A Process Approach to Mental Strategies by Ann & Johnny Baker

Mathwise: Teaching Mathematical Thinking and Problem Solving by Arthur Hyde & Pamela Hyde

These books also will help teachers make changes in traditional math lessons: J. Stenmark's *Assessment Alternatives in Mathematics* and *Family Math*, Neil Davidson's *Cooperative Learning in Mathematics*, and Ed Labinowicz's *Learning from Children: New Beginnings for Teaching Numerical Thinking*.

Readers' Workshop

Remembering Teaching Reading

As a teacher during reading time, I spent a lot of time feeling guilty, hearing and reading about things I knew I would never do as a reading instructor, things like teaching all the new words first, in isolation, out of their context in the reading passage, things like making sure all kids were reading all words. Things I didn't think would teach kids how to love books.

We don't really want to just teach kids to read. We want to teach them to love to read. And we learn to love to read by being satisfied by reading. We learn to love to read when it keeps us from being lonely, when it helps us to share in the world, when it links us to our friends and family, when it serves for us a meaningful purpose.

Reading, like writing, like typing, like adding, is a skill, learned to serve a purpose. Whether that purpose is to fill my hours with friends in a book, or to take away my troubles by giving me someone else's, or to get me thinking hard about things I care about, or to give me peace when I'm troubled, reading serves a purpose.

I have always been a whole language learner. I learned to read because I wanted to, because the people I was bonded to did it, and because it helped me to function in my developing world. When I learn anything, I work on the whole thing first and last, "taking a detour" (Clay & Cazden 1990) to a part only when something about that part impedes my ability to work with the whole. I read and listen to favorite books over and over. I approach organization in a generative way, one thing growing out of the thing before. When I don't understand a part of something, I work on that part just long enough to help me understand the whole. And then I go back to the whole. I solve problems in context, and try to avoid needless worry over things in isolation. When I have to learn something new, I drench myself in it, hanging around until I'm sure that I have a notion of the right moves to make. And I believe that we learn things for a purpose.

Being a whole language learner by nature used to make it very hard to teach, especially when I taught traditional, phonics-based, basalized, beginning reading. I began teaching in 1966, with my 35 kids, who sat in their seats and filled in papers. And so did I.

They changed rooms for reading—a departmentalized first grade with ability grouping. Because I was the last teacher hired, I got all the kids who couldn't read. Thirty-five kids, all expecting me, at 21, to teach them how to do it. It was a tough assignment. Especially because secretly I had always believed that children learn to read by magic.

That's how I learned to read. Back when I was three or four, or five, I learned to read from books. I was read to, and I read back, and together my folks and I read. To me, it was magic. But it was also expected. Everyone around me believed I would read. We read all the time and we had a lot of fun.

When it was time for me to start school, my mother took me to the superintendent and, using the first grade basal—a story about a little white house—I read to him. And entered second grade on my first day of school. From that day, my life in school was different.

I don't ever remember reading "round robin." I'm sure I must have done workbooks, but all I remember is being allowed to read what I wanted to, being in a group by myself, as it were. It's almost as if I was accepted as a full-fledged learner because I was a special kind of learner, one who learned from the whole language, all at once. I was in a group by myself. In Frank Smith's words, I had my own "literacy club" (1988).

When I taught reading, I tried to continue for all my students that feeling my parents had conveyed to me: you will learn, we all do. I wanted to share with students the holistic feeling that I think is essential to literacy development. My own experience as a learner and my years of teaching have continued to convince me that we learn from the whole language first and then sort out the parts we need to know more about. Learning to be literate should always be a joyful, successful occasion, full of a sense of wholeness and completeness. Reading—and writing—should only be atomistic when the reader chooses to be atomistic. Never when the teacher decides to sacrifice the learner to the completion of isolated parts.

I was never able, in 18 years of teaching grades 1–6, to get the "reading groups thing" going and keep it going. Traditional teaching of reading with reading groups presumes that students are divided into homogeneous groups according to their reading abilities as demonstrated on standardized tests. They are then assigned leveled basal readers to work in with accompanying workbooks, and the teacher works with each group for a few minutes each day at a small table while the other groups work independently at their desks, waiting their turns and depositing their completed papers in stacks to be corrected—sometime.

Right from the beginning, when I had groups, I never could get the hang of it. As a matter of fact, I had more luck with that huge group of non-reading first graders. Since they were already grouped, I never subdivided them. I didn't have a little table anyway. We all worked together, when we needed to. Mostly we worked silently anyway.

But when I tried to have groups, it never worked out. We'd start out all right, with the first group coming over to the little round table to review the passage they had read alone. We'd do our ten or fifteen minutes and then I'd wrap things up quickly, send the first group back to sit down to routine work guaranteed simple enough to be done alone, tell them to put the books we'd discussed away, and begin the same routine with the second group. And, hopefully, so on for four or five groups. By which time my planned hour of reading would have slid into an hour and a half. I usually made it through two or three days of this before the system collapsed.

It never made any sense anyway. Why would I work hard during "group" time to get readers excited about discussing what they had read, cut the discussion short, and tell them to stop and do something else? That's not what readers do. Readers read something that excites them enough to talk about it, and they keep on talking and sharing until they are talked out. And then they read some more.

And I hated dividing students up by ability and then telling everyone about it by calling them up by number or by "group name." Everyone knew what the levels of the groups were—the books were different colors. I had a hard time facing the students who were permanently marked as "group 4" or "the ones in last year's book"—or worse. I always tried to call the groups up by individual children's names but it didn't help. As Linda Erdmann, a special needs educator who teaches first grade, points out, imagine how it is for those who can't even qualify for the "low" group, the ones who aren't even able to stay in the room while the rest of us read, the ones who have to go "out" for reading. Homogeneous grouping at any age was never a system designed to promote confidence and love of reading. It certainly did not enable all students to think of themselves, in those magical terms, as doing what readers do.

Even when I stopped the group on schedule and sent them back to read the next section, it never really worked. They wanted to keep talking about the reading and all the things it reminded them of, their own experiences and other books they had read and speculations about what would come next. That's what readers do. And my readers usually did, too, secretly if they had to. Even way back in the days when talking outside of group was a no-no, they whispered about books.

Looking back on it I have to shake my head. The whole system—as I interpreted it—worked against everything I know about what readers do when they read and how they develop and fulfill a love of reading. The only time the reading group system ever worked right—that is, consistently and on schedule—was when we only did workbook pages. They were just right for that type of system in that type of time structure.

And the reason they worked is because nobody got excited about those pages. Nobody wanted to talk on about something special that the workbook page made them think about, nobody wanted to begin a discussion about how this page was like another page they had done and here's what happened on that page. Nobody said—as they do all the time about books—that they had read another book by the same author and here's what the author did in that book. Who would ever do that about a workbook?

Drifting Away From Basals

And so, as with writing, I gradually evolved other systems of helping students to be better readers. By better, I have come to mean students who can deal with ever-more difficult text, whose range of what to read expands, who become better and better at "talking like readers," at understanding and describing their own reading process, and better at interpreting and internalizing a variety of types of text.

My first breakthroughs came in the early 70s, when the "curriculum crunch" began to hit, when social studies and science became active parts of my elementary school curriculum. I found that I simply did not have time to work in science and social studies and also read a basal reader that had nothing to do with anything else we were studying—and that didn't even have very good stories. Abandoning the readers, I began using science pamphlets which came in different levels as reading materials. Students selected the ones they wanted to tackle, we read, we did the little activities that were on the sheets, we met to talk about the science topic. It was moderately successful as an instructional organizer, better than the reading kits which at that time were all that I could see as my other option.

Today, if I were drifting away from basals, I would have more help. I would first of all sit right down and read Regie Routman's *Transitions: From Literature to Literacy* (1988). This book was especially written for making the transition into "real" books from a more regimented and limited reading program. Regie focuses on helping teachers to make this shift.

I would also have in my classroom the "School Journals" published by New Zealand's Department of Education and available in this country through Richard C. Owen Publishers. These small, colorful, softcover books each have several kinds of writing/reading in them. In each there are stories, articles, a play, and poems. These provide a variety of models of writing and a combination of reading and pictures to support context. They cover a variety of content areas.

After teaching third grade, I never went back to the basals. And quickly— even during the year I used the science sheets—we slid into reading real books. They were, for all practical purposes, all that was left. We read and we talked. I suggested things that the students look for as they read. They told me—and each other—about what they were really interested in as they read.

All this happened when I was teaching third grade. I tried to read all the books that they were reading. All the literature and prevailing philosophy of reading instruction at that time told me it was necessary. I never succeeded. I would have been better off if I had spent the time listening—as I do now. There is nothing more powerful for a reader to engage in than to try to convince someone who hasn't read a book that their life will be forever altered if they read "this book that I just read—it's the best ever." That's what readers do.

Writers Who Read: Having "Author Dialogues"

In my classrooms we did have a time on my fall schedule devoted to reading, a time when there were certain specified activities we all did. However, during that time we slid out of specific reading time activities and into reading and researching in content, and into the reading/writing connection as the year went on.

One of the main reasons for the slide was that students who are reading think of themselves as readers and writers, authors on both sides of the text. I found with experienced authors that after the first month or so, while we were still fairly compartmentalized, we spent most of our writing time talking about reading and most of our reading time talking about writing.

During writing time, the authors-at-work were primarily concerned with how to influence future readers. They talked a lot about how they could get the readers' expectations of the story to match the writer's intentions. As writers they spent a lot of time—and their friends did too—trying to read the text the way a future reader would. Piaget calls this process ''decentering'' when small children do it. We decenter when we try to look at something from another's point of view. Authors of all ages decenter a lot about their writing. A book's success depends a great deal on the author's ability to decenter in terms of the text, to set aside personal perspective and assumptions and read it through someone else's eyes.

During reading time the authors-at-work also spent a lot of time talking about writing, about how the authors they were reading did what they did in their texts. That eventually became the main subject of discussion. Once I was working with a few sixth graders who had all been reading Mark Twain's *Prince and the Pauper*. We had gotten together in a literature group to discuss Chapter 3. Just as I was about to begin a discussion with a thought I had all picked out, Antonia said, ''Before you start, would you look at how Mark Twain started this chapter? Look at how he had the character talk about what was happening. You know, I worked all day yesterday on my story, trying to start a new chapter and here it was, a way to start. I could have looked at this chapter and seen how he did it.'' Here was an author working with a peer, Antonia ''talking to'' Mark Twain, a fellow author. Twain was a writer just like her and she could do what he did. A powerful thing to have happen in the classroom.

I abandoned my planned discussion and we talked for quite a while about how Mark Twain did what he did when he wrote. We looked at other chapters and talked about how he started them, how he wove the two stories of the prince and the pauper together. We always talked in terms of how we could do the same kinds of things when we wrote. I had forgotten for a moment that I was meeting with published authors who knew a lot about reading and writing as reversible processes.

These were what I call ''Author Dialogues.'' Sometimes they happened spontaneously like the one I just described. Sometimes I scheduled them and we all discussed things we had learned about how various authors seemed to work, depending on what we were reading. Sometimes we read accounts or listened to tapes of authors talking about their process. Accounts and tapes like this were often part of the materials we got from the educational book clubs available to students and teachers. Sometimes I talked about things I had read about how authors do what they do. I tried not to get too abstract in this, but rather to keep the discussions close to the work we were doing as authors ourselves.

The key to having Author Dialogues was that I was working with published authors, that is, the students in my classroom saw themselves as authors. They all had carried written works to fulfillment and the hard-won products were published in hardcover books on my shelves, and for some, in the school library. And it helped that I thought I was an author too. Then the Author Dialogue was authentic and fulfilled all our needs. We were all peers because once we were all writing, some of the students were as good at the process, as good at accomplishing their textual goals, as I was. We talked on equal footing.

And, as we have seen in Antonia's discussion, the authors we read were our peers too. Everyone who writes was involved in the same process with the same goals: to make meaning in print. A nice book to start Author Dialogues with is Joy Cowley's *Seventy Kilometres from Ice Cream: A Letter from Joy Cowley*. In this picture storybook, she tells about how she goes about writing. My students loved her work, having spent happy times with *Quack, Quack, Quack*, that beloved book of all upper elementary students who think they have ever been embarrassed by their parents.

In order to have Author Dialogues, a writing program must be in place on a continuous basis. This program must allow for the development of authorship and publication. At first, it seems overwhelming. But experiencing the impact on so many aspects of student-teacher interaction makes the initial effort worthwhile. Once a teacher-author is talking about reading and writing with student-authors, everything changes.

Readers' Workshop: Choice Reading

Developing a Readers' Workshop was my response to not being able to find a suitable rationale for running a discontinuous reading experience with students in homogeneous groups. I firmly believe that readers should be able to read what they want to, that classroom time and activities should support that proposition, and that my role should be to enable readers to act, talk, and grow as readers in a cooperative, supportive, non-competitive setting.

For those reasons, the central activity of my Readers' Workshop for the past few years has been what we call *choice reading*, readers selecting the books they want to read from wherever they can find them. Choice reading is done whenever readers can find the time and, in the fall, during the second hour of the day which is set aside for Readers' Workshop. Later in the year, when our day has become more integrated and subjects are sliding together, we may have Readers' Workshop later in the day, or read content material in the morning Readers' Workshop slot.

During Readers' Workshop three basic formal activities happened. I kept track of the books students were reading, they spent time reading alone or together, and they wrote to each other in reading journals. Last year I bought them blank books decorated with illustrations from J.R.R. Tolkein's *Lord of the Rings* trilogy and they wrote to each other about books in those.

As we began, readers notified me of the book, or books, they would be reading and how the reading was coming, and I wrote the title on individual lists. They told me when they finished a book and I noted that beside the selection on their list. It was not uncommon in choice reading for some readers to be working on more than book. Given a choice, readers do all kinds of things: some read a fiction and a non-fiction book at the same time; some read a long book and a short book together; some try out several books, reading a chapter or two in each before they make a final selection; some reread old favorites over and over.

In Readers' Workshop I kept a list of the books read each semester for each student and included it in the reporting done to the parents. This list was non-competitive because the chosen books were so different in length and reading level. The students all knew that and everyone also knew that readers, no matter what their ability, choose many different kinds, lengths, and levels of books at various times during the year. Many students shared favorite books and recommended books as the year went by without regard for whether the book was too hard—the main concern was how good it was.

This list represented a great deal of information about the reader. Students were very diligent about keeping it up and often came to tell me about books read at home. They felt these should be on the list too and I agreed. On that list we tracked the reader's growth. Some years, I copied all the titles onto bookmarks for holiday gifts for the readers. Some years, I kept a running record of pages covered between readings. They gave me the information, of course. But usually, I just kept a book list. Reading was an end in itself.

The main activity during Readers' Workshop was reading. I read too. Sometimes I read for school or for a course I was taking, but usually I read for pleasure. To an on-looker, Readers' Workshop would look like what is known as *silent reading* except that people might be quietly talking. Readers do that when they need to share an interest or when something excites them.

As it was set up in my classrooms, everyone read their own book or sometimes a magazine or newspaper. Some of them kept the book with them all day. It would be open on their desks, or under their knees on their chair— places where they could read a page or two when they found a minute. I found in the last few years that most of the students I worked with were happiest when they were reading and often asked to read all day, especially when it was raining. They had spent years in classrooms which emphasized and were geared to choice reading and it paid off. We had created compulsive readers— who could ask for more?

The final, formal activity during Readers' Workshop would be writing in a dialogue journal. Dialogue journals are notebooks in which two friends write back and forth to each other about a special subject, in this case, reading. About once a week, each student would write to me and I would reply, dialoguing with them about the reading we were doing. That gave me a chance to see how the interactions, the reading, and the writing were going and to write to a friend about books.

During Readers' Workshop, it was common for me never to get to my own reading because of students coming to chat with me about books they were reading or concerns about books they were thinking about starting. Since many readers shared books, they also shared reactions. That's what readers do.

I had a lot of books in the room, some from the library, some from educational book clubs, some accumulated from yard sales over the years. I had a good collection of picture story books and a complete set of *National Geographic* magazines from the early 1970s. I brought in the local paper every day and on Wednesdays we each got our own copy of the paper. I purchased a nearly complete set of Matt Christopher's fiction books on sports themes. They were very successful with many readers, especially those who had difficulty finding books that interested them. Some students made their selections for choice reading from the book shelves in the reading resource room with the help of the reading specialist.

All students wrote in their journals every day. Here are typical interactions (*see* Figure 46):

> To Charlie–In the past 20 pages, the Tucks are still trying to convince Winnie to keep their secret a secret. Also the guy in the yellow suit who witnessed the capture and the story is blackmailing Winnie's family, to get the woods by her house. Signed, Jack
>
> To Jack–I think this story is getting much better but I wish I knew the name of the man in the yellow suit. From Charlie. P.S. What page are you on?

(Figure 46 transcription)
Laura–I haven't read much, just up to page 61. But it is a good book. I want to read all day but we can't. Are you reading a new book? What's it called? Bye, Martha

Dear Martha–I am reading an Agatha Christie book. It's called "Hallowe'en Party." I am on page 2. It's pretty good. I am reading 3 books, "Hallowe'en Party," "Amy's Eyes," and "Secret Garden." Bye, Laura

Sometimes if students were stuck for a book to read, I might ask them to preview a book that I was considering using as part of an upcoming social studies unit. Here's a dialogue between Randy and me about a fiction book that looked in the catalog like it might be good for use in the Egypt unit (*see* Figure 47):

(Figure 47 transcription)
Dear Mrs. C: You couldn't learn anything about culture in the book because they make everything up except the two gods. They also buy cheap vases and pretend they're something special. Randy.

Dear Randy: So you would say that the only thing Egyptian about this book is the name? Are there real Egyptian names in the book? Or names of Egyptian things? I guess we didn't have any luck with this "pig in the poke." Mrs. C.

Literature Circles

When we found novels that contributed to what we were learning in social studies, I located multiple copies and several of us read and discussed them together. We called these Literature Circles. Students usually read these books right along with their choice books, although some preferred to finish a book for the Literature Circle before they read a choice book.

That always raised a problem for me. Nobody read the book the same way. Some readers really got into the story and wanted to finish it as soon as possible, some read a little of one book and a little of another—that's what those readers always did—and then there would be some who weren't crazy about the book for Literature Circle and were involved in another book.

When I first started the Circles, the various reading styles interfered with my notion of how Literature Circles ought to go—a notion derived from my old ideas of reading groups. I was taught that we ought to get together to discuss the same chapter or section and nobody should have gone any further because that might come up in the discussion and ruin it for the rest of us. Also, nobody should be behind the rest of us because that's not how it was supposed to be.

But that's not what readers do. Readers read as they need to and want to. Again, I found myself doing things that didn't make any sense, things that worked against my larger purpose. And my larger purpose was always promoting a love of reading and a sense of being readers. It didn't make any sense to say to a committed reader, "You have to stop on this page no matter

'I haven't read much Just up to page 61. But It a good Book. I want to read all day but we cant. Are you reading a new book? What's it called?

Bye

Dear

I am reading an Agatha Christy Book. it's called "Hallowe'en Party." I am on pg. 2. It's pretty good. I am reading 3 books, "Halloween Party", "Amys eyes" and "Secret Garden".

Bye,

FIGURE 46

Oct 16. 1989

Dear Miss C.
    You couldn't learn
anything about culture
in the book because
they make every thing
up exept the two
gods. they also by cheap
vases and prentend there
something special.

10/15/89   R
Dear Randy,
    So you would say that the only
thing Egyptian about this book is
the name? Are there real Egyptian
names in the book? Or names
of Egyptian things?
        I guess we didn't have
                    luck, will
                    this "pig in
                    a poke."
                    Love,
                    Mrs. C.

FIGURE 47

what," or "You can only discuss Chapter 3 no matter how far you've read." I didn't even want to do it that way.

So, quite soon after I began having Literature Circles, I realized that I had to adjust my expectations and, as usual, question my assumptions. Once again, the way I had been taught did not help me to teach. The eventual success of the Literature Circles eventually boiled down to this: I stopped asking questions and they started talking. I stopped trying to control the dialogue and we talked forever.

We still did get around to talking over things that I thought older readers should consider—characterization, the influence of description on the narrative, the development of story—but we talked about these things in a generative way, when they came up, from different parts of the book. We talked like readers sharing books we liked instead of students in a reading group.

The irony in my concern about "covering the reading curriculum" was that these things were all discussed in depth when we had Author Dialogues. How writers were accomplishing all these things was what we as fellow writers wanted to explore. And the level of our talk was much higher than that I knew from my old, traditional reading group days. It was higher because we were very informed reading-writing people—we were authors reading.

When we were having Literature Circles—and sometimes we only had choice reading—I would select multiple copies of three or four books at different reading levels. Anyone could choose any book. I informed them about the book, told them whether I thought it was hard for a sixth grader or not, and then they each made a selection.

Thus, the Literature Groups were heterogeneous, with students at different reading levels sharing accounts. Sometimes students of similar ability would all choose the same book, creating for that selection a homogeneous grouping. But then with the next set of selections the groups would be different. Readers chose books to read out of interest, not because of whether or not it would be too hard for them.

Students who opted to read a book, knowing that it would be hard for them, were assured by me of my continuing support. If need be, we would read it together, orally, taking turns, each with our own copy. Sometimes students on their own would read this way, doing an older students' version of what is commonly called *shared-paired* reading with emergent readers.

During the evolution of Literature Circles and choice reading, we also read "books that students their age should read," as we said to each other. So in sixth grade we read books like *Where the Red Fern Grows, Tuck Everlasting*, and *Iceberg Hermit*. Some also read Agatha Christie, Stephen King, and Mark Twain.

Books to Help

My Readers' Workshop evolved gradually over time. All of what I have described was in place about four years ago. I learned a lot, however, when I read Nancie Atwell's description of the evolution of Readers' Workshop with junior high students in her book, *In the Middle*. She confirmed what I had done and gave me new directions and ideas. I strongly suggest that anyone who is anticipating making a shift like this read her book. She accomplished the shift quite quickly.

I also have learned a lot from reading Frank Smith's view on reading instruction. To get started, readers might begin with his *Joining the Literacy Club: Further Essays into Education*

On the practical, how-to side, two of the books cited in the chapter on writing will be useful. Don Graves' *Build a Literate Classroom* and Harste, Short and Burke's *Creating Classrooms for Authors: The Reading-Writing Connection* both demonstrate strategies and techniques, like Readers' Theater, to use when working with authors-in-progress.

Dorothy Watson's *Ideas and Insights* and John Stewig and Sam Sebesta's *Using Literature in the Elementary Classroom* have ideas useful in upper elementary classrooms. David Hornsby, Deborah Sukarnäh and Jo-Ann Parry's *Read on: A Conference Approach to Reading* is a step-by-step guide for beginners.

Finally, for those who would like to reconsider the nature of the reading process and need a book designed to be understood, there is Connie Weaver's *Reading Process and Practice: from Socio-linguistics to Whole Language*. In this excellent volume, Connie teaches us about the reading process and its instruction at all levels.

Reading Content Material

A major reading agenda for upper grade students in elementary school is how to learn to deal with non-fiction, often difficult material. This is the stuff of student research much of the time.

My main goal for upper elementary students in this area was to give them insights into their continuing growth as readers, and their developing understanding of their own reading process as they encountered more difficult, often nonfiction, often non-choice reading. To this end I followed the perspective expressed by Nancie Atwell (1990) in her introduction to her edited volume, *Coming to Know: Writing to Learn in the Elementary Grades*. She says: "Writing in the content areas does not have to be a test of reading, a performance for the teacher that demonstrates whether the student located and reassembled someone else's information" (p. xii).

Although her volume focuses on writing, she expresses the heart of the issue of reading in content: who are we reading for, why are we doing it, how will our learning be expressed? The essays in *Coming to Know* are primarily written by teachers and those in the first section are useful to teachers introducing their students to the research process. The essays in the last section of the book discuss uses of writing as a way of "coming to know" what we are reading.

In asking children to approach reading in content, the first step for me was to look at my own approach and levels of assistance. As the International Reading Association (1989) points out in *Cases in Literacy: An Agenda for Discussion*:

> Felicia, for example, works hard as she reads about the causes of seasonal changes in her social studies book . . . Not surprisingly, Felicia learns a few terms but has trouble fitting them into her prior, informal theories about the seasons . . . she has thus developed a fundamental misconception about what it means to reason and learn within new domains. Ironically, her teacher would not have approached the reading of a short story in the same essentially uncritical fashion. (p. 34)

So, part of my task is to establish conditions that promote teaching and learning in content as related to, as the International Reading Association puts it, "the learning of literate behaviors." Just as readers in Readers' Workshop were enabled to consistently see themselves as readers, so in content, we try to enable readers to consistently see themselves as literate scientists, literate students of social processes, literate mathematicians. We want them to see themselves as doing what scientists, social scientists, and mathematicians do when they are reading and writing. Such people "generally use language in a variety of complex ways that are at the heart of the . . . process" (IRA, p. 33).

There are three theoretical perspectives that I use to guide me in practical ways:

1. I believe students should read for authentic purposes.
2. I believe I should provide plenty of time for reading in content areas.
3. I want students reading in content to work successfully on the outer edges of their ability.

Reading for authentic purposes

In the first perspective, I establish contexts so that students read in content for an authentic purpose. This is usually done in the guise of someone else whom they have selected, a made-up, grown-up identity that allows them to read as that person might read for a special reason, usually as part of a job to be done.

So a sixth grade student involved in trying to do research on Egypt would also try to become a classroom "expert" in that subject in the role of Fellow at the Royal Archeological Institute of Cairo (RAI), a mythical institution invented by me. In an artifact of research, a "letter to the Director of the RAI," a "research Fellow named Samantha" discusses her recent, collaborative research effort on a topic chosen by her, designed to result in a report to the "Institute" and also to prepare her and other Fellows for a trip to Egypt:

My Summary by Samantha Brown

My summary is all about family life (in Egypt). I have finished my report, thank goodness. In this I put all of my sources and told about what good resources of information each one was to me. I enjoy writing reports and summaries as I did.

Family Life is a good subject because when we get to Egypt we will understand their customs and culture of how they all live. Charlie and Jason are doing a great subject, diseases. But it's hard to find sources for it. Both Stacey and I are doing Family Life. I think studying their family life will be one important thing for when you arrive in Egypt. You don't want to make a fool of yourself!

Stacey and I share information from books. We run things off for each other (on the copying machine), too. We are both glad we are doing the same subject.

Samantha's development of expertise as a Fellow, working with "Stacey," another Fellow, resulted in a research report supported by six sources, including books, the encyclopedia, and videos. In her "Final Report to the RAI," Samantha appraises each of the sources she selected so that other readers might have a starting point:

- The encyclopedia gave me about a page of information.
- I liked this book and its information plus I like the pictures in the book. I thought this book was very useful.
- I really do think I could have found something a little better (than this book) but I don't know what else I could have used, so I just used this source.
- In this book I think the words were easy to understand for kids that can't read too well. This book was a good source because it was easy to read and good to understand.
- This was a very useful movie.
- This was a pretty good movie in my opinion.

After each annotation, Samantha includes page numbers for information she used. The report includes, as all do, a full bibliography. Later she writes:

> Egypt is an interesting subject. You can learn so much from it. All my summaries that I have done have something different in them. I didn't really tell about all I learned but, trust me, I learned a lot.
> This has been a pleasure. Sincerely, Mrs. Samantha Brown

Here is a sample of the topics which Fellows became experts on, and some of the reasons they were selected:

The Nile River, the Soul of Egypt

Tropical Diseases

Mummification

The Nile River of Egypt, Part I: The Distribution of the Nile to its People.
Part II: The History and Changes of the Once Changeless Land; Advantages of the Dam; Disadvantages of the Dam; The Suez Canal"

The Architecture of the Pyramids of the Ancient World–"I chose the topic of the architecture of the pyramids because I thought it would be interesting to find out why the Ancient Egyptians built the Pyramids. Because of dedicated archeologists this has been discovered."

Don't Be Sick in the Tropics: The Tropical Disease Guide–"So if you are planning a vacation to the tropics, read this manual first so an illness won't be your downfall for your vacation and remember, make your vacation a safe vacation."

Archeology–"An archeologist is like a detective."

Life in Modern Egypt; Life in Ancient Egypt; School in Egypt; Life on the Nile

Archeology: Working in the Field

Government in Egypt

These represent a vast array of topics, each with three to six sources in the bibliography, the result of experts in search of knowledge to share with other experts. Reports were contained in a word-processed, spiral bound format grandly entitled "Final Reports, 1989–90, Royal Archeological Institute, 1111 Pharoahs' Boulevard, Cairo Egypt" and in an all-school volume of student writing on the topic of Egypt.

Nancy Martin, Peter Medway and Harold Smith (1976) write of speaker interactions in content that are examples of genuine communication: "There has been a real reason for saying everything that has been said" (p. 27). The value and power of this authentic communication is evident here in the comments of the Fellows, such as: "I hope anyone who read my report learned something that you didn't already know—and I hope you enjoyed it." Martin, Medway and Smith say, "The speakers have made available to their listeners ideas, views and responses which were available only from them, which they thought to be original and valuable and which (they thought) their listeners would be glad to hear" (p. 27).

Provide plenty of time

The second perspective for promoting the translation of the reading process into content areas involves providing plenty of time and opportunity for verbal interaction: "We might have more success . . . if we deliberately made provision for this thinking, chewing-over part of learning to go on openly: which is to say, in language" (Martin, Medway and Smith 1976, p. 17).

Thus Charlie and Jason worked closely together as "expert Fellows" at the Institute. They spent several hours in the school library, poring over a rather grisly set of volumes, entitled *The New Illustrated Medical Encyclopedia*, finally settling on volumes 3 and 4. From time to time, they would ask me to help them understand something they were reading. One of the initial hurdles for them was to learn how to tell which diseases were tropical. Once they mastered that form of classification, they were off and running—together.

They both finally settled on describing separately in two reports the causes, symptoms and cures—if any—for these diseases: Intestinal Obstruction ("sort of like a clog in your intestines" writes Jason); African Sleeping Sickness ("Watch Out For—two-winged flies that look like big horseflies with a long beak. They fold their wings flat on their back" says Jason); Amabaisis ("An infection from a one-celled parasite" says Charlie); and, their favorite, River Blindness ("This is a disease carried by river crabs. The flies lay their eggs on the crabs and turn into worms and when you step on them they burrow into your feet" according to Charlie. Jason points out: "Don't worry about this disease. There should be a ban on infected waters.")

Together, through interaction, they learned what they needed to. Then, through talk, the process of translation and internalization began for each of them. We see the by-product of the learning—the report. Martin, Medway and Smith write: "Information is not just taken on like cargo. Nor is it like being given something, as if you now have something where before you had nothing . . . information is received" (p. 16).

Working on the edge of their ability

The third perspective is Lev Vygotsky's idea of growth in learning taking place in what he called "the zone of proximal development." This is that area of supported interaction where children perform at the edge of their ability because of the structured support offered by the adult or a more able peer. It is what Newman, Griffin and Cole (1989) have dubbed "the construction zone."

In the research efforts of young readers we see a great deal of their work in the zone of proximal development, understanding on the edge of their understanding, demonstrating, as Courtney Cazden says, "performance before competence." And this happens because they are involved in social interactions with "adults or more capable peers."

So I read material with students, sometimes with the whole group, and sometimes we work it through in tandem. We look at videos designed as travelogues for adult travelers and we stop and "translate" what has been said, rewording the adult language into phrases that connect to the younger world of the students.

As we talk about what we think is in what we are reading, we continually work at reorganizing what we know. Thus Patrick was able to compose a page-long report with three bibliographic sources, all cited in the report. His report was written in his own words, on the edge of his zone of proximal development, in the company of me and "more capable peers," in spite of any difficulties he might have been having with reading the language. He knew what he had learned, the information learned interactively with support in "the construction zone" had been internalized.

"Felisha" knows that she had dwelt successfully in the zone of proximal development and has learned knowledge that was hard to learn. In her final report, she tells all about Egyptian food and concludes:

> I thought it would be interesting to find out a little more about Egypt so I decided to research and find out about Egyptian food. My reason for that is because I found out a little bit about it at first and then I really got into it. I really wanted to just learn some more interesting things about it so I did.

Jason constructed his own zone of proximal development in his study of tropical diseases. As an "expert" on this topic, he did what experts do— consult other experts. He went out and spoke with people who were experienced travelers in tropical climates, interviewing them about what he needed to know. In the process of doing this, he created a zone of proximal development in which adults spoke to him on the edge of his understanding and, through interaction, helped him to raise the level of his learning.

Here's what he learned from "Interviews with various travelers:"

1. Bring a bottle of Pepto-Bismol
2. Bring a bottle of Kaopectate
3. Only drink bottled water
4. Don't eat uncooked foods
5. Try to get a 4 star hotel
    a. the rooms are free of germs
    b. they have water purifying systems
6. Be aware of rabies
7. Drink Pepto-Bismol every day for one week before you go

Thus, through practical application of these theoretical perspectives, I try to begin upper elementary students on a process of growth in reading in content, what Don Graves (1989) in *Investigate Nonfiction* calls "direct access to well-chosen information" (p. 90). A key factor is sustaining their belief that they are readers, that they know how to proceed.

In this "research without tears" approach, the hidden agenda is success and improved self-esteem. Or what "Tiffany Ross" expresses at the end of her expert Fellow report to the Royal Archeological Institute of Cairo: "This has been fun and an educational experience. I had a lot of fun and learned about Egypt."

Thanks, Tiffany, you made my day.

Content Learning
with Trade Books

Remembering Text Books

I mainly remember one thing from my year as a sixth-grade student. You'd think the really big, neat things would stand out in my memory—raising a rabbit, growing some beans in the closet and some on the window ledge and comparing them—but in my mind those are short, sunny images, nothing more.

What I really remember is copying a picture out of my social studies book. It was a picture of the inside of an igloo with the Eskimos at home. I was a good copier. Long before sixth grade I had identified myself as not good at art. But I was really good at copying pictures and I sure enjoyed that activity. Maybe it was the final activity for the chapter. Maybe we put the pictures up on the brick walls. I don't remember. Those things weren't important to me.

Working with the picture was the important part. I can see that picture now as clearly as I saw it then: the rounded shapes of the rectangular bricks; the little shelves on the wall with vague, cloth things on them; the man in the parka bent over his spear; the fire and the cook pot and the rest of the family. The picture and my concentration on it told me more about the Eskimos than all the compulsory reading and test-taking that had gone before.

Looking back now, I am struck with the impact of that picture on my learning. Certainly some of the textual information I acquired is still available to me. But my appreciation of Eskimo culture, my understanding of their family ways, and my affinity for their common, daily life—my conjunction with them—springs from that experience with the picture.

I don't know if the Eskimo picture of my sixth grade experience was good art or not. Certainly one thing that made it work as a learning tool for me was my engagement with it. As I copied it, I fantasized and "fell into" the whole topic.

"Dense Print" Books Versus Picture Storybooks

From about third grade on, once children are on their way to becoming independent readers, pictures in text begin to dwindle. Those that remain are often drawn by unknown artists for a specific textbook chapter. Few pictures in basals or textbooks are quality reproductions of good art. Most are small, and worked in minimal color. Few are inspiring. Compared to the richness available in today's content-oriented trade books and picture storybooks, the pictures in most "schoolbooks" come out a poor second.

Further, most books used in grades three through six and up are "dense print," only words with perhaps a picture on the cover. Many books available and required for students beyond eight years old are entirely text. This applies in both literature-based and basal-driven programs. In our concern for turning out readers, we have forgotten that people learn from many things in a book. "Dense print" is one medium for the transmission of information, but books have other avenues as well—pictures, captions, diagrams, maps—all convey information. It is the integration of learning through all media that produces full cognitive understanding.

In working with my own students, I tried to bring some of that understanding to them. I did this through the use of trade and picture storybooks as an integrated part of the social studies and science curricula. I tried to bring pictures back into content.

In working with trade books I hope upper elementary students will develop further the process of reading and writing content material. Using picture storybooks as models, students can analyze how information enters text and how learners derive meaning. These books can be seen as a bridge between fiction and academic writing, between texts commonly viewed by students as personal and contentless (i.e., made-up stories), and those viewed as impersonal and wholly content (i.e., reports and term papers).

I used a broad range of trade books with upper elementary students, including picture storybooks, to develop an appreciation of the beauty and richness possible in texts. Trade books can become text models for students learning to produce content writing of their own.

My friend, Mary Ellen Giacobbe, a great lover of children's picture storybooks, warns me to be careful about saying that I ''use'' books in one way or another. And she is right. We must be very careful about what we do with good literature and beautiful pictures in our classrooms, we must be careful how we ''use'' them. At the point when we have forgotten the story, when we pick up the book just to ''use'' it for something, when we have lost the love of literature, then we must stop and read. We must sit down, put our feet up, and renew our love of the book for its own sake. This is what must be shared with children.

So I will talk about ''using'' children's books, but I will monitor myself very closely. In my work with books I will ''use'' them only to the extent that we enhance our appreciation of the fine literature.

Trade books were always a part of my classroom, especially the dense print kind at the upper level. Upper level teachers whose reading programs are literature-based, like mine was, are quite good at helping children to appreciate this kind of trade book.

But in teaching grades four, five, and six, I worked a lot with children's picture storybooks, developing a personal library of them for classroom use. There are four main strands of my work with picture storybooks with upper elementary school children: picture storybooks for all ages; picture storybooks as text models; picture storybooks as models of creative products; and picture storybooks as a way of learning how to learn from books.

Picture Storybooks for All Ages

The most powerful way I found to use picture storybooks was simply to restore them to their place in the world of literature in my room. When I left off teaching small children, I left off enjoying picture storybooks and making them accessible to readers. And yet many of these books are written to readers with some experience of the world. For instance, one of my favorites is Ann Turner's *Dakota Dugout*. It ends like this:

> Talking brings it near again,
> the sweet taste of new bread
> in a Dakota dugout.

how the grass whispered like an old friend,
how the earth kept us warm.

Sometimes the things we start with are best.

I have read this book to many grown-ups in workshops and college classes
and they often write back to me about the impact this simple oral history has
on them. Upper elementary students, children on the edge of adulthood,
appreciate these books, too.

Once I began buying picture storybooks again and bringing them into my
sixth grade classroom simply as good literature, my students and I discovered
our passion for their beauty and lyrical language. Now I have a large collection, including "Big Books," those oversized picture storybooks advertised
for grades K–2. In my sixth grades, we loved them. We also indulged our
passion for pop-up books and discovered that many are written for grown-
ups, like Raymond Hawkey's *Evolution* and Ron Van Der Meer's *Majesty in
Flight*. We learned a lot just from the "paper engineered" pictures.

Picture Storybooks as Text Models

The second strand of picture storybook work relates to helping students to
work with books as text models—to study how the author used a particular
format or writing style to teach information, but in an interesting way, so that
we could try to do it too. We looked at how authors of written fiction compose
a story, how they manipulate language, how they use characterization and so
on, as a way of helping us to try to write our stories.

Many students get story ideas—plot and beyond into details—from books.
Annie Dillard says in *The Writing Life*, "He is careful of what he reads, for
that is what he will write."

One student, Bob, told me how proud he was that his uncle, who knew
that Bob sometimes read books to get ideas for writing, thought that one of
his books was an imitated idea. Bob said, "I felt proud because I thought of
it myself."

Richard Kolczynski, in John Stewig and Sam Sebesta'a *Using Literature
in the Elementary Classroom*, writes of a little girl who reads to help her learn
to write, but mostly had to do it at home because in school they were only
allowed to write reports. She said, "I don't want to write about books; I want
to write books" (p. 76).

I've used Robert Lawson's *Ben and Me: An Astonishing Life of Benjamin Franklin As Written By his Good Mouse Amos* . . . as a way of talking to upper elementary students about the possibilities for writing content material they have learned in the style of historical fiction. When we tried to do this, instead of simply writing a report, we tried to write for younger children, often using an author's device like Lawson's mouse as a way of writing nonfiction content into fiction so that it would be interesting to read.

Sometimes we did this in the upper grades ''to help our school,'' to teach younger children basic information on a topic that we wish we had known when we started the unit. We'd say, if younger children read our story, they will be ready to learn more when they are in our grade. So, a student might decide to write a story told by Paul Revere's horse which told—in an interesting way—some of the information which has been learned in a study of Paul Revere's ride. A sixth grader I worked with wrote a story about a boy who ran in the original Olympic Games, containing learned content information about Greek culture.

In the last chapter, we saw an aspect of this use of trade books as text models when Antonia, speaking about Mark Twain, drew directly on how he had started a chapter to help her start a chapter in her writing. Here we have authors using published trade books as a way to help them learn how to make a match between their author intentions and the story expectations they hope to generate in their readers.

Only recently have I thought to turn to the rich world of picture storybooks as a way of helping youngsters consider alternatives for writing—and reading—content. The writing of Byrd Baylor, lyrical and sparse, is inspiring to writers struggling with the problems involved in writing large amounts of text by offering them a model of condensed, expressive content text. Byrd writes about fossils this way on a page of *If You Were a Hunter of Fossils*:

> Maybe
> you
> are a hunter
> of fossils.
>
> Maybe you
> are the one
> who turns
> the dark earth
> of a flat
> Kansas wheatfield
> and touches
> a fish
> in a stone.

Or students might turn to the poetic language of Joanne Ryder in *Lizard in the Sun*, part of her "Just for a Day" series:

> Lean green lizard
> you feel the sun
> singing inside you
> and you run . . .
> Dashing down a hot wall
> you leap into the bushes.
> You run from one branch to the next—
> A jungle of leaves flashes by you—
> And you rest tucked inside a bush.

These kinds of texts, written so well in children's picture storybooks, offer alternatives for conveying information in subject areas.

Picture Storybooks as Models of Creative Products

The third strand of my work with picture books at the upper levels relates to helping young authors renew their creativity, to enable them to work with books that are designed to promote joyful engagement. The lyrical language of Byrd Baylor's books is supported by the beautiful drawings of Peter Parnell. And Joanne Ryder's poetic, science books about animals like lizards are completed by the beautiful paintings of Michael Rothman.

As children get older and become more and more steeped in literacy, visual creativity and the active enjoyment of it become compartmentalized during art time, usually taught by a specialist and completely separated from the classroom and its curriculum. Picture storybooks, especially those in content, provide a means of developing visual creativity in the regular classroom at the same time writers are developing literacy.

The longer I taught, the more I became concerned with children's apparent lack of creativity in a forum obviously designed to promote maximum creativity: the publishing of student-made books for classroom and personal use.

In the writing program in the school where I taught, children were given ample amounts of time to learn to write (see, for specific information on writing process: Harste, Short & Burke 1988; Calkins 1986; Parry & Hornsby 1985; Graves 1983). They were schooled in writing process from kindergarten to sixth grade. They wrote what they wanted to; they revised at length in teacher-and peer-conferencing sessions; they edited and used publishers' worksheets to prepare the manuscripts for publication; they word processed on computers to prepare a final text; and, finally they bound their stories up into cardboard covered books. In my room, students bound a "shelf copy" to keep in the classroom library. I have nearly 75 of these student-made products.

Classrooms operated as process writing workshops not only map the writer's process onto creativity components, but also match Delores Gallo's definition of a creative learning environment: "a psychologically-safe, non-authoritarian, stimulating, responsive environment, which would provide opportunities and requests for the free expression of thought and feelings" (1983, p. 93).

The initial impetus for establishing classroom time for student writing workshops was to free students from what Don Graves (1984) described as writers standing in the welfare line waiting for a handout from the teacher.

But while the writing process program provokes this positive vision of self-as-author, it fails to promote a broad role for creativity. The students I worked with were very creative in words—their stories, mostly fiction, were highly imaginative, well-developed pieces of text. If their written products had been turned in to me on white lined paper—the way I turned in writing when I was in elementary school—then I would have concluded without a doubt that this writing process program developed a great deal of creativity in children.

But these author/publishers went beyond the traditional "writing of a story on white paper for the teacher" and produced a real book, with cover, title page, dedication, publishing information, author biography, even a library card and a number in the Dewey Decimal System.

Students have many creative options available to them in publishing: the type of book they will publish, type of binding, size and style of book, options such as foldout books or pop-up books, structure and placement of text and pictures on each page, "bookish" features drawn from student observations of text models—all these and more are choices available to the author-turned-publisher.

Still the creativity is unilinear. The books on my shelf had mostly plain covers—title, author, nothing more. A few listed an illustrator, a few had a drawing. One had comments from reviewers and a summary on the back. Inside, many had a few words at the bottom of each page but no illustration to fill up the rest of the page. A few had simple illustrations, carelessly drawn. A few were well done in every respect.

In short, many of the books on my shelf were terrific stories, but visually uncreative books. The authors did not seem to view themselves as artists or even graphic designers. Books for them seemed to be only the stories in them and not the wholeness of a creative text, produced to appeal to several senses.

I have student-made books in my collection from students in kindergarten all the way up to sixth-graders. Up to third grade, most of the books have some kind of illustration. From fourth to sixth grade, illustrations virtually disappear.

Many emerging writers begin their writing process by drawing (Matthews 1988; Calkins 1986; Graves 1983; Bissex 1980). This persists up through the primary grades. It is common to find several children in a primary classroom who draw before any writing takes place, who use drawing as a self-made writing "prompt." Sometimes these drawings are pasted into a final product, sometimes students want to redraw them before they go in the book. Sometimes the "prompt" drawing cannot be used in the final product because for the student the act of drawing was itself a three-dimensional experience on a two-dimensional surface. Thus the picture been overdrawn as the student "acted out" the story on paper before writing.

Between second and third grade, drawing begins to dwindle as a writing prompt. Lucy Calkins observes,

> For most second graders, talking rather than drawing can provide a horizon and a supportive scaffolding. Just as in first grade, where the goal was to have writing catch up to drawing, in second grade the goal is to have writing catch up to talking. (p. 70)

Beyond second and third grade, drawing is seen in a different relationship to writing by student authors. For many of them, it appears that writing and drawing entirely take leave of each other at this age.

However, in their student-made books, many young authors—even up to sixth grade—continue to structure the page *as if* a picture will be drawn. That is, the text is a narrow band at the bottom of an otherwise blank page. When this is pointed out to them, some students reply that this makes the book longer. Some look puzzled and move the thin line of text up into the middle or to the top of the page. A few decide to put more text on the page. In the same vein, I have seen many third graders continue to do first drafts on primary "picture paper"—large paper with lines at the bottom and a blank at the top for a picture—and never draw pictures. It is as if they do not notice that the drawings are gone.

The absence of drawings at any stage of writing for older children may occur because of the child's own developing sophistication with symbolic language.

> One thing only is certain—that the written language of children develops in this fashion, shifting from the drawing of things to the drawing of words . . . The entire secret of teaching written language is to prepare and organize this natural transition appropriately. (Vygotsky 1978, p. 116)

Thus, it may be that sometimes as a natural part of symbolic development, drawing disappears from writing, that the pendulum swings too far for a moment in a child's development, thus eliminating art as a creative feature in the company of writing.

Or it may be that children develop the adult reader's perspective that meaning is carried in words. Young children seem to view all text the way good picture storybooks, cartoons and comic books are written: meaning is shared between drawing and print. But in writing process conferencing, adults may convey the view that meaning should only be contained in the words. Thus pictures, for a child, become redundant.

Coupled with these possibilities are other more practical, pedagogical matters. As children become older, adults may insist on "more writing and less drawing." Drawing may come to be seen as a waste of valuable writing time, or a child's way of stalling.

Also, art and creative endeavors are commonly compartmentalized in today's public schools, thus setting them apart from the classroom skills. Interaction is limited.

Further, grades four through six are commonly referred to as "the content grades." Creativity seems to take a backseat to factual knowledge and the ability to manipulate symbolic and alphabetic language. And, as already noted, upper elementary books become more and more textual with fewer and fewer drawings.

Finally, we have Torrance's (1965) report on "the fourth grade slump," a phenomenon associated with the way in which "nine-year-olds become greatly concerned about peer pressure and give up many of their creative activities" (p. 174). Torrance further cites Pulsifer's 1960 position that the "abandonment of creativity at about age 5 . . . is not a natural developmental change but is due to the sharp man-made changes . . . rules and regulations" (p. 175). Torrance agrees and expresses

> . . . unwillingness to accept the assumption that the severe drops in measures of creative thinking ability are purely developmental phenomena that must be accepted as unchangeable . . . children needlessly sacrificed their creativity, especially in the fourth grade . . . many of them did not recover as they continued through school. (p. 175)

Such a slump, coupled with the possibility of a youthful sensitivity to peer pressure, might account for lack of creativity in student-made products. Kagan (1984) cites "a major hallmark of a creative person" as "some indifference to the humiliation that can follow a mistake" (p. 222). Perhaps the lack of illustration is a reaction to the possibility of a "mistake."

Linked to Torrance's noting of "the fourth grade slump" also may be issues of identity. By a fairly young age, children are identified and identify themselves as artist/not artist, singer/not singer. Most sixth graders speak of themselves as not artists, unable to represent in pictures. I remember about an equal number of boys and girls over the years—no more than one or two per class—who were identified as "the class artist." These artists become the official illustrators of the classroom, trading artwork for publishing chores like typing and sewing.

Three additional factors might be of relevance:

1. We know that creativity flourishes best in a value-free atmosphere. But one can hardly call the general school atmosphere free of external evaluation. Even though writing process workshops try to be value-free and intrinsically motivational, factors which promote creativity, these workshops cannot help but be influenced by the general tone and tenor of the school climate, which is quite value-laden and extrinsically-motivated. Further, even when upper level students are working in a positive writing environment, they may come to that setting laden with baggage from previous years of schooling and home response.

2. Time is always a precious commodity in the school day. Although it seems that every effort is made in these process writing classrooms to accommodate and forestall this demand, it may be that in fact, students feel pressured to produce writing rather than books.

3. It may simply be that these students see only a writing task—the composing of a story—and for them the task is over when the story is completed. Publishing the book may only be an afterthought, an addenda to the larger, more crucial process.

Because of my ongoing concern over this dilemma of how to promote creative products in student-made books, I took a two-pronged approach. First, I went directly to my students and asked them: What does it mean to be creative? How can I help children to be more creative in the books that they produce?

The students had a good grasp of the concept of creativity: "ideas nobody thinks of," "to think of things in a different way. To be creative is to be unique," "even be a little crazy with their ideas," "when you get an idea that is really weird," "To differ from the others . . . adding pizazz to make something dull more interesting."

Some students had suggestions about how people get to be creative, "to be spaced out and you think of an idea and it is impossible." A pretty good definition of the defocusing that characterizes some creators' processes.

Student suggestions on how I could help students to be more creative ranged from:

> *the practical*: "give them more colors," "do the cover with spattered paint"

> *to the directive*: "close them in a room with no TV or radio or anything, only with a pen and pencil"

> *to the hostile*: "I had no idea that our class had a problem with this"

> *to the ethereal*: "Try to surpass the ordinary (in every way!)"

> *to the defeated*: "There's no way that I can think of that would make a kid creative in his publishing. It would only work if he would want to" "I think that you can't help us on our writing. I think it is impossible to help us with our creative writing."

I particularly liked the responses that suggested specific strategies I could try: "introduce them to new subjects . . . it would expand their mind . . . that would also make them unafraid to try new things" and "just show them some really good published books" "Let them know it is okay to be creative and that people will appreciate it more than the ordinary. Make them explore new ways of doing things . . ." I thought these kids got the idea.

The second prong of my approach was to share a broader variety of trade books with my students. I tried to balance the text-only books I read to them, books like *Where the Red Fern Grows*, and *Iceberg Hermit*, with the reading and sharing of picture storybooks.

These picture storybooks are often heavily rooted in content and information, often with a fictional overlay. I hoped to inspire the creativity in my students by showing them simply beautiful books, books with illustrations, collages, photos. As we did this, we also bridged the gap between "straight fiction" and "straight information," or between books read and written for pleasure and books read and written for information.

I did all this because I was concerned about many implications for a loss of creativity at an early age. I see shadows of a negative attitude toward product and the creator's responsibility for it. Children who create products become adults who create products; if the intrinsic motivation toward perfection was not present in the child, it will likely not be born in the adult. As Delores Gallo (1983) points out:

> . . . the crucial element in fostering creative thinking is attitude: to nurture creativity one must foster a positive attitude toward the creative enterprise, and toward the individual as a source of competence, worth and that enterprise. (p. 119)

When I worked this way with picture storybooks as models of creative products, I discussed how these books were put together, what the author intended, and how we learned from them. I hoped to show students that books are never words alone, that learning occurs to many senses at once.

I worry that this loss of creativity is more far-reaching than simple student-made books: Do we see in these products the decline of multi-faceted creativity at an early age, and its sublimation into a single form of symbolic expression?

Picture Storybooks as a Way of Learning How to Learn From Books

Finally, the fourth strand of my work with picture storybooks at the upper elementary level was to help students understand how we learn from books, how authors put information into books, and how readers go about getting it out. For this is what content reading is all about, understanding the nature of a certain kind of text designed to teach. Many picture storybooks teach, too, many have a strong content component. We started with those to help us work up to the tough stuff.

Don Graves (1989) in *Investigate Nonfiction* says:

> Picture books are a good place for children to begin to explore their subject. Authors of picture books . . . have chosen essential information underlying basic concepts. They have often touched on the most elemental areas and introduced broad, general knowledge related to the child's interest area. Some teachers may reason, ''Why, this is easy reading; the children should be challenged.'' But there will be time enough for challenge. What all readers and writers need, at any age, is direct access to well-chosen information. (p. 90)

I started work with picture storybooks for older students by posing six questions which we considered during the study of how we learn from books:

1. What could be learned from this book?
2. How did the author get information into this book?
3. How do readers get information out of this book?
4. Could you use this book as a model for your own writing?
5. Do you think other children your age would like to read this book?
6. Do you think we could use this book as a text for learning about this subject?

We started in sixth grade by reading and talking about Robert McCloskey's well-known *Make Way For Ducklings*. It is an old favorite for many of the children. But some of them never heard the story of Mr. and Mrs. Mallard and their search through the city of Boston for a good home for their babies, Jack, Kack, Lack, Mack, Nack, Ouack, Pack and Quack. Some children have always known and loved the book and have it on their book shelf at home. Some hadn't heard it for years and smiled and nodded as I read it to them. Some remembered it vaguely from first grade, but they couldn't read then and missed out on it and by the time they could read it wasn't part of the upper elementary classroom library.

When I tell some teachers about this way of beginning to investigate content in books, they say, "Don't the students laugh at those books as baby books?" I have never had this happen—and I have even used this book with grown-ups. A lot depends on the teacher's attitude in introducing books into the classroom and also how the work with the books is framed. Most listeners seem to enjoy hearing the story and look forward to their turn to have the books in their hands when I pass it around. Susan Hall points out in her "Introduction" to *Using Picture Storybooks to Teach Literary Devices* that the reading level of many of these books may "reach sixth grade and beyond."

I started out by asking listeners to consider what could we learn from a book like this, what do little kids learn when they hear it, is it "just a story" or is it a book that teaches? I know that there is a great deal of content information in *Make Way for Ducklings*, beyond the story, as there is in many children's picture storybooks. Joanne Ryder, in the beginning of *Lizards in the Sun*, thanks James P. O'Brien of the Department of Herpetology, California Academy of Sciences, for "his expert reading of the manuscript" and has an author's note all about lizards. Other books in that "Just for a Day" series have undergone similar readings by scientific experts. Her book, *The Snail's Spell*, was honored as an "Outstanding Science Book for Young Children" by the New York Academy of Sciences. Many authors and illustrators of children's books research their topic heavily before beginning the enterprise.

So we at sixth grade listened to the books for enjoyment but also to begin to get at how one learns from books. I would rather have done this introductory study with younger children so that I could have continued into harder material with sixth graders. But that was the grade I was teaching at the time I began the work and the students had not looked at picture storybooks in this particular way.

After we read and discussed *Make Way for Ducklings*, I asked my sixth graders to write about what they had learned from the book and what they thought of it. Figures 48 and 49 show two of their responses.

I started with *Make Way for Ducklings* because many of the students

Make way for Ducklings is a fun book to read. It's about two ducks who are looking for a place to live and have their babies. It's really good book!

I think you could learn about how ducks hatch their eggs, how they teach their ducklings to swim, and avoid danger. Mostly you learn about just in general ducks' ways of living.

I think Robert McClosky is a good author, although I have only seen one of his books I think he's a good author!

FIGURE 48

One thing you could learn is how a bird might think. Another thing you could learn is how birds pick their nesting place. You could also learn how birds live, like how the hatch their eggs.

I think it is a great story for all ages Robert McClosky is a great author, because he tells about the birds, but in a fun, nice way. THE END

FIGURE 49

I learned some things about Canadian-geese. One of the things is, how they explained the information, I felt like I was in the book. The second thing is when the book talked about how geese open and close there webbed feet to swim through the water. Another thing I didn't know about geese is that they fly in a "V" shape.

FIGURE 50

---

associated it with the early grades, with reading for fun, and stories that were just for little kids. I wanted them to realize that all books teach information in some way and that even books we think of as far behind us taught us something when we were young and may be able to teach us something new with a rereading.

We then moved to a reading of Joanne Ryder's *Catching the Wind*, part of her "Just for a Day" series. In this series, children "change just for a day" into another kind of creature to experience life as that creature lives it. In *Catching the Wind*, a little girl leaves her room and flies with the wild birds, the geese. Michael Rothman's oil paintings drew me into the story when I picked up the book for the first time. Beautifully done and reproduced, they take the reader into the experience.

I asked the students to write about what they had learned that they hadn't known before. Figures 50–52 show a few of their responses.

One student, George, demonstrated in his writing something we had been emphasizing, the identifying of information in the text itself. In learning to read and report in content areas, one of our goals is to help students understand how to locate literal information and distinguish it from textual inferences. George wrote:

> 'Real Information'
> One thing I learned from *Catching the Wind* was how geese swam, that geese oil themselves, and how they talk to each other. These things were on pages 7, 14, and 18.

Here, in noting the page numbers for his facts and conclusions, this serious student moves directly toward the work we must someday do: research. For

> Learning from books
> In the book Catching the wind
> you can learn many things about
> Canadian geese, you Just have to
> listen. In this book you can learn for
> Instance that geese have speacial feathers
> on their body, they swim with thier
> webbed feet and how they fly in a
> Vee.

FIGURE 51

this is what students in secondary education and beyond must do—document their sources. This young learner showed that such thinking can spring from any source.

We then worked with the Big Book by David Drew, *Postcards from the Planets*. In this book, a family goes on a vacation through the solar system and visits the planets. They send back photographs from the planets to their relatives on earth. The book is illustrated with large photographs of the planets themselves.

I asked my students to write about three things: what the book was about; what they had learned; and how they might use it as a text model for writing in content, how they might make a book like it to teach about a subject they had researched. Figures 53 and 54 show excerpts from their writings

We read many other books as the year wore on, always talking about how we could learn from them, how information was put into them, and how we could get it out. We worked with David Drew's Big Book, *Millions of Years Ago*, to see all the different ways he had put information to be learned onto the pages, with charts, diagrams, text, labeled pictures, and a time line along the bottom of each page, similar to a very fancy textbook.

We looked at his Big Book, *Tadpole Diary*, to see how to keep scientific observations in "a fun, nice way." We particularly looked on the back of the book, where there was a large calendar chart of the observations over time.

And we spent quite a lot of time with Joanna Cole's "Magic School Bus" series, *The Magic School Bus at the Waterworks*, . . . *inside the Earth*, . . . *inside the Human Body*, and . . . *in the Solar System*. We reveled in Bruce Degan's illustrations and my students said I looked like the teacher, Ms. Frizzle. I decided to take that as a compliment.

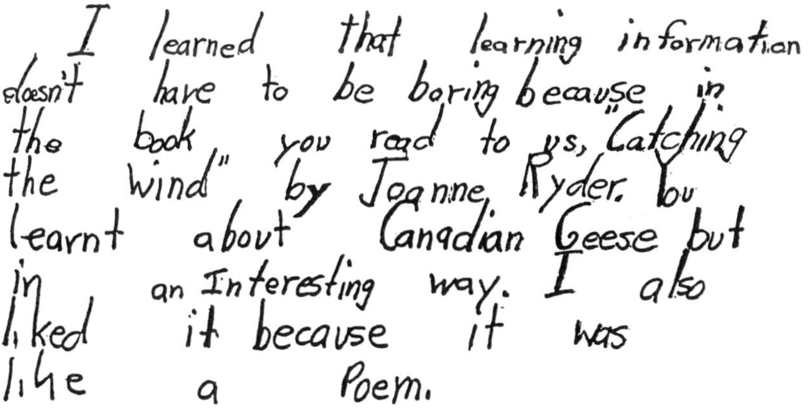

I learned that learning information doesn't have to be boring because in the book, you read to us, "Catching the wind" by Joanne Ryder. I learnt about Canadian Geese but in an Interesting way. I also liked it because it was like a Poem.

FIGURE 52

We discovered that we liked to read the series out loud together, with different people taking different parts. It was a natural, authentic time for me to hear how oral reading skills were proceeding without the drudgery of traditional oral reading.

We spent a lot of time looking at how we learn information from a book like one in the "Magic School Bus" series. Some people only read the children's reports in the book, some people never read them. Some people skipped the main text completely and only read the conversation balloons, like a comic book. Almost everyone looked at the pictures first.

The power of pictures on our learning process is vastly underrated in upper elementary classrooms, those bastions of print. I often take a survey of groups of teachers when I am sharing these books with them. I ask them how many have read a *National Geographic* and usually all indicate that they have. I ask all those to raise their hands who, when they first look at the magazine, go through it completely, only looking at the pictures. Nearly everyone raises their hands. Then I ask how many first go through the whole magazine, only reading the captions. I raise my hand and once in a while someone else does too. Not many people do this. Finally, I ask how many select an article and read it and usually one or two indicate this option.

I then ask of those who look at pictures first how many look at all the pictures from the back of the magazine to the front. Usually, many raise their hands. This is the most common way of beginning to learn from the *National Geographic*. Most people set out first to learn from the pictures, without regard for their context. Some deliberately upset the contextual framework of the illustrations by reading the book backwards. It's an eye-opener for those

The plot of this book is about
a family who goes on a huge space-
-ship from earth to all the other
planets. Two kids send post cards to
their relatives on earth.
    In this book you can learn abt
about all eight planets Just from the
facts on the post cards. I think
this is a very educational.
        If a person wanted to write a
story in this format he/she could
very easily write one about a sea voy
-age or a trip any where. I really liked
this book.

FIGURE 53

of us at upper elementary who have been proceeding on the assumption that
people learn from print.

I also point out to teachers their own excitement at looking at these books.
That is the joy of engaging in beautiful literature. Many nod and smile.

Picture Storybooks With a Difference

Not all picture storybooks are lighthearted and written for everyone. Although all good ones are beautifully illustrated, some differences in content
do exist.

We did find some picture storybooks that were too hard for us at sixth
grade. Some of our pop-ups were hard to read and had more information
than we were ready to absorb. Also, Ruth Heller's picture storybooks about
grammar were advanced learning. We were all right through her book on
collective nouns, *A Cache of Jewels,* and we did pretty well with the compara-
tives and superlatives in her picture book on adjectives, *Many Luscious Lollipops,* although the part about predicate adjectives left some of us in a tizzy.
But when we got about halfway through her book about verbs, *Kites Sail
High,* and into the subjunctive case, we realized that this was a picture book
for high school, far beyond what we wanted to know, and so we put it away
until we were older.

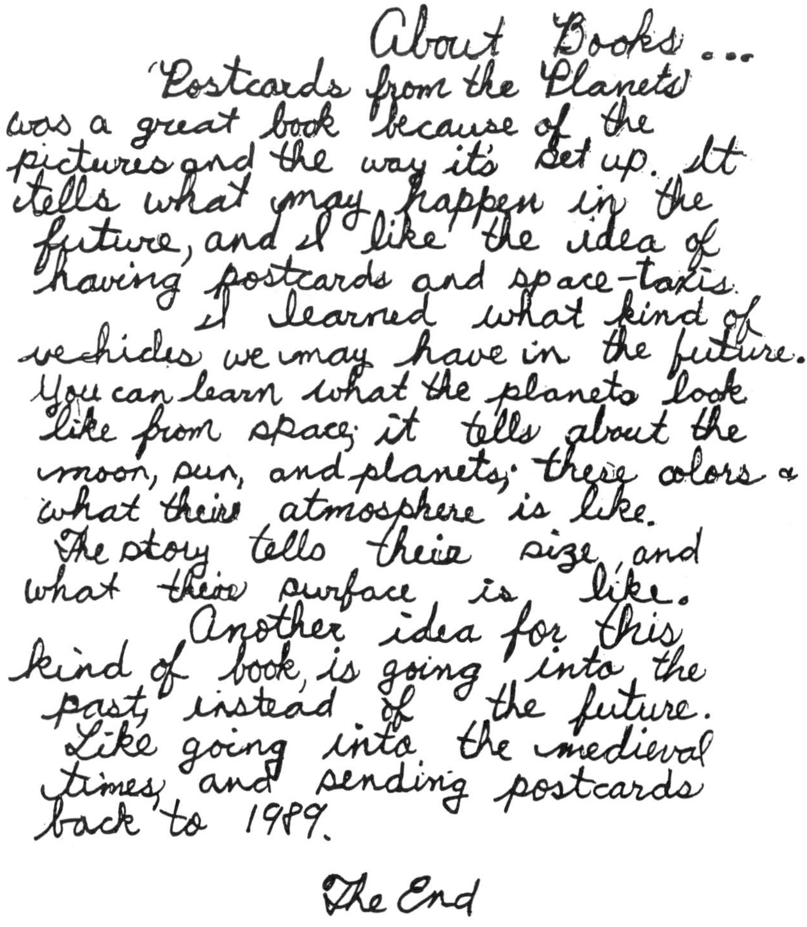

About Books ...

"Postcards from the Planets" was a great book because of the pictures and the way it's set up. It tells what may happen in the future, and I like the idea of having postcards and space-taxis. I learned what kind of vehicles we may have in the future. You can learn what the planets look like from space; it tells about the moon, sun, and planets; their colors & what their atmosphere is like. The story tells their size, and what their surface is like. Another idea for this kind of book, is going into the past, instead of the future. Like going into the medieval times, and sending postcards back to 1989.

The End

FIGURE 54

Also, there is a genre of picture storybooks that deals with difficult topics. In these, material which is hard to approach in common conversation is approached through beautiful illustrations and lyrical words. One set of this genre deals with death, both of pets and people. Typical books include: *The Tenth Good Thing about Barney*, about the death of a favorite pet; *Badger's Last Gifts*, about the death of an old badger and his lifetime gifts to his friends; *I'll Love You Forever*, about the aging and death of a parent.

A more recent set of picture storybooks deals frankly with the difficult issue of war. Included in this set are: *Faithful Elephants*, about the destruction of animals in the Tokyo Zoo during World War II; *Rose Blanche*, about a young girl in World War II Germany and her experience visiting concentration camps; and, *Hiroshima No Pika*, about the bombing of Hiroshima as seen through the eyes of a young Japanese child.

Sources and Booklists for Picture Storybooks

There are several sources and booklists for picture storybooks, each designed for a specific purpose. The list of my personal collection appears in this book as a Bibliography. It reflects only the books that appealed to me and my interests, the books I simply had to own and couldn't leave on the shelf, and books bought because they taught in a certain way. Anyone visiting the children's sections of bookstores could develop an equally interesting list.

I have resisted classifying the books on my list into science and social studies as some teachers have asked me to do. There are too many books that travel on the boundary, like *Millions of Years Ago* and *Catching the Wind*. My goal is integration, not compartmentalization.

I have also resisted classifying them by age—that would defeat the whole point. Picture storybooks can be used and enjoyed in different ways at all ages. We are always learning something new from them because we are always new learners.

For professional literature, I find Susan Hall's book *Using Picture Storybooks to Teach Literary Devices*, to be a good source list for children's books. It sounds like it was designed for high school English classes, but when I looked into the classification of "literary devices" I found many categories that were useful to me in my work with children at grades four, five, and six: analogy, flashback, foreshadow, point of view, pun, and stereotype/reverse stereotype. All of these elements were devices we talked about in my classroom either as authors or during discussions of critical thinking skills and strategies. So I highly recommend this annotated bibliography. The essays that precede the literary categories are informative and thought-provoking. The picture storybook titles are annotated well, sources are given together with examples from the text of the literary device, and suggestions for other literary devices which can be amplified by the text are given.

In Nancie Atwell's *Coming to Know* there is a fine bibliography of trade books and picture storybooks classified by subject area. In Donald Gallo's compiled *Speaking for Ourselves: Autobiographical Sketches by Notable Authors of Books for Young Adults*, titles are listed in each author section. These book are classified by readability and type. These are learner-centered bibliographies. David Russell's *Literature for Children* has children's book award winners listed in the back and a variety of bibliographies listed throughout.

I was pleased to note the books on the picture storybook section of the International Reading Association's "Teacher's Choices for 1991." All of them are picture storybooks in content and would be quite useful in my own work with learners. Here is the list:

Dream Wolf, Paul Goble, Bradbury Press
The Empty Pot, Demi, Henry Holt Pub.
Feathers for Lunch, Lois Ehlert, HBJ
The Great Kapok Tree: A Tale of the Amazon Rain Forest, Lynne Cherry, Gulliver/HBJ
Great Northern Diver: The Loon, Mary Brown, Little Brown Pub.
Osa's Pride, Ann Grifalconi, Little Brown Pub.
Thundercake, Patricia Polacco, Philomel
Totem Pole, Diane Hoyt-Goldsmith, Holiday House
Urban Roosts: Where Birds Nest in the City, Barbara Bash, Sierra Club/Little Brown
The Wall, Eve Bunting, Clarion

These books are all listed for K–2 on the IRA list, probably because they all contain little print. There are many fine books listed as "Intermediate—Grades 3–5" and "Advanced—Grades 6–8" and some of those have pictures, too. But I call attention especially to the beautiful books on content listed for grades K–2 because we might otherwise overlook them, thinking them too simple for our advanced ideas of literacy. For all the reasons I have given in this chapter, these books are not just K–2, and I'm sorry we keep classifying them that way. They are picture storybooks for all ages.

The best living bibliography of picture storybooks is the children's section of a good library or bookstore. There we can revel in the current explosion of beautiful picture storybooks. And we can help our students at all ages to reflect, as one sixth grade girl did in writing about how we learn from books (*see* Figure 55).

I Learned that writers can really write Anything. Like poetry, regular books and more. I like the rhyming, matching words. I also learned about how I could get ideas for my book that I'm finishing up with only Illustrations left.

FIGURE 55

11

Strategies for Informal Writing in Content

Remembering Academic Writing

I was always very proud of being a teacher in a self-contained classroom, one where my students and I could range free through the curriculum for hours on end, learning fully and in depth. It took a student-written content report to make me see that I had inadvertently worked against my own goals.

Nat was a good writer with a strong personal voice during writing time, working on pieces of fiction for days on end, conferencing, revising, doing what writers do. He would never have expected to produce a story that he liked in a short time, without input. But he thought maybe it was possible to do that in social studies. He had asked me if he could write a "report." He wanted to try out academic writing and see how it felt to write it. We had talked in class about this kind of writing, what it looked and sounded like and why people work in that genre. Here is the report he produced at home, overnight:

The Early Explorers

Centuries ago the sea-faring sons sailed their frail little galleys to the undiscovered islands and wild coasts of half the world. They ranged from cold, brisky and foggy harbors . . .

This is not how sixth graders talk—or write. Nat and I agreed that this was certainly not like anything else he had written.

After we read, I asked Nat, as I always did when I worked with writers, what he thought of this piece of writing.

"I don't like it," he said.

I asked him why and he said that he hadn't really learned anything from writing it and he didn't think that anyone would learn from reading it. Nat knew his own writing.

I did what I usually do during writing time, and said, "Let's see if we can process this writing a little—tell me more about this part about the undiscovered islands."

Nat said that he didn't know anymore about the harbors—that's all it said in the book.

Nat did go back to work on this. He knew as a writer that maybe somewhere buried in there was writing that was his. Eventually he shortened it, trying to find his own voice in the encyclopedic words, and then he abandoned it.

Ann Brown and Jeanne Day, in their research-based article, "Macrorules for Summarizing Text," warn about the dangers of enabling students to get good at what they call copy-delete as a summarizing strategy. *Copy-delete* is just what it sounds like: writers using this strategy copy out some the text they are reading, delete the next part, copy some more and so on.

Brown and Day found that the copy-delete strategy is reinforced just enough by teachers and others to support inexperienced writers in their use of it. However:

> . . . there is evidence that partially adequate strategies such as copy-delete are not just way stations on the road to expert strategies; they may actually impede progress. Copy-delete is a partially adequate strategy in that it results in a product that is recognizably a summary, an outline or a set of notes, and teachers will accept the product as adequate. (p. 13)

In order to develop mature writing strategies involving the consolidation of text, what Scardamalia and Bereiter (1986) call "knowledge-transforming" as opposed to "knowledge-telling," writers will have to reject strategies like copy-delete. It will not be sufficient to count on simply teaching them more efficient habits—we will have to help them undo partially adequate strategies like copy-delete that they may have practiced for many years of hasty, elementary school "report" writing.

In thinking about all of this, I took the problem to be mine. Without realizing it, I had compartmentalized my writing program, encapsulated the process of writing in the first hour of the day. During the rest of the day, I had not continued to work with writers, even though they were there all the time.

As a writer, I would never approach a major piece of writing like this book without having done some preliminary scribbling about the topic or without having talked to my friends about what I thought I wanted to say. Student writers do these same things as a way of getting rolling on a piece of writing.

During writing time, Nat scribbled and wrote too, but faced with content writing on his own, he did not do what writers do. He somehow expected that this text would magically fall together on its own without input from his writing process.

I believe Nat was responding to a model of academic writing that seems to float around in the air. It says that academic writing has many long words and complex sentences. In it the writer is invisible, without voice.

But that's not what Nat is really good at. And that's not the model that I want student writers to fall into. Nat is really good at telling about what interests him and arousing the readers' interest. He is very good at description. He knows what he likes in his writing.

When I realized how I had compartmentalized the writing process, limiting writers' experience to the world of personal narrative and fiction, I saw what a disservice I was doing to my students. This is exactly what secondary teachers have commented to me—that students are good at reading and writing in certain personal areas but are unable to transfer that knowledge over to reading and writing in academic domains.

Freewriting in Content Areas

I began a sequenced plan to help writers see themselves as writers in all domains by drawing on the work of Peter Elbow (1983, 1981), who in working with students unable to write, evolved a use of "freewriting." Elbow found that older students who had suffered failure in writing benefited from a writing activity that enabled them to write without stopping, without concern for appearance, writing that was only to be seen by the writer.

Sometimes called *rapid-writing* or *writing on*, freewriting simply means putting pencil to paper and keeping it moving with whatever comes to mind.

If what comes to mind is "Tired—tired—tired" then that's what will be written.

Processing a freewrite means going back and looking for ideas that have sprung out of writing on, for parts that are well-written, for parts that readers respond to, for parts that get the writer's mind going on what to really write about. When readers share freewrites, they may only read aloud the best parts—or they may add ideas that come to them as they read. Freewriting is a way of helping a writer use writing to learn.

I use freewriting as a way of helping students begin to think about a content area and I usually give them a focus to get them going. That focus might be a picture, an experience, or perhaps a word. I once had a very successful focused freewriting working from the words *assembly line*. These words were unknown to many of my students who then began their study of the Industrial Revolution by exploring in writing what might be involved in an assembly line.

I use focused freewriting as a way of getting a lot of thoughts out in the open. In my classroom, we sit in a circle and, after writing, students read out loud what they have written—or portions of it—without comment, one after the other. This gets a lot of words in the air about the focus.

If a visitor, the principal or someone from another school, is in the room during a freewrite, we ask them to write and "read-around" with us. Freewriting is a time when readers need to be in a secure setting. It is not a time when they need someone sitting and watching or someone wandering around looking over their shoulder. Freewriting is a time when everyone needs to be involved in sharing ideas.

I am also interested in finding out what interests learners about the topic we are beginning. If my focus is a good one, I begin to get a sense of how different students' minds work and what they respond to. In working in content areas in my classroom, each of us is always involved in developing an area of expertise within the topic. A focused freewrite gives students a chance to begin to think about what they might like to study and research.

Through use of a focused freewrite I am able to find out what connections students are making between the knowledge they carry with them and the topic we are working on. I am most interested in helping learners to achieve useful cognitive, or learning, connections between new and old knowledge. For we know that the way new information enters long-term memory storage is by being taken in, "reworded" into the learner's own terms of understanding, and then by being connected to something, some memory or piece of knowledge, already stored.

I am interested in knowing as much as I can about what the new knowledge I hope to convey will be connected to. For it is by those connections that students will retrieve knowledge.

Personally, I have found that getting knowledge into my head is not a problem—I am a good reader and a good listener. Getting it out again, retrieving it, is another matter. I am a terrible trivia player—my husband is much better. My cognitive connections, those linkages between old and new knowledge are terrible and I have trouble in the memory search. It would have helped me as a learner if my teachers had been more concerned with the duration, the strength, and the nature of my memory connections than with the neatness or quickness of my replies.

I was doing a demonstration once with third graders who had been studying "Southeast Explorers." That's what the teacher told me they knew a lot about and so that's what we were using as a database for learning about writing to learn. They had all jotted down (a strategy we'll talk more about later in this chapter) something they thought was important to know about Southeast Explorers and I was writing their ideas on acetate on the overhead projector so we could all think about them. For my part, I was glad that I didn't have to provide the list because at that moment I couldn't think of a thing about Southeast Explorers. For that matter, I couldn't even think of which Southeast they might talking about—Southeast Asia? Vietnam? My more recent "Southeast" learnings, the news about Vietnam, were better connected and thus more retrievable than my old grade school learning.

But as the list grew, I began to remember. Of course, they were talking Florida, Georgia, the explorers in the early development of the American continent. And then one student said, "Ponce de Leon." As I wrote it down and the next student spoke, I was suddenly taken with the knowledge that I could spell this foreign name. And in the back of my mind I could see myself, sitting at my fifth or sixth grade desk, staring at my textbook, at the picture of the explorer in his bloomers—those puffy, slashed, short pants they all wore in the textbooks—and being fascinated with way his name was spelled.

I was a good speller and it was the first time I had run into "ce" being a syllable all its own and the small letter "d" as part of what to me was a last name. Good old Ponce de Leon went right into my spelling bucket—what I call that part of my brain where I store spelling words. And that's as far as I got with him. As I sat there in fifth or sixth grade, fascinated with the spelling, making my own cognitive connection, I apparently didn't hear anything else about him. That's what learners do. Say "explorers" to me and you won't hear about Ponce de Leon. Begin to talk about spelling, and probably eventually I'll tell about my fascination with Spanish spelling.

I was telling a teacher I know this story and she said that I must get hold of a recent magazine because there was a wonderful article about Ponce de Leon in it—I'd really like it. I searched all over and finally found the magazine. The article was on Hernando Cortes—we all have this problem.

When I use focused freewriting with students I want to enable some useful cognitive connections. I want to bring their knowledge to the forefront in the freewrite so that I can use that to help them make connections that work for them between old and new knowledge.

I also want to get some text to process. Ideally, students would build up a reserve of freewrites and other shared, processed, informal writing on a topic so that they would have something to draw on when they wanted to construct a report. This is what writers do. As we saw with Nat's report, "The Early Explorers," not all text can be processed by the writer even with help and conferencing.

My sixth graders called focused freewriting a way of "letting everyone talk at once." And it was the only learning strategy I ever saw them consciously use in a social way. Several times when we had come in from recess and there had been a disagreement, everyone would talk at once, trying to tell me "the real truth" about what had happened. Eventually someone would say, "We should do a freewrite." And so out would come the freewrite books, small, student-made notebooks kept just for this purpose, and everyone would fall silent and write their version. Then, as we always did in using focused freewriting in content, each student would read in turn while everyone listened. Thus I got all the stories and everyone got "to talk at once."

When I share this strategy with teachers, I ask them to look at a reproduction of a Winslow Homer painting and then freewrite for three or four minutes. Many write for longer. One teacher said it was the first time she ever felt comfortable writing. In this painting, a lone fisherman in a dory, his face weathered and lined, rows against the waves toward a faraway ship. It is a moving portrayal, one which evokes a wide range of responses in writers young and old.

I used this picture as a focus to get students going at the beginning of a social studies unit. Here is Bill's response as he wrote and read it aloud:

> This picture is a really good one painted by Winslow Homer. There is a man in this boat trying to row back to the mother ship. It looks like he was dory fishing. And I think he's caught about two or three good hallabits. It's getting very rough out there and I think he'll probably have a hard time getting back to the mother ship. It looks like it's not a great day, cloudy, and maybe a little foggy. I think this guy (Winslow Homer) is a great artist.

I think this is a beautiful piece of writing. Bill's voice comes through clearly and lyrically. I was excited to get a sixth-grade boy interested in studying about art—it's not something I would have tried for or predicted.

Bill also has constructed a very complex sentence, one every bit as complex as any sentence he might try to construct in academic writing. Here, Bill has written "It looks like it's not a great day, cloudy, and maybe a little foggy." That, to me, is a beautiful sentence, quite complex (it would be difficult to diagram for those of us who remember how), and it is just how Bill talks. He talks in complexities as we all do and, given free rein to write things important to him, those complexities emerge.

Once a teacher in a workshop said of the freewrite, "That's a vocabulary lesson, isn't it," thinking that I was trying to turn it into something else. I assured her it wasn't. The words weren't on the board waiting for sentences. That is not how I spell "halibuts."

What did happen here was that as we began the focused freewrite, the students, who knew me well, asked me questions and I, contrary to my usual custom, answered them:

They asked: "What's the name of that boat back there?"

I replied: "I don't know—I think it's called the mother ship."

Someone said: "Is that a dory, like in dory fishing?" (They knew this from another unit we had studied.)

Someone else asked: "What kinds of fish are those?"

I replied: "They look kind of like halibut, but they might be big flounder."

And off we went to write. Those words that I had said showed up in most of the writings. And from my point of view, that was bad and that was good.

It was bad in that everyone using the same words narrowed the responses. Many of them sounded the same and concerned the same kinds of things. I didn't get the spread of response that I usually got when starting a topic. It might make it harder to decide on individual expert fields in the thematic unit we were starting.

But it was good in that it showed me clearly that writers want to use the best vocabulary possible when they write. I have always had this notion of vocabulary development that implies that teachers have to lift up students' thinking caps and pour in vocabulary words, that they have to be visible, on the board and mandated for use. But that's not the case at all. Here, faced with the possibility of writing about anything at all, students chose to use vocabulary. We need to remember that.

Another student showed me a lot about how he thinks and taught me about people and their interests. Joey wrote and read:

> . . . the Mother ship. A hat on. In the ocean. A little fishing Dory. Oars in both hands. Windy seas. Looking out. Sometimes I feel left out and away from the bigger people. Like this fisherman away from the Mother ship. St. Peter was a fisherman. Men like the guy in the picture looked up to St. Peter. This relates to my topic because since my topic is religion I thought it had something to do with the picture.

Here, Joey shows me that he thinks in phrases. I do too so it's good for me to know that we think about things in the same way—it will help our communication. Joey also shows me he knows that people write in phrases for certain purposes—here, to help him think something through. Not all students know this.

I believe that we in school teach the form of the sentence very well, over and over. This is understandable to me because in my studies of how children learn to punctuate in writing, the linguists' point about the uniqueness of every sentence spoken really came home. Each sentence we create is a new one and, as writers trying to punctuate in standardized fashion, we must match it to the most similar model we hold, a model which may be much simpler than our newly created sentence. For as we improve as writers, speakers and thinkers, we create more and more complex sentences. It is no wonder then, that students must constantly be refreshed on the nature of the sentence—they keep upping the ante on themselves.

And so we teach the form of the sentence over and over. I believe that by the time they leave school some children believe that adults write in sentences all the time. But that is far from true. Many of us write in phrases a lot. I have written whole letters to people I didn't even know and, when I looked back over what I had written, found that there were no subjects in any of the sentences and some of them didn't even have verbs. They were all phrases.

Joey knows that he uses phrases to help him think and that in this kind of writing, phrases are appropriate. As a matter of fact, I have shown here a recopied form of his writing. When he wrote it for himself it had a lot of dashes, no periods and no capital letters. But when I asked him if I could use it as an example of a focused freewrite, he put in the periods and capital letters. He thought teachers would expect to see them.

Joey also taught me about people and the power of their interests. He knew that when we worked in content areas, we selected individual expert fields. Before we began this particular unit, he told me that he wanted to study religion, no matter what the topic was going to be. This Winslow Homer was not the prompt I would have picked to start him off on his topic of religion.

But he taught me that when people are interested in something, they find it everywhere. We as teachers don't have to work to develop their interest— we simply have to find out what their interest is. And now that he has made the connection between this particular painting and religion, I have seen it ever since.

This was not the part of his freewrite that Joey was most interested in, however. He was interested in the part where he writes, "Sometimes I feel left out and away from the bigger people. Like this fisherman away from the Mother ship." That was the part that caught him up, the part that we conferenced about, and the piece of this focused freewrite that he chose to expand on.

I have taken the old doryman to many, many teachers and students, asking them to do focused freewrites and I continue to be entranced with how one painting can mean so many different things to so many different people. Several writers have responded to the odd cloud formation at the right of the horizon in the picture. Some see in it the outline of World War I German tanks and the end of a way of life in Europe. One woman was simply fascinated by the shape and, try as she might in her freewriting—"I'm going to think about the rest of the picture now," she wrote at one point—was unable to tear her attention away: "Those clouds—they look so strange."

An eighth-grade boy wrote forcefully and lyrically about the man in the dory who "doesn't have much to work with but he keeps on going . . . I think that's what the world's like—you have to keep going even if you don't want to." I saw in the boy's reading and writing a vision of how life is for the determined.

Many people respond to the doryman with a personal story. This illuminates for me the cognitive connections that I could use in beginning a unit. Antonia wrote and read:

> The guy looks tired and he seems to want to go back to his ship because he is looking at the boat and it is getting rough. He looks worried that he won't get back to his ship. And I don't think he does. I wouldn't want to do dory fishing but at least I would have food because of the fish.
> Once I was in a small, red, sailboat and we went sailing in the lagoon to see some of the reefs and the wind started picking up. We almost banged into a reef but we got away in time. We got out the oars and changed tack so that we could get back to the boat. It was hard though but we finally got back and had hot cocoa.

One of the most important things for me to know is if students have their own agendas in a topic. Like me and my daydreaming about the spelling of Ponce de Leon, something in a topic can set a student's mind to wandering so that they miss the rest of what's talked about. And if what the student's mind goes wandering to has a powerful emotional content, as Antonia's sample seems to, then a great deal of the teacher's intent for content may be subverted or missed altogether.

As the teacher, I need to know these things right away and not later on, after we have worked on a unit for a month. It would be the best of all possible worlds if I could sit down and chat with students individually about what they each know about the topic but that is not possible. Reading focused freewrites has been the best way for me to gain insight into students' minds.

Informal Versus Formal Writing

We're looking at a view of writing which is somewhat different from traditional writing in content areas. Freewriting and related strategies are specifically designed to help writers think about the topic at hand. The writing is not designed to stand alone or to serve anyone but the writer. It is a kind of writing I am calling "informal." Here is a chart which contrasts informal and formal writing in my view:

INFORMAL	FORMAL
Writing for the writer	Writing for a reader
Writing which needs the writer nearby	Writing which stands alone without the writer
Writing as a tool for thinking	Writing as a tool for communicating
Writing for articulating ideas	Writing for communicating ideas

James Moffett in *Teaching the Universe of Discourse* (1968) draws a distinction in how we represent our view of reality as we abstract from it. He says that it is a two-pronged process, abstracting *from* the world around us, a process done for ourselves, and abstracting *for* an audience. He sees these as two aspects of the same process, distinct but intertwined, particularly in composition.

Here, in my distinction between informal and formal writing, Moffett's distinction is useful. Informal writing follows his category, abstracting from, because it is writing done to help the writer understand and draw from the subject. Formal writing follows his category, abstracting for, because it concerns the I-you relationship, the communication prong of composition.

As Moffett points out, both categories are essential components: "we must use these two dimensions of abstracting as coordinates with which to map the universe of discourse" (p. 32). But making students aware of the distinction and enabling them to focus first on one and then on the other allows them leeway to do what writers do, to choose which dimension is their current focus.

When I was in school, the informal category was altogether missing. I do not remember writing to help me learn **from**—I was always in the dimension of learning **for** someone else. Writing, especially in areas of content, was never exploratory, to find out what I knew or what I might like to learn, but always a proof, to show that I was trying to approach the teacher's level of knowledge.

For there is one powerful peculiarity about writing in content in school:

writers are always writing *up* to someone who knows much more about the topic than the writer. It is a proposition which carries the seeds of its own doom and one which does not prepare the writer for real writing in the adult world. In that world, writers who find themselves doing serious composition in a formal dimension most often are doing things like composing letters to the Social Security Administration, explaining why the wrong number went onto the W-4 form two years ago and now the accounts are all mixed up. Real, formal, adult writing is often to an unknown audience that knows nothing about the writer's particular topic.

So I work with students in content writing in the informal writing category to help them to explore what they know, what they think they know, and what they need to find out. In the process, I learn about their learning.

Sometimes the informal writing is processed into formal writing, but often it serves only the writer. Often it remains the voice of the writer whispering in the writer's own ear, not for public consumption.

Jotting Things Down

I add one more informal strategy to the writers' battery of ways to think on paper. I ask my students to jot things down—just like grown-ups do. Jotting is one of the best kept secrets of the mature writer's storehouse.

Grown-ups jot things down for two reasons—to help them put their thoughts into words and to remember. It's a commonly used strategy in the adult world, little notepads are sold just for the purpose. There's even one available with a giant suction cup so grown-ups can jot things down while they're driving. I once bought my mother a special pen with a light in it so that she could jot things down in the middle of the night. Clearly, none of these special items are intended for extensive, formal writing to communicate. The notepads and the car pad with the suction cup are quite small. The pen had a tiny little light, just big enough to see the end of the pen—not very good for extended composition. And now, for several thousand dollars, one can buy a laptop jotting computer on which the writer can jot away to heart's content and on the press of a key, the computer will convert the scribbles to typed copy. But the screen is not very big. These items are intended to hold little fragments of writing, jottings, not sentences, not revision.

When grown-ups jot things down so they won't forget them, most often the jottings are telephone numbers or lists of things to buy. But sometimes grown-ups jot down ideas so they won't forget them. I jot down ideas on little scraps of paper, scraps I often lose. But jotting down the idea seems to help me remember it a little better.

Grown-ups often have to teach themselves to jot things down to help their understanding of what they want to say. Anyone who has ever written a difficult sympathy note and written it, the first time, right on the two dollar, store-bought card knows that sometimes the message of sympathy doesn't look the same out there, in print, as it did in the writer's head. Sometimes the writer has to throw away the card after seeing how the thought looks in print if it hasn't been jotted down first.

And so we teach ourselves as grown-ups to jot things down on the back of an old envelope first, to try them out before we commit them to formal communication. It takes a lifetime of learning for some of us. On my sister's last birthday, I bought a card I really liked and wrote right into the inside, without jotting it down first. I don't remember what I said, but it looked terrible in print. I had to cut off that half of the card and send her the front. It was very embarrassing.

But what about students? Do they know about jotting things down? Are they given the opportunity to jot things down if they want to? Do they even know that this is something that people do, that writers do, that kids could do?

I think that school is about the worst place to have an idea. What do you do when you get an idea and you're a student in school? In many classrooms, you can't turn to the person next to you and tell them your great idea—you'll get in trouble for interrupting the flow of classroom talk. You certainly can't lift up your desktop and get a piece of paper to write it down, if writing it down even occurs to you. Opening the desk any old time is frowned on in some classrooms. Writing your good idea on your desktop is out of the question. What do you do with it?

Mostly students forget the idea. I've asked them what happens. It's a rare student in a classroom who has a place to write things down in a handy, unobtrusive way. But clearly it is a strategy that children should learn to use if they are to function as literate, thinking adults.

I had students keep a pad of paper clamped to their desktop. Some students preferred to tape a large piece of manila drawing paper over the entire surface. Thus, they had somewhere to write whenever they needed to. Did they doodle? Sometimes. But I think that doodling serves its own purpose in supporting thinking. I've seen copies of Presidential doodling that were accounted to be quite interesting as visual evidence of the thinking going on below the surface.

I'm not convinced that I know all about how people learn. I know that as a graduate student—with paper available and expected—I doodle and jot a lot, not just classnotes, but ideas of my own. I'm quite pleased when it happens.

I think we need to consider why we have tied learners' hands behind their backs by denying them one of the most forceful ways of learning—jotting down ideas—experiencing informal, immediate literacy.

Having liberated my students into literacy, I make use of jotting as a classroom strategy to help me get a quick handle on what students are thinking. Thus, after we have tried to learn something, I might ask everyone to jot down what they learned and do a quick, uninterrupted "read-around" so that I can see what they made of what I said.

I also often ask all my students to jot down a response to a question I need answered. Thus, I use jotting as a way to get all students thinking about my question. Then, those who always raise their hands, the class spokesmen, can respond. But everyone in the room has had an opportunity to think about the question. No one can drift away.

I use jotting and reading-round to find out what pops into learners' minds. If I were using the old doryman as a way to begin a unit on Portugal, for instance, I might ask students to jot down some connection they could make between that picture and Portugal. Out of the resulting list, I would begin to form my experts list by connecting students with similar interests.

If someone made no connection between that picture and Portugal, then I would want to know that right away, too. Often I fall victim to my own assumptions, thinking that everyone responds the same way I do. Jotting and reading-round help me to remember that everyone sees something different, everyone makes their own connections.

If, in the jottings, I find out that someone spent the last year in Portugal and is a genuine resident expert, I want to know that as soon as I can and not after I have been talking and teaching for days.

I try to use jotting in the classroom to keep me from being in the position of the man in the *New Yorker* cartoon, looking up at the sky, talking on about it to two children, while one young listener says to the other: "That's not what Carl Sagan said." I try to find out as soon as I can if I am working with students who know more about a topic than I do. I ask my students to use informal writing to help us all to learn.

REFLECTING
AND
ASSESSING

12

Taking Time to Do Philosophy with Kids

Remembering Philosophizing

My first strong memories of philosophizing are from when I was about eleven. I remember having a powerful revelation about how the universe had no edges. That's what some of us believed in those days. It took me many days of hard concentration trying to picture something—flat?—that had no edges, that went on forever, before I gave up and settled for something that got kind of milky in the distance. I was very two-dimensional in my visual thinking in those days and flat was easiest to work with. Besides, having no edges took up a lot of cognitive space and there was only room left for flat. The best image I could muster was a mind full of a flat disk with sort of a fog where it disappeared into the distance at the edge of my mental space.

Of course we never did this stuff in school. These were just things that I thought about when I was on my own. In school we did schoolwork and sometimes we went down to the school basement where the cafeteria was and practiced what to do in case anyone ever dropped a bomb on the building.

Those "atom bomb drills" were responsible for a lot of private philosophizing on my part—and maybe for my classmates, too. I wouldn't know, I don't ever remember discussing the subject. But those drills and my reflections on their implications resulted in a lot of long-term philosophic decisions.

The idea in those days—in the early 1950s—was that we would protect ourselves from the bomb by holding our arms over our heads. It sounds silly now, but anyone who has seen the documentary, "The Atomic Cafe," knows how it was and how naive we were about things like atom bombs.

At any rate, every so often the teacher would get some sort of signal that it was time for an atomic bomb drill. We would all line up and march downstairs to the cafeteria. It wasn't really in the basement—it was sort of half underground. When you looked out the windows you could see the grass on the playground at the bottom of the windowframe. But it was the best we could do for a bomb shelter.

I don't remember exactly how it happened but the next thing we knew, we would all be on the floor, under a table, curled up on our knees, with our arms folded over our heads. This was supposed to protect us from flying glass. And in that cafeteria there would have been plenty of that.

We stayed there for a while and then we all lined up again and went back to work. We did this quite often while I was in fifth and sixth grade, at least as often as we went outside and stood in the weather to make sure we wouldn't get burned up in a fire.

I used to think about a lot of things after one of these drills. I thought a lot about practicing for war. When I was a baby, we lived in England and Scotland during the bombing of World War II. I was a "blackout baby," raised for two years in the blackout conditions prevalent through Britain at that time. I grew up hearing about how it was "during the war" and it was well into my life before I could sleep in a lighted room. And here we were, getting ready for war again I thought.

I thought about the future—how it would be in the world if the bomb was dropped—and in those days we only thought of the atomic bomb—and how it would be for people. I worried about my children. And maybe then I decided not to have any. There's no way of measuring the impact of a childhood experience.

As a child, I reflected on the things that were happening to me. At the time, schools were not prepared to deal with children thinking, only children responding. But I was concerned philosophically about the world around me and my changing role in that world. The time spent thinking about the edges of the universe taught me about the limits of my mind; the time in the bomb shelter taught me about the limits of my life.

The philosophizing that went on for me would have benefited from guided interaction with my peers who were going through the same experiences. I knew by fifth and sixth grade that I learned by talking, even if it was forbidden, and sharing philosophic thoughts on these major topics might have helped me to better understand the world around me. In the early 1950s the world was changing. Talking about those changes would have helped those like me who would eventually prepare others for greater changes yet to come. Learning to "talk philosophy" would have been a good model for teaching present-day youngsters to "talk philosophy" about the twenty-first century and what will be possible for them.

Doing Philosophy

Unless we make a space for it, we have no way of knowing the impact and philosophic effect of events in the lives of our children. Many major life decisions get made at upper elementary, I think, and they may play themselves out in various ways. It is a crucial time in the life of a child and not a time to shut down the free exchange of ideas.

Some of my most enjoyable times with students have been when we dwelt for a while in the realm of the speculative. Sometimes this occurred when we debated newsworthy issues, like war and peace, life and death. Sometimes these discussions were spontaneous and the result of incidents that occurred during simulations or during our classroom life, or that came from a book we had read. Sometimes discussion of moral dilemmas arose from our own reading and writing.

We often found ourselves discussing moral issues of great significance, discussions that Lipman, Sharp and Oscanyon call "educational means that are meaning-laden" (p. 9). Children care a great deal about gaining meaning. Gareth Matthews in his books, *Philosophy and the Young Child*, says:

> For many young members of the human race, philosophical thinking—including, on occasion, subtle and ingenious reasoning—is as natural as making music and playing games, and quite as much a part of being human. (p. 36)

In fact, I have found that this kind of debate gives students particular pleasure and is often requested. As Gareth Matthews says, "(Philosophy) is often play, conceptual play" (p. 11) which is to say, children enjoy it. They enjoy talking about things that are really important to them.

One year, several sixth-grade students read Agatha Christie's *Death on the Nile*. This group then made a presentation to the whole class on the main characters and certain evidence which might or might not prove important. We all then got to watch a video of the movie. Agatha was a big hit. We spent quite a long time predicting the outcome, assessing the evidence, and critiquing the plot.

For a follow-up, all viewers wrote a short paper on "The value of trusting what you think you see." In *Death on the Nile*, the crucial link hinges on the detective, Hercule Peirot, (and all of us) believing that one character was shot to death *before* his wife was murdered. In fact, he was not shot at that time but used a blank. He then shot his wife and killed himself later.

The assumption that he was shot first provided great fodder for writing and discussing whether one can truly trust what one sees. And this, of course, provides a natural link to the world of reality and appearance. These students naturally drifted into this phase of the discussion. Once the debate about Agatha had been settled, the discussion generalized itself, and students began spontaneously to discuss whether one could *ever* trust what is seen. And this led to a brief but deep discussion of the external and internal world of perception and reality.

Philosophizing About Topics Like 'Honesty'

Children—even our grown up ones—speculate on matters such as reality and illusion. They also think deeply about social and moral obligations such as honesty. John Ruskin wrote: "To make your children **capable of honesty** is the beginning of education (In *Time and Tide*, letter viii). I recently came across a letter I wrote to Arthur Millman, Professor at University of Massachusetts at Boston. It was part of an assignment for a course I was taking on doing philosophy with children.

> Dear Arthur,
> You ask me philosophically, What is wrong with modern education? Today I came out of a late afterschool meeting, and backed into some poor guy's car. And I thought to myself, what *is* wrong with modern education? No wonder teachers get a bad name, he was right there and I never saw him: "Those teachers are in space," they say.
>
> For one thing, I'm too busy to think, and so are my kids. We don't take a lot of time to think things through completely and when we do, we don't have any place to record the results. And a lot of the job is accountability. I'm accountable in many ways and so are they, so a lot of what we do is a reaction to that accountability. Most of the time and energy left over is taken up with what I think is important to education. The slight remainder left is given over to what my kids think is important to learn with me.
>
> You ask us to read Socrates. I think Socrates and his poor family could have never survived had he decided to make his way as a public school

teacher. He would have received poor evaluations, would have been marked down on "Uses time wisely", and "Covers all subject material adequately" and would have been fired. We public school teachers don't have the time that Socrates did to wander around a subject, to pin it down, to squash it flat.

Besides, when I have a Socratic-type dialogue with my students, they all respond at once. I mean, they all talk to me at the same time—in mixed chorus. I have so convinced them that I am interested in every thought they have, that they respond with great self-centered trust in my listening abilities, at the same time, with different thoughts.

I wish that I **could** sort out what they say, for it seems the best way to get the most information. It is a response system which allows everyone to express ideas without being afraid of what others will think (How can anyone else think about what you're saying when they're talking at the same time)—and, everything about the subject is on the floor at the same time. But, alas, I cannot always decipher all the ideas at once.

We had a philosophic discussion which evolved into a formal debate to fulfill an assignment which had come from the Citizenship Committee. Each month we have to elect a Citizen of the Month from each class, someone who demonstrates a particular characteristic. This has never been easy for my class, because we see many aspects to some of the qualities, and many classmates who fulfill those aspects. This process sometimes tends to oversimplify difficult concepts, and sometimes, as my students pointed out with the quality 'friendly,' it may be a back-handed compliment—as in, "You're friendly this year."

This time we had to elect someone who we thought demonstrated 'honesty.'

We began our selection of our honest person according to our critical thinking precepts by setting up criteria:

> Tell the truth
> Don't lie
> Don't steal
> Don't squeal
> Don't frame anyone
> Don't cheat anyone
> Be fair
> Take only your fair share
> Don't be dishonest

This led to a discussion of whether anyone never lied. The conclusion was that everyone lies sometimes. This led to an extended discussion of whether it is ever right to do wrong, or to lie. One girl said, "If my mother is just ready to go out, and she asks me how I like her dress, and I don't, I tell her I do anyway. Because if I tell her that I don't then she'll be all worried and she'll run around trying to find something else when she's supposed to be gone, and things will really be bad. So it's best that I tell a white lie, a little lie."

This raised the issue of whether all wrongs were the same. What happens when you answer in partial truths? What happens when you only answer the question even though you know that the person intended to get at some other information. We discussed the concept of 'moral dilemma.'

The discussion continued for two days and many examples and analogies were given. These sixth graders raised and informally debated the following:

Is it possible to never do wrong?

- Impossible
- Sometimes you do wrong by accident
- All here agree it's impossible

Are there different degrees of wrong? All agree there are. "It's different if you're always doing wrong than if it just comes up once in a while."

Lies build up. "What a tangled web we weave when first we practice to deceive."

Wrong depends on the situation you're in.

Degrees of wrong can come in (extremes) like this: life and death decision versus a chocolate bar.

At first these students chose the whole class as being "The Most Honest Person," saying that no one was more honest than another. But this didn't satisfy everyone, so a revote was called for, and some asked to hear more arguments.

They decided that one argument in favor of the whole class was that no one in the class ever tells lies to get someone else in this class in trouble. Debate: How can we know this for sure?

But we could vote for just one person because it is possible to tell or say if one person is more noticeable for being more honest; you can see it in them. Debate: How?

Could we use as a standard whether or not you could trust someone? No, you can trust someone the most, but they don't have to be honest all the time. It's impossible to have someone who's honest all the time.

Maybe we should take into account what someone thinks of him/herself. So we could elect someone who seems honest to us all the time but doesn't see him/herself as honest. No, that's too contradictory.

They finally decided to elect someone who we think is honest all the time and who is willing to admit that they are as honest as they can be. And so they did.

In all the hours that went into this debate no larger issues of morals or authority ever came up. This discussion emanated from self-imposed standards and not from laws, rules, commandments. No mention of punishment was made. No mention of church was made although almost all my students attended catechism and had done so ever since kindergarten.

All students essentially agreed. No one stood out as seeing any of these issues differently.

All were willing to think this through as far as it would go. Many said that they really enjoyed talking about such things and would like to again. I wondered if they ever had these discussions anywhere else.

This took a lot of time, this Socratic exploration. It's hard for us to find time like this. We have a very busy schedule. But the opportunity it afforded for these students to think things through, to hear each other's thoughts, and for me to catch the drift of the current tide was invaluable. We practiced the art of debate. We learned how to honor each other's ideas. We fully explored a topic that concerned us all.

We don't have a place for "doing philosophy" on our "State Chart of Recommended Minutes for Each Subject." Because I've been around teaching for awhile, I wrote it up in my plans as "Time to Do Something Worthwhile." Otherwise I would have probably called it "Health and Nutrition."

Your student, Pat

Reflections

We can keep in mind Lawrence Kohlberg's (1973) Stages of Moral Development as we work with upper elementary philosophers. They are:

Stages 1 and 2: egocentric, what is fair is based on one's need
Stages 3 and 4: societal, what is fair is based on agreement
Stages 5 and 6: individual, what is fair is self-determined and reciprocal

Kohlberg held that we proceed through these stages in order, without omitting any or reverting to an earlier stage. We may have a mix of stages at the upper elementary, but part of our goal in doing philosophy is to help students to recognize their own stage of moral development and move on.

But we should also consider the research of Carol Gilligan. In her book, *In a Different Voice: Psychological Theory and Women's Development*, Gilligan points out that Kohlberg's theories were drawn from a 20-year study done of 84 boys, a study in which "females simply do not exist" (1982, p. 18). Gilligan thus questions the validity of Kohlberg's stages for work with girls. She also points out that in Jean Piaget's 1932 study, *The Moral Judgement of the Child*, the word, *girls*, is listed in the index with "four brief entries" (p. 18), while the word, *boys*, does not appear at all in the index because, according to Gilligan, Piaget's ongoing reference to *the child* is assumed to be male.

What does this mean to us in the classroom? We will consider our upper elementary learners in light of Kohlberg's stages of moral development while keeping in mind that there may be great variations for half of our student population, the girls. Gilligan concludes that in their moral dilemmas girls seek resolutions in "a mode of thinking that is contextual and narrative rather than formal and abstract" (p. 19). When we observe girls and boys on the playground debating which rules to follow, who's right and who's wrong, and whether a rule should be changed, we will think of Gilligan's observation about the play of girls before we assign Kohlberg's stages: ". . . girls subordinated the continuation of the game to the continuation of relationships" (p. 10). To girls, playing the game was less important than being a friend.

What is most important in this for teachers is the concept that the students we work with are in formation, they are not complete. What we must not do is pigeonhole them into any stage of any kind. Rather, we must see them as always in transition. And in that dynamic, fluid state of transition, the most important thing we can give them is the opportunity for feedback.

Some might think that philosophic concerns are too "grown up" for young children. In fact, Plato believed students should be given ten years of pure mathematics before beginning work in abstract reasoning and moral problems (Cornford, 1945). But in *Philosophy and the Young Child*, Gareth Matthews writes about "doing philosophy" with very young children. He finds as a philosophy professor that "my task as a college professor is to reintroduce my students to an activity that they had once enjoyed and found natural, but that they had later been socialized to abandon" (p. vii). We can foster this "doing natural philosophy" by structuring curriculum around a life theme, or philosophic concerns and moral dilemmas relevant to the simulation which are also concerns of real people in real life.

"Life themes" are what Bobbi Fisher and I took to calling those recurring themes in literature, themes like "Are you my mother," "Who am I really," and "Does this person wish me well?" Books for people of all ages explore these life themes, things we worry and wonder about from childhood on. Most life themes reflect our ongoing exploration of self in the world.

What are the implications for curriculum and classroom practice? We continue thematic learning but now we do it for a larger purpose. We explore with children their concerns for self in light of the theme. One of the main activities of curriculum designed around a life theme is philosophic discussion and activities which enable children to relate themes to self. One of the main goals of schooling should be to "do philosophy," to arrive at a higher order of thinking using the content and literate tools at hand to promote the furthering of the human spirit.

If we are doing developmental curriculum, the life themes and the connections they promote arise from children's interests and concerns as they are expressed in the classroom, not as teachers conceive them the summer before school starts.

Thus, when the sixth grade "went West," we faced many dilemmas which required philosophic discussion and moral decision-making. When cholera struck some of the wagons, the decisions for how to deal with the sick and yet continue on the trail raised philosophic issues regarding responsibility to individuals versus the general good.

When we read in actual women's diaries from the time period about decisions that were made to bury lost loved ones in the prairie along the trail, far from home, those decisions were reflected in student writings: "I pray we will make it safe without any trouble," "Grandma and Grandpa are going with us. (I have my doubts about them goin', they might not make the trip."

Heathcote writes that classroom instruction should hold as its goal the enhancement of children's lives: "to keep people's experiences 'real' . . . to bring about a change, a widening of perspective, in the life of the real person, as well as to offer systems of learning and knowing" (p. 106).

In our work with children, we should not neglect philosophy. It takes time, this thrashing out of ideas. But through it, people grow.

13

The Theory behind
the Practice

Developing Theory

This is a chapter for those who want to know more about why I am doing what I'm doing, those who wonder whose ideas helped me. The minute we begin to ask "why," we are in the world of theory. I have heard a debate about whether or not teachers need or want "theory." And I thought there were legitimate arguments on both sides.

One side argues that teachers are practical people, that what they really want is something to put into place in their classrooms tomorrow and they will take it from there, that they live in a world of practice. This argument holds that teachers don't want or need the theory behind what they are doing, that theory often dwells in an ideal world and doesn't account for the realities of classroom life.

The other side of the argument says that teachers need to know why things are being done the way they are so that they can extend and deepen the surface activities learned "for tomorrow." This argument holds that to give practice without theory is to slight teachers, to keep them from growing professionally. To give only the activities is to continue the rote model of the old teachers' editions: do this without understanding why.

These are both valid perspectives and the debate will probably continue.

There is, of course, always a theory behind the practice. Although some of us began the practice and then developed or learned the theory. That's what happened to me. The day came when I needed theories—both my own and other people's. I didn't know where to go next without them.

Human beings run on theories. Theories are built by learners in the process of learning. Theories are cognitive constructs, frameworks and mental structures that support, explain and account for our observations and actions. They help us integrate our perceptions of phenomena in the world around us and make accurate predictions about what might happen next. Eleanor Duckworth points out that it is only when we have a theory about something that "a result can contribute to the development of . . . understanding" (1987, p. 45). For it is when our results are not what we predicted that we reconsider our theory and revise it in light of our experiences and observations.

The way this book is organized tries to model how it is with theories: theories evolve as the result of experience and are confirmed, denied or modified with further experience. So theory in this book comes **after** some practice and before "moving on" to more practice. This is how we develop our own theories. And as we develop our own, we add the theories of others to ours.

I reached a point in my career when I needed to sit down and think about what seemed to be happening in my classroom and the changes I was bringing about—that was my own built theory. To this I added reading about what others thought would be good to have happening. Those were the learned theories. Here are some theories I read about, added to, and developed to help me develop my Whole Learning concept, a combination of built theories and learned theories.

Developing a Theory of Conditions of Learning at Upper Elementary

Throughout this book, I have stressed the importance for me of setting up the best possible conditions for learning to take place. In Chapter 1, I referred briefly to Brian Cambourne's conditions of learning theory but supplemented it with what I know about how adults learn. Students—young men and women—in upper elementary school are on the edge of adulthood. They are deep in a stage of practicing how to be a grown-up. They exhibit some characteristics of adult learning, acting more within what I call the adult performance model. Also, they are learners with a history, be it good or bad.

They do not come to us with a clean slate. In this, they are more like adults than children.

All of this must be taken into account when developing a Whole Learning classroom in the upper elementary grades. We cannot adopt wholesale a model of learning drawn from infancy language acquisition. We must account for the distinctions in the population we work with. And our classrooms must reflect this awareness.

Brian Cambourne's Conditions of Learning

In his book *The Whole Story*, Brian Cambourne describes a set of optimal conditions which promote the acquisition of literacy learning and which can be applied across other kinds of learnings. Reacting against what he calls "a model of learning that has imprisoned the majority of teachers . . . habit formation" (p. 18), Cambourne outlines conditions for learning "based on the way that human brains create meaning in the real world of language use" (p. 27).

Cambourne's (1988) conditions of learning describe an optimal learning model, using as a starting point those natural conditions present as children acquire their native language. The conditions of learning model builds on language acquisition studies done by McShane (1980), Snow & Ferguson (1977), Greenfield & Smith (1976), Halliday (1975), Bruner (1975), and others. From these infancy studies, factors were isolated which enable children to learn to speak. In these optimal conditions, acquisition is facilitated, never forced. Don Holdaway (1979) points out that "learning to walk and talk are learned almost universally with great satisfaction" but not learning to read and write (p. 11). Whole Language looks to the language acquisition model as a set of principles for providing optimal learning conditions for all literacy.

Cambourne's conditions are:

1. *Immersion:* Under optimal conditions, the learner is immersed in what is to be learned. Children learning to speak are surrounded by their native language, and from the confusion of sounds around them, they take what they are ready for.
2. *Demonstration:* Under optimal conditions, what is to be learned is demonstrated by an expert to whom the learner is bonded. Thus, the learner is predisposed to want to be like the teacher to whom the child is bonded. Children learning to speak spend much time watching people demonstrate speaking.

3. *Engagement:* Under optimal conditions, learners try out what is to be learned, often in private, until they feel secure in their performance. Children learning to talk often babble and play with words, practicing on their own. Cambourne points out that in order to engage, learners must see themselves as doers, must see a potential use for the new learning, and must feel that the risk involved is tolerable. Further, learners are more apt to engage with a person with whom they are bonded.

4. *Expectations:* Under optimal conditions, there is an expectation that the learner will succeed. Children learning to talk enjoy an atmosphere which expects that this will happen. Such an environment is "secure and supportive, providing help on call and being absolutely free from any threat associated with the learning of the task" (Holdaway, 1979, p. 23).

5. *Responsibility:* Under optimal conditions, learners make decisions and choices about the learning they undertake. They are placed in a position of trust. Infants learning to talk are left to take what they need from the language flow around them and are trusted to find their own best sequence.

6. *Approximation:* Under optimal conditions, learners' efforts which resemble correct form are rewarded as if they were correct. Sounds made by children learning to talk are heralded as if they were real words. Experts to whom children are bonded willingly translate and respond as if the approximation were correct. Thus, the learner is gradually led closer and closer to the proper form.

7. *Use:* Under optimal conditions, learners are allowed time to "play around" with and use what they are learning. This element of play permits the self-regulation necessary to a successful learning experience. Children want to perform and share successful results. Children learning to talk are eager to display newly-acquired skills. This confidence is the result of much self-regulated practice.

8. *Response:* Children learning to talk are given a "no-strings" response—immediate feedback that lets them begin to work with the language they are learning. This response allows children to use all their naturally occurring, self-regulating mechanisms. A learner gradually fine-tunes approximations until satisfied. Children learning to talk develop judgment about correct form through response by self-regulating.

In these optimal conditions, acquisition is facilitated, never forced. Here we look to the language acquisition model as a set of principles for providing optimal learning conditions for all learning, especially for the learning of big ideas. As Brian Cambourne puts it, "I find it . . . satisfying to believe that there is a single, unitary, very effective process of learning which is exemplified by learning to talk . . . and that most learning . . . proceeds most effectively under these conditions" (p. 42).

I do a workshop with students and teachers that I learned to do from Bobbi Fisher. In it we all describe something we have learned because we wanted to learn it. I ask participants to think about something they have learned lately simply because they wanted to learn it. I then have them describe how they went about it, what conditions were important in their own learning process.

In the workshop, as the descriptions grow, I jot down words that respondents use to describe the process they went through in the learning. What emerges on the chalkboard is the list of Cambourne's optimal conditions tempered by certain characteristics peculiar to adults.

The Adult Performance Model

The adult performance model is the logical outcome of the growth of Cambourne's conditions of learning, a model of learning which is the foundation of much of Whole Language philosophy and practice. Because we learn real, meaningful things through natural learning when we, as children, learn to talk, we make use of the same components when we perform meaningfully as adults.

The adult performance model is practical, realistic, and reflective. Adults cross-check and verify results, adults work together and consult; they problem-solve cooperatively, and perform authentic tasks in an atmosphere of communication.

Whenever they can, adults select tasks which are appropriate and possible for the performer. Adults know themselves as learners. Adults are allowed to find out things they don't know. They need to be encouraged to succeed. Adults utilize constant feedback to fine-tune their actions and decisions, and they are rewarded for performance.

Cambourne's (1988) conditions of learning describe an optimal learning model, using as a starting point those natural conditions present as children acquire their native language. They lead naturally to the adult performance model, *with some variations*. This is important to those of us dealing with children on the border, at upper elementary level, caught halfway between childhood models and adult models. These children incorporate features of both.

The similarities in the conditions of learning are:

1. *Immersion:* Adults who took Spanish in high school but never lived in a Spanish-speaking country know how the principle of immersion works. Most of us remember little if anything of the learning we did in isolation. Like children learning their native language, adults learning by choice prefer to drench themselves in the thing to be learned.

2. *Demonstration:* In the adult performance model, learners are bonded in some way to the demonstrator. Because adult differences are pronounced, it may be more difficult for them to make a successful teacher-student match (Cross 1981). They may hire a coach, they may learn from a friend, they may even learn from watching a child, as has happened to some of us who became computer literate while teaching and learning in the classroom. Many of us have learned from watching a child perform.

   As David Hornsby points out, we do learn from individuals we are not bonded to, but not always what we are supposed to. And without demonstration, learners have no inner vision of what is to be accomplished. For adults, this means that a task not demonstrated may not be tried. Without a vision of how performance is supposed to look, an adult may simply avoid trying to learn. People used to ask me to play miniature golf with them, but I had never really watched people play it and I didn't even know what it looked like when someone did it. I never tried. I would need to have time to look carefully, knowing that I would soon try it myself. I would need a lot of time.

3. *Engagement:* Anyone who has tried as an adult to learn something new knows all about the need and conditions for engagement. Adults are apt to suffer a lowering of risk-taking behavior and a heavy reliance on prior learning (Cross 1981). Going down the hill on skis, standing up on skates, even trying a new dance step all require practice and may be best done in private the first time. Adults forcefully decide on the time to engage in their own time, in their own way.

4. *Expectations:* Adults usually are very sensitive to lack of positive expectation; they are aware of being tagged as inefficient learners and are victim to their own prior learning experiences (Kidd 1973). Some adults have spent time in negative learning climates or have been ridiculed for failed attempts. Many adults know a lot about how hard it is to learn something when no one thinks you can do it. To be successful learners, adults must be encouraged in positive self-perception (Lovell 1980).

For instance, it has been only in recent years, thanks to supportive students with positive expectations, that I have tried to "make a basket" by throwing a wad of paper into the nearby trashcan. Under the watchful eye of students who I'm bonded to, I'm getting pretty good.

5. *Responsibility:* Like children, adult learners do best when they are allowed control of their learning processes. Given an opportunity to learn to knit, for instance, most adults know and seek out their own best mode of learning. Some watch expert knitters carefully, some get a step-by-step lesson from one they trust, some give it a trial-and-error approach, still others buy a book called "How to Knit." Successful adult learners proceed at their own pace, appreciate encouragement, and return for more teaching at the point when they are ready to learn more. Successful learning depends on an internal locus of control. All learners need choice in the learning experience; adults may demand it.

6. *Approximation:* Adult learners often need to be persuaded to accept their own early approximations. Often schooled in perfectionist systems, adults have grown accustomed to getting one piece of paper for writing, one chance to read out loud. Adults are apt to focus most on accuracy (Cross 1981). Given a private opportunity, however, adults are likely to approximate. Go to any dance floor and see the power of adult approximations.

7. *Use:* Adults need time to learn and opportunity for extended use and play. This permits the powerful mechanism of self-regulation. Once an adult decides to learn something new, self-regulation becomes the key to eventual successful performance. Some adults, like some children, may talk out loud to themselves during use (Vygotsky 1962) as they self-regulate.

Adults who have achieved success in a practiced skill or routine can be as excited as children about sharing it. Once confident, adults proudly present a special dish they have just learned to cook, display the new bookcase they just built, or even play you a piece they have just learned on the accordian.

8. *Response:* Response is important for adults. Adults need immediate sensory input from performance (Lovell 1980). However, some adults may need a long period of use before response is risked. Adults describing their own optimal learning processes are quite specific about how and when they show their new learning to another. They choose the viewer carefully for specific reasons, most often for the quality and type of response. Adults constantly monitor their own performance, regulate their behaviors, and perfect techniques.

These are the similarities between the conditions of learning as observed when infants learn to talk and extended into classroom practice, and the adult performance model seen when adults learn a new skill. Both children and adults learn best when they are immersed in the task to be learned, when it is modeled, when they are allowed to practice, are given feedback, and required to perform only when they are ready. Like children, adults learn best when everyone expects them to do well and when their "near misses" are heralded as sure signs of future success.

Comparing and Contrasting the Models

Do any differences exist between the conditions of learning and the adult performance model? Surely there must be some differences between the learning model which facilitates a child learning to talk and an adult learning, say, to windsurf. These differences would be observed in pre-adult, upper elementary students already past emergent literacy but on the border of adulthood. We can use these distinct characteristics of adult learners as guideposts for working with upper elementary, experienced students who are learning "by doing what adults do."

The greatest difference is a cognitive one. Older learners benefit from degrees of abstract thinking. That is, they are able to think about thinking and are able to use words as a means of concept formation (Vygotsky 1962). Skills learned after the development of logical and hypothetical thought can never be developmental stages leading to formal operations, as they are for children. For adults, abstract thinking enables subsequent concrete learning. "In fact, formal operations are ingredient to (skilled motor activities learned later) in ways impossible to the child" (Howard 1982).

This ability to conceptualize with the word permits the more formal education which is characteristic of adult learning (Lovell 1980). Bruner (1978) was impressed with the 'logic-like' and rational quality of adult thinking when learning new tasks. He found that adult thinking was inefficient but thorough; adults searched for information while demonstrating awareness of environment, personal limitations, and risks; adults were able to use minimal clues to make "highly predictable conclusions."

But this strength of adult learning can also be a weakness, for it subjects adults to possible overloading (Lovell 1980) and slows down information processing (Cross 1981; Kidd 1973). Also, adults are more attentive to a variety of things in the environment (Reason 1977), thus creating interferences with learning. Adults may have a hard time learning new information because they have to unlearn old strategies (Rogers 1971).

In working with people learning to word process, Daiute (1982) found that while both children and adults needed to learn in context, adults found the process more arduous. They learned linguistically, and wanted to know why operations work the way they do. "Adults want the systems to make sense, to relate to their experiences and theories" (p. 141).

In the long run, Daiute found, adults learned more than children. By initially resisting isolated learning of commands, adults used their own "ways of relating knowledge, models and experience stored in long-term memory to provide a home for isolated pieces of new information" (p. 143). She concluded that adults need more structure when they learn. Lovell (1980) also concludes that the most important factor for adult learning is how the information is organized:

> Perhaps the most important contribution a teacher can make to the adult's learning of cognitive information is to select, organize, present and translate new material in such a way that the learner can appreciate its relationship with ideas he already has clearly established in his memory. (p. 54)

Another significant difference in place for some older learners is the fear of failure (Kidd 1973). Adults and experienced students at upper elementary are more aware than infants of the possibilities of failure and may have undergone it themselves. This impacts on the learning process by making some learners more secretive, some more reluctant. It lengthens the period of Use. Even pre-adult learners, experienced in schooling, may need a long period for very private "trying out."

A final difference is the role of social indicators. From pre-adult years on, learners are deeply involved in learning communities. They may be in the learning community—if they are successful learners—or they may be out of the learning community—if they have tried to learn and failed. They may have accepted themselves as permanently outside the learning community. Frank Smith says that people "learn to read and write successfully only if they are admitted into a community of written language users . . . the 'literacy club' " (1988, p. 2).

Older learners are also involved in social communities (Knox 1978). To the extent that they are successful with a particular task, learners will be accepted into the chosen social community. Further, to the extent that the task to be learned is accepted in the social community, learners will try to succeed at learning it.

Applying Both Models to Upper Elementary Learners

All these distinguishing features of adult learning can be observed in the learning behaviors of pre-adults to a lesser degree. Children in the upper elementary grades are on the edge of abstract thinking; their use of pseudo-concepts (Vygotsky 1962) introduces them to the still-to-come, adult use of conceptual thinking. Like adults, pre-adults need structure to relate new material to old material already stored in long-term memory, even though they have less stored than adults. Many children also have experienced failure in life and past schooling; and, like adults, upper elementary students' learning and social bondings are strong. Differences in the learning model between adults and pre-adults are differences of degree, not kind.

Other differences occur on an individual basis. Some upper elementary children, like adults, may not be able to accept their own approximations. Others may need encouragement to believe that the teacher holds a positive expectation for their learning. Some children may not see learning as meaningful if it is not on a worksheet. Teachers at the upper elementary level—like adults suddenly in a positive learning environment—may have to play catch up with their learners.

Adults and children on the edge of adulthood also share features usually attributed specifically to the adult learning model, although the impact differs in degree. Those of us teaching at the upper elementary can look at the following features generally attributed to adult learning and see elements of our students' behavior:

> Adults need to feel confident that they are learning what is needed to meet their own goals; they have a variety of goals for learning; they enter the learning experience with a wide variety of experience and background; learning rate, style and preferences all vary (Knowles 1979).

> Adults have a deep need to know why they are learning something; they are task-oriented; and, they have a deep pyschological need to be self-directing (Knowles 1983).

> When learning, adults must be given time, opportunity and means to relate new information to old information already stored conceptually in long-term memory (Cross 1981; Knox 1978; Kidd 1973).

> Adults need immediate sensory performance, information about the achievement expected and information about the consequences of choices (Lovell 1980).

Upper elementary children display some features of the childhood learning model and some features of the adult way of learning. There are more similarities than differences between the two models at the upper elementary level. For example: all learners share a common concern with learning tasks for a reason which impacts on their own lives; learning styles vary for both groups; new information is acquired by being related to older information already stored, for this is the nature of learning; and, both groups benefit from reward.

We can observe elements of both Cambourne's conditions of learning and the adult performance model at work as we watch pre-adults learning to play softball at recess. Skills to be learned are acquired in immersion, are being demonstrated constantly, learners are deeply engaged, in use, and self-regulation. There is a lot of approximation going on. Learners are deeply bonded to each other and to those who model expert performance.

What may vary from the conditions of learning is the degree and form of response. Not everyone on the ball field learns in an atmosphere of positive response. Some learn in a hostile, threatening climate. How this affects the quality of the learned skill is difficult to measure, but "teaching by yelling at each other" has been a feature of pre-adult recess sports interaction ever since I can remember.

As teachers, we fight this trend, charging students to encourage each other, to support each other's efforts. But I suspect that some pre-adults learn some skills out of fear of ridicule and negative response. This is a major departure from the optimal conditions of learning. It foreshadows a negative possibility in the adult performance model, that of learning a skill so as not to be fired from a job. I know adults who have learned to play golf, not because they loved the game or because there was a positive expectation that they could, but because they needed that skill as an entry pass into a social or working community. Knox (1987) lists these social factors as "modifiers of learning" for adults; clearly they are present in learning experience at upper elementary.

Holdaway (1989b) adds "joy and laughter" to the list of features associated with natural, and optimal, learning. Children learning to talk do so in a climate of happiness, surrounded by bonded experts who are entranced with the child's efforts.

For adults, learning is not always accompanied by joy and laughter. In the adult performance model, there is a level of privacy and shyness not part of the childhood learning model. But in those things they have chosen to learn, adults demonstrate a level of joy and laughter appropriate to their social surroundings. When they are bonded to a mentor, adults may share a happiness in learning that is reminiscent of the conditions surrounding a child's first words.

Together with these principles, the optimal learning conditions presuppose "a high level of positive prophecy" (Holdaway 1989b). Going beyond the principle of expectation, this high degree of positive prophecy is the excitement which the bonded expert conveys to the learner: "I know you can do it!"

Upper elementary students, like some adults, may not expect classrooms to be places for joy and laughter or places where students can expect Holdaway's "high degree of positive prophecy." In this way, they are already more versant in the adult performance model. They have already become suspicious of negative possibilities in the learning experience.

By attending to these two models of learning, we can develop a theory about what kind of learning conditions are optimal for students in upper elementary school. The prime prerequisite will be to take into account the nature of learners on the edge of adulthood. Still children, learning to be adults, these learners will have characteristics of both extremes.

Learning from Lev Vygotsky

Lev Vygotsky, a Soviet psychologist who died young in 1934, was an interactionist. He had read the works of Jean Piaget, and decided to take things a step further. Like Piaget, Vygotsky believed that children were active learners but unlike Piaget, he felt that this learning did not proceed in stages, biologically, but rather was the result of particular interactions. He believed that learners could not be separated from the social, cultural, and historical context of what they were learning. Vygotsky's thinking, which I learned about while working with Courtney Cazden at Harvard University, has influenced me more than any other thinker.

I have read Piaget, too. As a matter of fact, we read and learned and discussed Piaget extensively one year for in-service training in the school in which I worked. But Piaget bothered me. I saw too many children who were at different Piagetian stages, depending on what they were working with. I discovered upon introspection that I was pre-operational *and* concrete when it came to economics. I couldn't make the stages match the years. Piaget's biological perspective troubled me. I was eventually able to look beyond Piaget's reputation as a stage theorist and consider his ideas more broadly, thanks to working with Eleanor Duckworth at Harvard. But in the meantime, I had read Lev Vygotsky, his critique of Piaget, and his own interactionist perspective.

I guess if there's one thing I am for sure, it's an interactionist. And from the work of Lev Vygotsky, I drew three main ideas which focus my thinking to this day. They are:

1. Learning occurs first *interpsychologically* before it is internalized *intrapsychologically* as development.
2. Learning occurs best in the *zone of proximal development* where young learners work in the company of adults or more capable peers.
3. Concept development is the result of the meeting of *scientific* learning, which proceeds downward, and *spontaneous* development, which proceeds upward.

Inter-to intrapersonal learning

Vygotsky believed that learning occurs first *between* people, interpersonally, before it occurs *within* the individual intrapersonally. To me this means that in order to be successful, a learning experience must include a chance for people to interact and this must occur somewhere near the beginning. When people are learning, there will be talking. Vygotsky wrote: "All the higher functions originate as actual relations between human beings" (1978, p. 57).

When activities that involved concrete manipulatives like Cuisenaire rods and base ten blocks entered the classroom world of mathematics, we began to recognize the need for interpersonal learning. In part we responded to Piaget's widespread belief in the need for concrete activity before abstract representation but we also honored the need for interaction. Many of the activities that preceeded abstract learning were games that children played and talked about together, as when they learned to add by playing chip-trading games together. The use of learning centers as places for concrete experiences in mathematics often presupposed a social interaction at the learning site.

Vygotsky thought that as learning takes place, operations that have been performed externally are reconstructed internally. Learners need to think things over and make learning their own. And he felt that this happens over time. He wrote: "The process being transformed continues to exist and to change as an external form of activity for a long time before definitively turning inward" (p. 57). This means to me that I won't expect children to "get it" right away, that after an interactive learning experience I will give them a long time to internalize what they have learned. I won't expect to see the transfer of the learning for a while.

The zone of proximal development

Vygotsky's exploration of what he called "the zone of proximal development" was an analysis of the time and place when interactions between people actually happen. The "zone" is the interaction itself, usually between a child and the teacher but sometimes between a child and a more able peer. Conferencing during writing time can be such a zone. The "proximal development" is what happens to the child's learning during that time. When working in this zone with a teacher or more able peer, a child can be enabled to do things during the interaction that the child could not do alone. Courtney Cazden calls this "performance before competence" [1981]. Vygotsky describes the zone of proximal development in this way:

> It is the distance between the actual development as determined by independent problem solving and the level of potential development as determined through problem solving under adult guidance or in collaboration with more capable peers. (1978, p. 86)

When we know from observation or measurement what children seem to be capable of doing alone, and then we help them to perform a harder process or think about a harder concept by working with them, we have taken them into their zone of proximal development. We have taken them one step further **because they worked with us**. Central to working in this zone is its social nature and the fact that we mediate, or interpret, the learning for the child.

When we work in a writing conference with a child who feels that a story is finished but fails to recognize that the storyline is out of sequence, we must take that child into the zone of proximal development if we are to help him/her learn about sequencing. As we work with learners who understand the form of the written division algorithm but are all mixed up on the part that hangs down in the problem, below the bracket, we take them beyond what they know. And these learners are successful because we work with them, because of the interaction with an adult or a more capable peer.

Denis Newman, Peg Griffin and Michael Cole have thought a lot about working in the zone of proximal development and have studied the nature of what happens there. They have reported their ideas in a book called *The Construction Zone: Working for Cognitive Change in School*. They have dubbed Vygotsky's zone of proximal development, "the construction zone," the place where knowledge is constructed, and offer many analyses of how teachers are able to take learners beyond their range. In his introduction to this book, Sheldon White calls the "construction zone":

> . . . a magic place where minds meet, where things are not the same to all who see them, where meanings are fluid, and where one person's construal may preempt another's. (1989, p. ix)

Spontaneous versus scientific concept development

Vygotsky believed that conceptual development occurs in two ways, spontaneous and scientific. Spontaneous concept development happens as learners interact with their environment and each other. It is how we learn from practical and personal experience. Scientific concept development originates in the classroom, is mediated by instruction, and may be outside the learner's experience. He used the term, spontaneous, to refer to any learning acquired through experience and the term, scientific, to refer to abstractions acquired through mediated instruction, or school learning.

To be learned, scientific concepts must have a foundation built of spontaneous concept development, Vygotsky said. In Vygotskian terms, to learn a "scientific" concept like "justice," a learner must have some practical and personal experiences, some "spontaneous" concepts, in which to embed the scientific concept. Like a seed which must find fertile ground, a scientific concept must find a spontaneously-founded base of the concept. In order to learn the concept of division and the attending algorithm, a child must have developed a clear notion of dividing. Vygotsky said that "the development of the child's spontaneous concepts proceeds upward and the development of his scientific concepts downward" (1962, p. 108).

Once the foundation is in place, scientific concept development spurs greater learning spontaneously: "the development of scientific concepts runs ahead of the development of spontaneous concepts" (p. 106). That is, once the process has begun, school instruction can help a learner to understand personal experiences more deeply. Once the two types of ideas have met, knowing about the abstract concept will help the learner to interpret day-to-day experiences that relate. "Scientific concepts . . . supply structures for the upward development of the child's spontaneous concepts toward consciousness and deliberate use" (p. 109).

Vygotsky and integrated school learning

Lev Vygotsky was a firm believer in school instruction. He believed in the interaction between school subjects and the need for learners to explore all of them: ". . . all the basic school subjects act as formal discipline, each facilitating the learning of the others: the psychological functions stimulated by them develop in one complex process" (p. 102).

He argued that integration and linking between domains of learning was a key to clear intellectual growth and believed that learning in different subject areas contributed to a unitary whole in intellectual development. He was concerned with the "revelation of this internal, subterranean developmental network of school subjects" (1978, p. 91).

Vygotsky believed that instruction in one subject area influences all growth, beyond the limits of individual disciplines and disputed what he called the "traditional view" that when a child masters an operation or learns the meaning of a word, developmental processes are completed.

Such detailed studies as the arithmetic operations resulted in extended cognitive development: ". . . initial mastery of, for example, the four arithmetic operations provides the basis for the subsequent development of a variety of highly complex internal processes in children's thinking" (p. 90).

Learners need to interact in a guided setting in a linked integration. He wrote that "learning awakens a variety of internal developmental processes that are able to operate only when the child is interacting with people in his environment and in cooperation with his peers" (p. 90). The linking between concepts is the key to the development of higher functions: "Concepts do not lie in the child's mind like peas in a bag, without any bonds between them" (1962, p. 110). In fact, he believed that the very links between concepts enabled cognitive growth. It is crucial that integration across the school subjects and the school day be accomplished if we are to follow the findings of Vygotsky.

Lev Vygotsky held out high hopes for the role of school instruction in the life of the child. He wanted teachers and their teaching to be flexible and receptive to the reality of the processes in a child's mind: "Development in children never follows school learning the way a shadow follows the subject that casts it"; rather, development reflects a "dynamic relation" that cannot be contained by a rigid, "unchanging hypothetical formulation" (p. 91).

He encouraged us in our teaching efforts, giving us a motto to teach by: "We have given him a pennyworth of instruction, and he has gained a small fortune in development" (1962, p. 96).

14

Assessment and Evaluation

Reflecting on Assessing

Throughout this book I have emphasized the enabling of students and teachers to engage in productive self-evaluation—of progress, of process, and of product. And so, in considering the assessment and evaluation of whole learning processes, this emphasis continues. Much of the work done by my students and me in evaluation, both ongoing and final, hinges on structures which encourage the fruitful assessment of our own processes.

Linda Rief, in her article "Finding the Value in Evaluation: Self-Assessment in a Middle School Classroom," says,

> Learning to make meaning in reading and writing is not objective, as our evaluation systems would seem to indicate. We must become more flexible in our assessment of students' work . . . When we trust them to set goals and to evaluate their learning in progress, we will begin to realize that they know much more than we allow them to tell us through our set curriculums and standardized tests. (p. 29)

Most schools use testing and evaluation instruments such as Linda describes—set curriculums and standardized tests. Most schools have reporting systems—grading scales and checklists—that may or may not serve the instruction being evaluated. All of these systems are changeable, but change comes slowly in this area of education.

As of 1992, we seem to be moving educationally in evaluation in two directions at once. While there is evidence and a demand for the value of productive self-evaluation and assessment in a reflective mode, there is also a proliferation of standardized testing. The political climate seems to support the idea that good learning is the result of testing. But, as I have heard Yetta Goodman put it ironically, some must be surprised to find that when we don't test them, they grow anyway.

My mother told me that when she lived in India, she sometimes saw a sign in a shop window that gave the owner's name followed by the credential, "B.A. failed." This said a great deal about the shop owner. This was someone who had proceeded through the entire Bachelor's degree, with whatever level of success, but had failed the final exams. This was an educated person unable to pass exams. I personally knew highly intelligent people who were unable to attain degrees in such a system because of their inability to undergo examination and whose lives were profoundly affected.

In the British system which spawned the credential known as "B.A. failed," the final exams were the measure of success for the entire program and were largely based on memorizing information. India was once part of the British system and this aspect of the degree program persisted. All the hard work, all the learning could be nullified by poor test results or inability to face a test. And "B.A. failed" became a valid credential.

I think the United States needs to consider carefully whether it wants to move further in this direction. There is no doubt that some drift is already apparent. Do we want the test to be the substance of the credential for learning?

It is important for teachers and administrators to continually assess the assessment going on in their educational systems. Evaluation instruments and policies need to be continually held up against program to be sure that one supports the other. If, for instance, the traditional language arts program has modulated in favor of 40 minutes of process writing a day, incorporating the old language arts focus, the reporting system should be flexible enough to cope with the transition.

Of course, it never is. And teachers find themselves grading children on defunct educational programs by lockstep procedures. So what I do at all levels is to enlarge the scope of the reporting. Bound by the old systems in place, I have added new components to reflect what I think is important to know in evaluation. I have increased the feedback to those interested in learners and included aspects which respond to my instructional emphasis on self-evaluation and growth in process.

I have done this through two primary avenues, the use of student-constructed portfolios and the use of self-evaluation instruments. Both of these aim at providing an evaluation forum for one's own assessment of growth in learning and are provided in addition to any traditional reporting instruments and standards which may be in place.

Portfolio Assessment

Portfolio assessment is a visible, concrete means of documenting more abstract assessment. In a portfolio, one would find evidence for the letter or number grade and for any checkmarking of criteria on a reporting instrument. In portfolio assessment, students or teachers put together a collection of work representative of growth during a certain period of time. In evaluating process writing, for example, a student would select from work done during a term. Selected pieces of work would demonstrate facets of growth that were important to the student as well as to the teacher.

When students put together writing portfolios in sixth grade (*see* Figure 56), they included a wide variety of written products to show at the conference.

When Marcia put together her portfolio, she elected to be at the conference to explain it. Otherwise she would have included written comments about why certain items had been selected. She included a word-processed copy of finished writing, a draft of a speech she gave during a simulation, both the draft copy and the final product from a practice session for a state-mandated writing sample, a final draft of an essay she had written in content from a writing prompt, research notes, and jottings on a scrap of paper that might someday be a poem.

Marcia had papers available because we saved our work. We did this for two reasons: so that we would have it available when we wanted to demonstrate growth in process, and so we could use it to learn new skills.

Once students have put together their own portfolios, they begin to look at their work in progress differently. It was not uncommon for me to hear students assessing something by saying, "I wonder if this should go in my portfolio?"

Once items were selected for a portfolio, I took the time to talk to students about why those items were selected. Sometimes I asked them to write out the reasons and make it part of the portfolio. We did this so that those who attended a reporting conference could be informed as to why items were seen as important.

For instance, Marcia told me that she selected some writing as final and some as draft so that her mother could see how her writing changed when she worked on it after conferencing. She included a computer printout to show her facility with word processing. She put in the draft and the final copy of

AdKins Debate

Side One: "Pro-Euthanasia"

In the case of Janet Elaine Atkins I rule that, Dr. Jack Kevorkian, under the circumstances that Mrs. Atkins pressed the button that terminated her deseased life, and that she initiated the 'suicide', by contacting Dr. Kevorkian, is innocent in any and every way. ~~Docto~~ A person's life is irreplacible, +only lasts for a while. But, if the person should choose to expire his/her life that is totally their decision, and nothing, especially Doctors or the government, should prevent that person (Atkins) from ~~the~~ fulfilling his/her demands

Side Two: "Anti-Euthanasia"

(Since I see no reason why anyone should not be able to die at their desired age, it would be hard for me to debate both sides But since I am, I only have a few reasons on why someone would be for "Side Two: Anti-Euthanasia".)

A human life is a mortal one, a short amount of time to experience and fulfill your fantasies, dreams, +wishes. Why would anybody wish to terminate his/her life?

In the act of deciding to die, they are obviously acting selfishly, ignoring how their non-existence will break the hearts of all the people that loved that person dearly.

THIS SHOWS HOW I CAN TAKE DIFFERENT POINTS OF VIEW.

FIGURE 56A

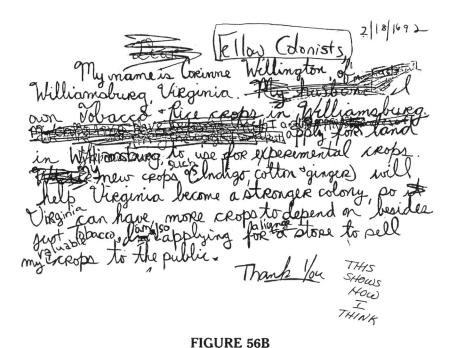

FIGURE 56B

the practice writing sample to show how a piece of writing grew and also because a test-situation writing sample shows "what I can do under pressure." She put in the quite messy draft of the simulation speech because she said it would show her mother how she thought. The research notes were to show that she was getting ready for hard work in high school. And, finally, the tidbits of a poem were to show that she tried all kinds of writing.

As Linda Rief points out in her article, one reason why portfolios are effective as evaluation instruments in her classroom is because students determine their own criteria for what will be included, what she calls the "internal criteria" (p. 24). They are valuable program assessment instruments because the teacher has the opportunity to see what is important to students in their own learning and to make a comparison between their standards and those of the teacher.

I have used portfolios as assessment instruments in a variety of subject areas. Students can display growth through products and artifacts in any subject area that is included in evaluation—math, reading, even spelling. The purpose of these portfolios is to support, explain, and amplify traditional reporting through conferences, grading, checklists, and anecdotal comments.

Recently some graduate students and I tried to make a list of all the options that are available in putting together a portfolio. The primary option available

THIS SHOWS HOW I DO AN INTERVIEW
AND THE WRITE IT UP.

So far I have done four interviews
the ones I have done are,
    1) my Dad
    2) my mom
    3) my older sister
    4) And my younger sister.
I did my younger sister because I
wanted to see her point of view of
this problem. So far what I've learned
is that their is alot of congestion in the
downtown are that I wasn't reconizing before.

    The most important problem in the
downtown are is that the traffic is getting
worse.

FIGURE 56C

was who would put the portfolio together and we isolated three primary choices, only the teacher, only the student, or the teacher and the student together.

We divided the list into categories, starting with Linda Rief's distinction between external and internal criteria. External criteria were defined as "options for *what* might be in a portfolio" and internal criteria were defined as "options for *why* things might be in the portfolio." Here is a sample of the lists:

External

fiction pieces	letters
several drafts of a long project	notes
journal entries	drawings and illustrations

THIS CROSS-CULTURAL FAIRY TALE SHOWS HOW I CAN USE RESEARCH IN FICTION

The Three Little Pigs In Egypt

Once upon a time there once lived 3 pigs, Ra, Hathor and Anubis. Anubis was rich. He had a nicely made brick house.

Hathor who had a wooden house was semi-rich. Ra was poor so he lived in a small hut around the Open Court. They all libed in Cairo. There was a man his name was King Ramses. He goes around and huffs and puffs your house down. A messenger came to town one day to inform us that King Ramses' was coming to Cairo. Ra did not know what to do. He did not have a sturdy house.

Hathor didn't know what to do either because he did not finish the roof. Anubis was sitting comfortable next to the fire. Anubis didn't worry because he had a beautiful sturdy house. The seconds passed. The suspense was on for Ra and Hathor. They were both sweating extremely bad.

King Ramses was here he yelled. First he went to Ra's house and huffed and puffed and it collapsed. Next Ramses went on to Hathor's and huffed and puffed and that house collapsed. And last but not least he came to Aunbis's house. And he started to huff and puff until he died of to much huffing and puffing. Anubis lived happily ever after. A few yrs. later Anubis made a statue of King Ramses to remember him by. The End

FIGURE 56D

THIS SHOWS HOW I CAN WRITE DIRECTIONS IN SCIENCE.

~~~~ Science: ~~~~

How to win at Island Survivors:
  The whole idea of Island Survivors is to make it through the year and leave the Island with the species alive and well balanced.
  How to do a month:
When you pick a what to do in your month, the first month you should usually have 1 person get food, (hunting + fishing give most supply of food) 1 person build a shelter +1 person collect firewood. It takes 2x to collect enough firewood +2 times to finish a shelter, so take 2 months for those.
  What species to sellect:
When sellecting land species, always select plants- grass is good for rabbits, but are not food for people. Acorns + blueberries are your best bet for supplying food for animals + for people. Bears supply lots of food, but become extinct very quickly, and hibernate in Winter. Rabbits supply a small amount of food, + bears help to eat them. →

FIGURE 56E

Internal

to show growth	only the best
risk-taking	variety of genres

Each list seemed like it could go on indefinitely. We then considered what options were available beyond the lists of criteria for content. One set of options involved why the portfolio was being put together. Here's a sample of that long list:

Why?

to demonstrate growth	to encourage and inspire a learner
to document evalua-tion	to fulfill an administrative mandate
	to evaluate program
to help a teacher learn	to give as a gift to parents
to pass to next teacher	

We thought about **When** a portfolio might be put together and/or be displayed: once a month, at reporting time, at the end of the year? And finally, we considered **Where** it might be kept and **Who** might have access to it: in a private file for teacher only, on the shelf for student and teacher, in a file for student only. And so on.

There were many, many decisions to be made around this topic of portfolio assessment. Teachers working together on this kind of assessment and documentation would make these decisions as a team. When I used portfolios, they were a new idea and in my classroom we used them as a way of helping all of us to understand how a particular student thought. My students and I developed the answers to all these lists.

Self-evaluation

The second assessment device I have used is written or oral response to specific self-evaluation questions. I originally heard these four questions from Don Graves at the 1989 National Council of Teachers of English National Convention in St. Louis, and I have found no way of improving on them. The questions are:

1. What can you do now that you couldn't do before?
2. What are you good at?
3. What do you need to learn next?
4. How will you learn it?

When I first asked students to respond to these questions, I made the mistake of rephrasing number 4. I said, "Who will you learn it from?" Inevitably, students answered "You, the teacher." In fact, I find that a great deal of what is learned in the classroom is learned from sources other than the teacher—from other students, from books and text models, from adults and sources outside the classroom, from a variety of media.

Now I am very careful to word question 4 in an open-ended way, a way which asks students to consider a multitude of learning sources rather than the traditional "teacher knows it all." In a whole learning approach, this teacher does not know it all nor do I want to imply that I think I do or that I think I should. What I do know is how to help people improve their own processes for obtaining answers.

When I use these four questions as self-evaluation instruments in conjunction with traditional reporting devices, I ask upper elementary students to write out the answers and include them with their portfolio. The answers are shared either in the report card or at the reporting conference. I usually ask students to respond to the questions in the three major "basic skills" areas, reading, writing, and math.

Here are Vicky's written responses to the questions in the area of reading:

1. **What can you do now that you couldn't do before?**
   Vicky: How to understand confusing sentences.
2. **What are you good at?**
   Vicky: Reading different kinds of books. Reading fast.
   Understanding big words.
3. **What do you need to learn next?**
   How to understand what some of the sentences mean, and faster.
   Reading more classics and reading different books.
4. **How will you learn it?**
   At school with my teachers and by myself at school and at home.

Here are Jerry's responses in math:

1. **What can you do now that you couldn't do before?**
   Before I didn't know much about decimals as in adding and I didn't know what some of them were called.
2. **What are you good at?**
   I am good at double digit and triple digit multiplication, addition and subtraction.
3. **What do you need to learn next?**
   I need to get better at square roots and at factors.
4. **How will you learn it?**
   I plan to learn it all in my mathematics books and in group sessions.

Some students took their responses home and typed them to make them look good for the report card conference. They knew the value of well-made products, in assessment instruments as well as school work:

1. What can you do now that you couldn't do before?

> Response: In writing, I did not realize that if you want a good book product, you have to work at it. In the years before, I made books and they came out well in the end. I thought my past books were great but now I see how well they can come out. I have also learned to take information and put it in my own words.

If we want to know about what students know we only have to ask them. All these years, I have tried to trick them into showing me what they didn't know. In fact, I really care a lot more about what they do know and how they know they know it:

4. How will you learn it?

> Response: I think there are a lot of sources of information. I plan to find anything I need to know from teachers in the building, including mine. Other ways are to read books, watch films at school or home televisions. I am not worried about where I learn my information as much as if I will learn it.

I have found through asking that students know a great deal about how they learn. I am only one resource among many that they suggest as options for learning a variety of things:

4. How will you learn it?

- By asking people who are familiar with it.
- Going to computer class and going to extra-curricular activities for the computer.
- By reading more.
- By watching other people and paying attention.
- I plan to learn to type better by using typing lessons from the computer.
- I'm going to practice more on my own time.
- I would like to learn it more at home.

Documenting self-appraisal serves two purposes: it allows us to provide authentic information in addition to more abstract traditional reporting methods, and it promotes a deeper understanding for the learner of one of the most important skills a learner possesses—self-regulation. In self-regulation, a learner utilizes a natural feedback system, "sensitive to what is going on both inside and outside the system" (Holdaway 1979, p. 86). Through portfolio assessment and self-evaluative questioning, learners can develop their self-regulatory skills, those internal mechanisms that help them to know when they're wrong and when they're right, what they know firmly and what needs to be learned next.

Ongoing Evaluation

My part of evaluation and assessment goes on over a long period of time. Teachers are constantly appraising the learning going on around them. Successful teachers have highly developed, sensitive self-regulating systems, which respond quickly to learners' expressed and unexpressed needs. Such teachers' sensors that tell them at an intuitive level not only what needs to be taught next to any given student, but how it ought to be taught and which part of it ought to be taught first.

I document my long-term observation, I do a lot of "Kidwatching" as Yetta Goodman (1985) called it. Kidwatching is "learning about children by watching how they learn" (p. 9). Evaluation through kidwatching involves teachers knowing "what to look for as signs of growth and development" (p. 11). The long-range purpose of anecdotal record keeping in kidwatching is "to provide profiles of the children's language growth in different settings, with different materials, and through different experiences" (p. 17).

I keep notes on learners—sometimes nothing important, just things I don't ever want to forget. Sometimes I keep a log of interactions or happenings for a particular student. I try to always do what Courtney Cazden calls "sensitive listening" (1981, p. 155).

I always keep lists of reading and writing activities, sometimes carrying a notebook around with me. Students entering into a writing or reading conference have hesitated, saying "You don't have your notebook, you know . . ." And sometimes I just sit and listen. Sometimes I need to give my students my full attention and rely on memory or recording soon after to help me sort out what I've seen.

Books to Help

There are some books on evaluation and assessment of the type of program we have been investigating. They are few, but there is a trend toward a more thorough and primary investigation of this crucial topic. Teachers might find these useful:

Evaluation: Whole Language, Whole Child by J. Baskiwell and P. Whitman. New York: Scholastic, 1990.
Assessment and Evaluation in Whole Language Programs, edited by B. Harp. Norwood, MA: Christopher-Gordon, 1991.
The Whole Language Evaluation Book by K. Goodman, Y. Goodman, & W. Hood. Portsmouth, NH: Heinemann, 1989.
The Administrator's Guide to Whole Language by G. Heald-Taylor. Katonah, NY: Richard Owen, 1989.
Portfolio Grading: Process and Product by P. Belanoff and M. Dickson. Portsmouth, NH: Heinemann, 1991.

Putting It All Together

One of the over-riding goals of my classroom is to promote a cooperative spirit wherein everyone wins, an atmosphere of trust, a climate of "positive prophecy." The additives I use to the traditional evaluation instruments are not only to help students understand themselves as learners but also to follow through on this commitment to cooperative support. Although grades are competitive and serve as the students' "pay," I believe it is still important to have structures in place which say, "I trust that you are here to learn, I believe you will, and I know that you understand that we are a learning community."

In evaluating and assessing in a Whole Learning Concept, we also need to consider how we will gather information about our children. At the upper levels, the most common means of gathering information has been testing, classroom-designed, textbook-provided and standardized.

As additives to traditional reporting, I have suggested methods for documenting our most valuable collection resource: the students themselves. I have suggested that our best and most fruitful avenue is to go to them and ask them—through portfolios and self-assessment questions. Our most profitable means of assessing and evaluating is through interacting with those being appraised.

I find it useful to envision the scope of evaluation and assessment as three, interlocking Venn circles, as shown in Figure 57.

The area we would like to grade from is in the shaded area in the center where all three categories intersect. Thus, we can make use of all tools and avenues of assessment and evaluation.

The last time I filled out an elementary school report card, it was very thick.

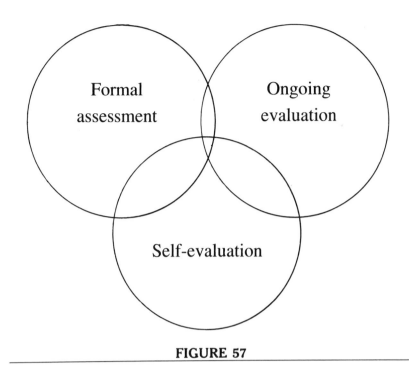

FIGURE 57

On the outside was the ''hard card,'' the old report card that had been in use for many years. Designed to be usable in many grades, its categories were so broad as to be meaningless for the learning I wanted to document and appraise: applies appropriate skills, masters material presented. The more grade levels the criteria must cover, the less specific they become. But few schools— perhaps for reasons related to the economy of bulk printing—have grade-specific report cards.

Inside the hard card were what we called ''the inserts.'' These were subject-specific photocopied sheets of criteria for subjects that had entered the curriculum after the hard card was printed, subjects like writing and computer literacy and critical thinking. Some of these were grade-level specific.

Together with the inserts I included the student self-evaluations, three for each student in the basic areas, reading, writing, and mathematics. And then there was my narrative account of the student's progress. Separate, and available to be hand-delivered, was the portfolio folder, together with student comments about the contents. It was a lot of evaluation.

We teach knowing we must evaluate. Teachers and students take evaluation seriously and work hard to make it meaningful and relevant. The packet that we mailed to the parents as the years went by got bigger and bigger. But it also gave more and more information about what we did from day-to-day and how teacher and learner appraised progress.

Don Holdaway would simplify the evaluation process by looking at the assessment value of performance in a natural learning model. In performance, we are granted insight into a learner's own self-evaluation. For when a learner chooses to perform, says, "Look at me, look at what I can do," then the learner demonstrates mastery and success. We don't need to test and evaluate it. They show us when they know.

Moving On

What Happens When We Move On

When I visited Baker, Oregon, I walked between the ruts made by the covered wagons during the Westward migration. My mother and I were driving across the country, following what we could of the old Oregon Trail. We had a book that describes where to find the Trail today and we sought out these ruts in Baker.

They were quite deep and clearly visible on the hillside as we looked across the fields of the pastureland. We drove up the hill to a marker commemorating the emigrants and I walked down the hill between the deep ruts.

Coming down the hill, the emigrants had looked out on the beautiful Powder River valley. The hillsides were colored with dried grass and sagebrush in July and the pastureland was tan. But far down, along the Powder River, was a ribbon of emerald green, wide and wandering, following the river. Beyond it stretched more pastures across the plains. And at the far edge of the plain rose the Blue Mountains, steep, rocky, lost in the clouds.

The emigrants wrote of mixed emotions as they came down the hillside where I stood. They were about to come into the beautiful Powder River valley, with food and water and a long rest. But ahead of them, still to come, were the Blue Mountains which had to be crossed to reach the Umatilla River and on to the Columbia River and eventually, for many, the Willamette Valley. It was late in the trip for these travelers. Short of provisions, they moved ahead out of the fear of being trapped by winter snows in the Blue Mountains.

The mountains were steep and rocky. So steep, in fact, that the wagons and the oxen had to be winched up and over them and down the other side. But the travelers didn't know that as they came down into the Powder River valley, down in the brightest green of the journey, onto the wide, flat plain between the slopes and the mountains.

I thought about all these things, walking down the hill between the ruts, heading down the miles to the river valley, dreaming of the minds of the pioneers and how it was for them. I thought a lot about moving on, what it takes, how it feels to look ahead at what is still to come. And I thought about why people do it.

People move on because they have a vision, they see a better life ahead, a better way of doing things, and new possibilities. It's hard, sometimes, being a pioneer. Sometimes the road ahead is not clear, mountains loom up, it takes a lot of work to make change. But sometimes you come into valleys that make it all worthwhile. Like the pioneers on the westward journey, people who move on in any way search for better ways of living and learning, trying to create better climates for a way of life that makes sense.

The emigrants on the westward migration had all the essentials for a Whole Learning environment. The life they lived was authentic, it was appropriate for their needs and wants, and they carried with them a strong sense of community. Lillian Schlissel quotes from Elizabeth Stewart Warner's 1856 diary: "It was a pleasure to travel then we had a very agreeable company not one jarr among us" (1982 p. 94).

The emigrants' greatest strength was their faith in themselves and their intuitive knowledge. They were taking great risks, but around them they built a safety net of friends and community. Lydia Milner Waters wrote in 1855: "I . . . learned to drive an ox team on the Platte (River) and my driving was admired by an officer and his wife . . ." (p. 84). Within themselves they built trust in their resourcefulness and good, common sense. "I do not wish to brag but I think we shall ere long be as well off for property as some of the family think they are . . ." wrote Mary Colby in 1849.

People who move on know that they are part of an adventure. The emigrants kept diaries and letters as records of this great history in the making, using their literacy to participate in the growth of a nation. People who move on know their role in the change process and set up conditions for themselves that make change possible and fruitful. They give themselves a Whole Learning environment.

Teachers and Their Moving On

Teachers are pioneers, too, working together to break new ground. Every time we look at the classroom life we're living and decide to try something new, we move on. Every time we share our reflections, we take part in the history of growth and change.

Moving on as a teacher begins with taking risks, learning in many new ways, developing understanding of students' understanding, and trusting the power of teaching and learning. As teachers begin to implement change in their own classrooms, as they move on, they must be supported in risk-taking and encouraged in self-reflection. Teachers-in-change "must first learn to reflect on their own everyday knowledge, especially to discover and to trust their informal ways of knowing" (Bamberger 1979, p. 2). We must enjoy optimal conditions of learning, too.

As Mary Holly (1989) reminds us "There is no Book of Teaching; the teacher writes it along the way . . . Teaching calls forth everything a teacher is . . . (p. 9). Dorothy Heathcote (1984) puts it this way:

> No one teaches a teacher how to teach. Teachers are made in the classroom during confrontations with their classes, and the product they become is a result of their need to survive and the ways they devise to do this. (p. 61)

We must value our greatest gift, our own intuitive knowledge. We must create teaching climates for ourselves which allow us to freely exercise our "complex, practically-oriented set of understandings which [we] use actively to shape and direct the work of teaching" (Elbaz 1983, p. 3). Successful Whole Learning teachers are ongoing learners, and much of the learning goes on while they are in the act of teaching.

Valuing practical knowledge can best be secured by granting teachers a larger measure of autonomy than many now experience. For me, the greatest asset I possessed which was granted by my teaching situation was respect and trust in my inherent and intuitive knowledge.

> I strongly believe in teachers' autonomy. Curriculum change is too often imposed from above, and teachers are recycled overnight to be mere executors (if not the executioners) of some else's decision. (Kamii 1985, p. xiv)

In a book about developing a generative curriculum, we should end on a generative note. In this book I have described what worked for me and my students. These were the attitudes, strategies, and activities that helped me to define what moving on meant for me as a teacher. But, like a generative curriculum, this generative plan can only describe the beginning of each teacher's personal growth. How moving on plays itself out for any individual teacher will be a reflection of that teacher's experiences. The particular path will be generated by what goes before.

If a teacher is implementing a generative curriculum, then many judgments, plans, and decisions will be the result of students and teacher learning together. Whole Learning and whole language are learner-centered, not curriculum-centered. But that does not diminish the role of the teacher. In fact, in a generative curriculum, the teacher becomes the key to the ongoing life of learning. My mother, who taught junior high for many years, believes that her most important asset was her creativity. While the child is the center of the classroom, the teacher is the most creative resource. And a creative resource that keeps on learning is always up-to-date. For a classroom will only be a successful learning place to the extent that the teacher is a successful learner and shares that learning while teaching.

By developing a respect for their own knowledge, teachers give value to the knowledge of their students. The teacher's search for learning becomes a model for the students' search. By validating themselves, teachers validate their students. As Whole Learning teachers, we constantly demonstrate the "power of positive prophecy."

> Teachers have a moral duty not to abandon hope—to be constantly in search of changes in procedures which will have the effect that they can teach those children they find unteachable, can initiate them into worthwhile activities into which they cannot yet see ways of initiating them. (Passmore 1980, p. 29)

As teachers begin to move on, they must seek and find support for their ideas and for their growth. Like the pioneers, they must build their own ongoing community. Such support most often comes from other teachers, teachers who are also in the process of change. Some teachers join active support groups which give them a forum for growing ideas. Whole language's TAWL (Teachers Applying Whole Language) groups and their national networking system assist many teachers to accomplish change in a supportive environment.

Like the pioneers, teachers in change are driven by a vision of what might be. I once asked my students what "having a vision" meant. They said it so well:

> I think a vision is like a dream. Usually when people have tried to make vision come true, they have only halfway done it. Because a vision (to the person) is so perfect it is impossible to make it come exactly true.

I think having a vision means something flashing through your mind and following that flash.

To me a vision is a large goal that could effect an entire population. Or even the world.

Like the pioneers, some teachers write to themselves—journal keeping, we call it—to give ourselves a "respondent" to our reflections. People who know they are part of a great adventure keep records of how it was. I look back in my journal and find myself thinking:

The kids did all different than I planned—Attended to other things than I thought they would. Hard not to feel that my good ideas were slighted— But they had other interests and eventually I got more interested in those than in mine. I keep learning from them. As I get older, they get younger.

Listening for Surprises

Meaning—and growth in learning—is constructed between us. Interactive learning in a social setting leads to intrapsychological growth and development, said Vygotsky. I find it so. I cannot grow and learn in teaching without my students. It is as if together we have created a whole learner.

And that is tremendously exciting to me. The mutual, active construction of knowledge between learners and me, the listening that goes on between us, is the most satisfying and fulfilling experience I could have. As teachers, we must always be ready for surprises and we must search them out and help them to surface in our children.

These surprises can be of many kinds. Some of them should make us question our own assumptions about children and their values. Some of them should make us slow down and listen. My sister told me that she remembers going on a walking field trip with her teacher and classmates when she was quite small, down to the pond in back of the school. It wasn't a big pond and with the first warm weather it always dried up. The day the class went to the pond, it was full of tadpoles, tadpoles who probably would not live to maturity before the pond dried up. My sister remembers being horrified at this prospect and being more dismayed at the teacher's inattention to this imminent natural disaster. In fact, no one but her seemed to care, she remembers.

This excursion left a strong impression on her, and as she tells the story today, there is a note of disbelief in her voice at the teacher's inability to relate to the concern of a small student. My sister went back to the pond after school to rescue some of the tadpoles, to do what she could for the natural world.

We can see the teacher, taking her small charges out for a walk on the first warm day, to see the seasonal changes around them. But we also see a teacher who isn't listening, who fails to participate in the learning going on around her. We see a teacher whose teaching overshadows her learning. And in the process, a child learns lessons that the teacher didn't know she was teaching. For in the growth of children's caring about the world we find the grown-up's environmental and ecological concerns.

Eleanor Duckworth (1986) says that the role of the teacher is "to make it absolutely clear that what they think is O.K. with you" (p. 42). And we do this by listening to what they think and learning from it ourselves.

A New View of My Faults

Things were not always the way I wanted them in my growth and change. As a teacher, I've always been very aware of my faults, all the things I should have done or should have done better, the things I should have left undone. I always thought of this self-critical view as productive, a good way for me to self-appraise and improve, even when my disappointment in myself paralyzed and depressed me. It was not always a productive situation.

Lately, though, I've taken a new view of my faults. I've been thinking about what the word "fault" means in nature. Sometimes I drive on highways where the road has been built by blasting through rock and the faults in the rock are quite clear to see. And as I drive I can't help but notice them. Because in these cracks in the rocks, in these faults, plants grow. The faultlines become catchbasins for soil and water and seeds. The faults become opportunities for new growth and development.

When my mother and I drove out west, we went to Neah Bay on the Olympic Peninsula in the state of Washington. On the highway into Neah Bay, there is a long stretch, several miles, with the bay on one side and a high, sheer, rock face on the other. And when we were there, that sheer rock face, going up thirty or forty feet, was covered with lupines. The whole face for several miles was a festival of flowers that were three feet high in all colors. It was a spectacular sight. And how were these huge plants growing on this sheer rock face? In the faults of the rocks. The faults were the occasion for one of nature's best shows, a vertical field of flowers.

Like the cliff in Neah Bay, a productive view of our faults can be the opportunity for new and exciting growth. Faults catch the eye and the mind. And as we reflect on them, we can begin to see new possibilities. For it is in those spaces between that new ideas catch hold and growth becomes possible.

I Move On

When I first began writing this book, I was a sixth grade teacher. As I finish it, I have moved on to teach in the elementary education department of a college, sharing my history with pre-service and in-service teachers. On this emigration, I am having a Whole Learning experience. I see myself as part of a great adventure, I share in two communities—my old school and my new college, my life is authentic and appropriate for me, and I have a vision.

I want to bring to college teaching all that I believe about Whole Learning, to follow Jerry Harste's thought at the Whole Language Umbrella Conference in Phoenix in 1991, that it ''would be a sin'' not to apply to the college classroom all that we know about good environments for learning. But all I have to fall back on are the old ways from my own college experience and that's not the kind of teacher I want to be. So I am making a basic shift without really knowing what the new terrain looks like. Much like crossing new mountains in an old wagon.

It has been hard to move on. Taking risks is a lot of work. I am making changes toward a new way of life without being quite sure what it should look like or feel like for me, much like any teacher who seeks to change old ways, like any pioneer looking on new lands. My moving on has been supported by my vision, developed in the elementary school classroom and still very much a part of my beliefs about teaching and learning. I share the ideal expressed by Vivan Paley in her wonderful book, *The Boy Who Would Be a Helicopter*: ''Was it not my own best-beloved teacher fantasy that led me to worry over every inch of the classroom in pursuit of the yellow brick road on which the children and I would skip along to the magic kingdom?''

I'm still in search of the yellow brick road, looking now in the land of the college classroom rather than in elementary school. But the search feels the same. I find parts of the perfect road through risk-taking and introspection. When I travel that road with my students, no matter how old they are, generating the path of learning as we go, learning and teaching become a powerful dynamic for me. Like Vivian Paley, sometimes I'm able to skip along with them.

When I'm interested in my own learning, when I set up conditions for learning not only for my students but for me too, I move on. When I engage in classroom interaction myself and collaborate with learners to design a climate that allows us all to be immersed in the learning process, I move on. When I share the building of a classroom that allows us all to teach and learn, we all move on.

Sometimes the process of shared growth in the classroom is so exciting that it takes my breath away, like the sight of a great mountain. When I was pretending to be the Director of the Royal Archeological Institute of Cairo and writing letters to my sixth graders who were writing back as Fellows on the archeological dig, I was constantly impressed with the depth of their involvement. Their dedication spurred mine and together we had a grand old time, generating an exciting learning experience.

And every so often someone would go beyond the norm and I would be astonished, for when that happened I saw students in the full flight of learning, under their own power. Once Dr. Aurelia Laschenova—a name invented by a sixth-grader-pretend archeologist—wrote me, the Director of the Royal Archeological Institute, a long and unexpected letter explaining why she hadn't written to the Institute for so long: she—in her mind as Aurelia—had moved to be nearer to her university, the one in California, to improve her research opportunities, to be better prepared for her trip to Egypt with the Institute. I have to shake my head in wonder as I think back on children like this, roaming in the realms of their imaginations, so deep in the joy of their learning that they generate work without even being asked, writing long homework assignments for the sheer pleasure and satisfaction of it.

One day when I came in from recess, long after the archeology simulation was over, I found a letter on my desk addressed to the Director of the Royal Archeological Institute. It read:

> Dear R.A.I.,
> I learned a lot about Egypt with the tough assignments you gave me and I
> just wanted to thank you for letting me be part of your great Institute.

It was signed "Sincerely, Dr. Charlie Coorlain," the adopted name of a student who reminded me that the best thing about teaching is learning. Thank you, Charlie, for letting me be part of your great life. You—and others like you—have given me some of my best moments. You inspired me to learn and reach and for that I will always be grateful. I love teaching and you're the reason why.

Bibliography

Armstrong, M. *Closely Observed Children: The Diary of a Primary Classroom.* London: Writer and Readers, 1980.

Atwell, N. *In the Middle: Writing, Reading, and Learning with Adolescents.* Portsmouth, NH: Boynton Cook, 1987.

————, Ed. *Coming to Know.* Portsmouth, NH: Heinemann, 1990.

Babbit, N. *Tuck Everlasting.* NY: Trumpet Club, 1975.

Baker, A. and J. *Maths in the Mind.* Portsmouth, NH: Heinemann, 1991.

Baker, D., C. Semple and T. Stead. *How Big is the Moon? Whole Maths in Action.* Portsmouth, NH: Heinemann, 1990.

Bamberger, J. "Music and Cognitive Research: Where do our Questions Come from, Where do our Answers Go?" Paper presented at the American Educational Research Association, 1979 Annual Meeting, April 8–12, San Francisco.

Barnes, D. *From Communication to Curriculum.* New York: Penguin Books, 1976.

Bash, B. *Urban Roosts: Where Birds Nest in the City.* New York: Sierra Club/Little Brown, 1991.

Baskiwell, J., and P. Whitman. *Evaluation: Whole Language, Whole Child.* New York: Scholastic, 1990.

Belanoff, P. and M. Dickson. *Portfolio Grading: Process and Product.* Portsmouth, NH: Heinemann, 1991.

Bezuszka, S., M. Kenney, and L. Silvey. *Designs from Mathematical Patterns.* Palo Alto, CA: Creative Publications, 1978.

Bissex, G. *GNYS AT WRK: A Child Learns to Read and Write.* Cambridge: Harvard University Press, 1980.

Bodanis, D. *The Secret House: 24 Hours in the Strange and Unexpected World in Which we Spend our Nights and Days.* New York: Simon and Schuster, 1986.

Brown, A., and J. Day. "Macrorules for Summarizing Texts." *Journal of Verbal Learning and Verbal Behavior*, 22, 1983, pp. 1–14.

Brown, D. *Bury my Heart at Wounded Knee: An Indian History of the American West.* New York: Holt Rinehart & Winston, 1970.

Brown, M. *Great Northern Diver: The Loon.* New York: Little Brown, 1991.

Brown, S., and M. Walter. *The Art of Problem Posing.* Hillsdale, NJ: Lawrence Erlbaum, 1983.

Bruner, J. *Toward a Theory of Instruction.* Cambridge: Harvard University Press, 1978.

————. "The Ontogenesis of Speech Acts." *Journal of Child Language*, 2, 1975, pp. 1–19.

Bunting, E. *The Wall.* New York: Clarion, 1991.

Burns, M. *A Collection of Math Lessons from Grades 3 through 6.* The Math Solution Pub, distributed by Cuisenaire Co. of America, New Rochelle, NY: 1991.

Calkins, L. *The Art of Teaching Writing.* Portsmouth NH: Heinemann, 1986.

Cambourne, B. *The Whole Story*. New York: Scholastic, 1988.

Cazden, C. "Active Learners and Active Teachers." In *Handbook of Research in the Teaching of English Language Arts*. J. Flood, J. Jensen, D. Lapp and J. Squire, eds. New York: MacMillan, 1991.

———. "Performance Without Competence: Assistance to Child Discourse in the Zone of Proximal Development." *Quarterly Newsletter of the Laboratory of Comparative Human Cognition*, 3, *1*, 1981, pp. 5–8.

Cazden, C., P. Cordeiro, and M.E. Giacobbe. "Spontaneous and Scientific Concepts: Young Children's Learning of Punctuation." In *Language and Learning: An Interactional Perspective*. G. Wells and J. Nicholls, eds. London: Falmer Press, 1985.

Cherry, L. *The Great Kapok Tree: A Tale of the Amazon Rain Forest*. New York: Gulliver/HBJ, 1991.

Clay, M., and C. Cazden. "A Vygotskian Interpretation of Reading Recovery." In *Vygotsky and Education: Instructional Implications and Applications of Socio-Historical Psychology*. L. Moll, ed. Cambridge: Cambridge University Press, 1990.

Coles, R. *The Call of Stories: Teaching and the Moral Imagination*. Boston: Houghton Mifflin, 1989.

Cordeiro, P. "Vygotsky in the Classroom: An Interactionist Literacy Framework in Mathematics." In *Interactionist Approaches to Language and Literacy*. V. John-Steiner, C. Panofsky & L. Smith, eds. Cambridge: Cambridge University Press, forthcoming.

———. "Problem-based Thematic Instruction." *Language Arts*, 67, *1*, 1990, pp. 26–34.

———. "Structuring for Success: Setting up a Whole Language Sixth Grade." *Teaching PreK–8*, August–September 1989, pp. 83, 85, 87.

———. "Playing with Infinity in the Sixth Grade." *Language Arts*, 65, *6*, 1988, pp. 557–556.

———. "Moonwatching: Teaching and Learning as a Scientific Enterprise." *Language Arts*, 63, *2*, 1986.

Cordeiro, P., M. E. Giacobbe and C. Cazden. "Apostrophes, Quotation Marks, and Periods: Learning Punctuation in the First Grade" *Language Arts*, 60, *3*, 1983, pp. 323–332.

Cornford, F., trans. *The Republic of Plato*. New York: Oxford University Press, 1945.

Cowley, J. *Seventy Kilometres from Ice Cream: A Letter from Joy Cowley*. Katonah, NY: Richard C. Owen, 1987.

———. *Quack, Quack, Quack*. San Diego: Wright Group, 1987.

Crafton, Linda C. *Whole Language: Getting Started Moving Forward*. Katonah, NY: Richard C. Owen, 1991.

Cross, P. *Adults as Learners*. San Francisco: Jossey-Bass, 1981.

Curtis, E. *Portraits from North American Indian life*. Outerbridge & Lazard, 1972.

Daiute, C. "Children and Adults Write Notes on the Computer." *Parents League Review*, New York, *16*, 1982, pp. 138–44.

Davidson, N. *Cooperative Learning in Mathematics*. Menlo Park, CA: Addison-Wesley, 1990.

Davidson, P. Personal communication. Critical and Creative Thinking Program, University of Massachusetts at Boston, 1990.

Delano, A. *Life on the Plains and at the Diggings*. Oginally printed 1854. Alexandria, VA: Time-Life Books, 1981.

Demi. *The Empty Pot*. New York: Henry Holt Pub., 1991.

Dillard, A. *The Writing Life*. New York: Harper & Row, 1989.

Donaldson, M. *Children's Minds*. New York: W.W. Norton, 1978.

———. *A Study of Children's Thinking*. London: Travistock, 1963.

Duckworth, E. *"The Having of Wonderful Ideas" and Other Essays on Teaching and Learning*. New York: Teachers College Press, 1987.

———. *Inventing Density*. Monograph published by Center for Teaching and Learning, University of North Dakota, 1986.

Edelsky, C., B. Altwerger and B. Flores. *Whole Language: What's the Difference?* Portsmouth, NH: Heinemann, 1991.

Elbaz, F. *Teacher Thinking: A Study of Practical Knowledge*. New York: Nichols Pub., 1983.

Elbow, P. *Writing With Power: Techniques for Mastering the Writing Process*. New York: Oxford University Press, 1981.

———. *Writing Without Teachers*. New York: Oxford University Press, 1983.

Ennis, R. "Critical Thinking and the Curriculum." In *Thinking Skills Instruction: Concepts and Techniques*. M. Heiman & J. Slomianko, eds. Washington D.C.: NEA, 1987.

Finn, J. Personal communication, 1991.

Fisher, B. *Joyful Learning: A Whole Language Kindergarten*. Portsmouth, NH: Heinemann, 1991.

Gallo, D. "Educating for Creativity." In *Thinking, the Expanding Frontier*, W. Maxwell, ed. Philadelphia: Franklin Institute Press, 1983.

———., ed. *Speaking for Ourselves*. Urbana, IL: National Council of Teachers of English, 1990.

Gamow, G. *One, Two, Three . . . Infinity: Facts and Speculations of Science*. New York: Mentor Books, 1947.

Gilles, C., M. Bixby, P. Crowley, S. Crenshaw, M. Henrichs, F. Reynolds, D. Pyle, eds. *Whole Language Strategies for Secondary Students*. Katonah, NY: Richard C. Owen, 1988.

Gilligan, C. *In a Different Voice: Psychological Theory and Women's Development*. Cambridge: Harvard University Press, 1982.

Gleick, J. *Chaos: Making a New Science*. New York: Viking, 1987.

Goble, P. *Dream Wolf*. New York: Bradbury Press, 1991.

Goodman, K. Talk given at conference, "The Whole World of Whole Language," sponsored by Richard C. Owen Publishers, Rye, NY, May 18, 1991.

———. *The Findings of Research on Miscue Analysis*. Urbana IL: National Council of Teachers of English, 1969.

Goodman, K., Y. Goodman, and W. Hood. *The Whole Language Evaluation Book.* Portsmouth, NH: Heinemann, 1989.

Goodman, Y. "Kidwatching: Observing Children in the Classroom." In *Observing the Language Learner.* A. Jaggar and M. Burke, eds. Newark, DE: International Reading Association, 1985.

Gordon, K. *The Transitive Vampire: A Handbook of Grammar for the Innocent, the Eager, and the Doomed.* New York: Times Books, 1984.

———. *The Well-Tempered Sentence: A Punctuation Handbook for the Innocent, the Eager, and the Doomed.* New Haven, CT: Ticknor & Fields, 1983.

Graves, D. *Build a Literate Classroom.* Portsmouth, NH: Heinemann, 1991.

———. *Discover your own Literacy.* Portsmouth, NH: Heinemann, 1990.

———. *Experiment with Fiction.* Portsmouth NH: Heinemann, 1989a.

———. *Explore Poetry.* Portsmouth, NH: Heinemann, forthcoming.

———. *Investigate Nonfiction.* Portsmouth NH: Heinemann, 1989b.

———. "Let's Get Rid of the Welfare Mess in the Teaching of Writing." In *A Researcher Learns to Write.* Exeter NH: Heinemann Educational Books, 1984.

———. *Writing: Teachers and Children at Work.* Exeter NH: Heinemann, 1983.

Greenfield, P., and J. Smith. *The Structure of Communication in Early Language Development.* New York: Academic Press, 1976.

Grifalconi, A. *Osa's Pride.* New York: Little Brown, 1991.

Griffiths, R., and M. Clyne. *Books you Can Count on: Linking Mathematics and Literature.* Portsmouth, NH, Heinemann, 1991.

Hall, S. *Using Picture Storybooks to Teach Literary Devices.* Phoenix, AZ: Oryx Press, 1990.

Halliday, M. *Learning How to Mean.* London: Edward Arnold, 1975.

Harp, B., ed. *Assessment and Evaluation in Whole Language Programs.* Norwood, MA: Christopher-Gordon, 1991.

Harste, J. "Curriculum for a Democracy", talk given at Second Whole Language Umbrealla Conference, Phoenix, August 2, 1991.

Harste, J., K. Short, and C. Burke. *Creating Classrooms for Authors: The Reading-Writing Connection.* Portsmouth NH: Heinemann, 1988.

Hawke, D. *Everyday Life in Early America.* New York: Harper Row, 1988.

Hawkins, D. "Enlargment of the Esthetic." In *Curriculum and Instruction in Arts and Esthetic Instruction.* Martin Engel and Jerome Hausman, eds. St. Louis: CEMREL, Inc, 1981.

———. "Nature, Man and Mathematics, 1972." In *The Informed Vision: An Essay on Science Education.* New York: Agathon Press, 1974.

———. "What it Means to Teach." In *Teachers College Record.* 75, *1*, 1973, pp. 7–16.

Heald-Taylor, G. *The Administrator's Guide to Whole Language.* Katonah, NY: Richard C. Owen, 1989.

Heathcote, D. "Dorothy Heathcote's Notes." In *Dorothy Heathcote: Collected Writings on Education and Drama.* Johnson, L., and C. O'Neill, eds. London: Hutchinson, 1984.

————. "Drama and Learning, 1975." In *Dorothy Heathcote: Collected Writings on Education and Drama*. Johnson, L., and C. O'Neill, eds. London: Hutchinson, 1984.

————. "Learning, Knowing and Language in Drama: An Interview with Dorothy Heathcote." *Language Arts*, 60, 1983, pp. 695–701.

————. "Material for Significance, 1980." In *Dorothy Heathcote: Collected Writings on Education and Drama*. Johnson, L., and C. O'Neill, eds. London: Hutchinson, 1984.

Heathcote, D., and P. Herbert. "A Drama of Learning: Mantle of the Expert." *Theory into Practice*, 24, *3*, 1985, pp. 173–180.

Holdaway, D. Personal communication. Denver: Regis College Whole Language Institute, 1989a.

————. Talk given at Massachusetts Whole Language Teachers Association meeting, Fitchburg State College, Fitchburg, Mass, May 11, 1989b.

————. *The Foundations of Literacy*. Portsmouth NH: Heinemann, 1979.

Holly, M. *Writing to Grow: Keeping a Personal-Professional Journal*. Portsmouth, NH: Heinemann, 1989.

Hornsby, D. Personal communication. Whole Language Teachers Association meeting, Sudbury, MA, 1989.

Hornsby, D., J. Parry, and D. Sukarna. *Read on: A Conference Approach to Reading*. Portsmouth, NH: Heinemann, 1986.

Howard, V. *Artistry: The Work of Artists*. Cambridge: Hackett, 1982.

Hoyt-Goldsmith, D. *Totem Pole*. New York: Holiday House, 1991.

————. "The Big Questions behind Whole Language," *Teachers Networking, the Whole Language Newsletter*, Richard C. Owen, Inc, 9, *2*, winter 1989c, pp. 10–12.

Hyde, A., and P. Hyde. *Mathwise: Teaching Mathematical Thinking and Problem Solving*. Portsmouth, NH, Heinemann, 1991.

International Reading Association. *Cases for Literacy: An Agenda for Discussion*. Newark, DE: International Reading Assoc., 1989.

Johnson, D., R. Johnson, E. Holubec, and P. Roy. *Circles of Learning: Cooperation in the Classroom*. Alexandria, VA: Association for Supervision and Curriculum Development, 1984.

Kagan, J. *The Nature of the Child*. New York: Basic Books, 1984.

Kamii, C. *Young Children Reinvent Mathematics: Implications of Piaget's Theory*. New York: Teachers College Press, 1985.

Kidd, J. *How Adults Learn*. New York: Association Press, 1973.

Knowles, M. "Malcolm Knowles Finds a Worm in his Apple," in *Training and Development Journal*, 37, *5*, May 1983, pp. 16–17.

————. *The Adult Learner: A Neglected Species*. Houston: Gulf Pub., 1979.

Knox, S. *Adult Development and Learning*. San Francisco: Jossey-Bass, 1978.

Kohlberg, L. "Continuities and Discontinuities in Childhood and Adult Moral Development Revisited." In *Collected Papers on Moral Development and Moral Education*. Cambridge: Moral Education Research Foundation, Harvard University, 1973.

Labinowitz, E. *Learning from Children: New Beginnings for Teaching Numerical Thinking*. Addison Wesley, 1982.

Lipman, A., A.M. Sharp and F.S. Oscamyan. *Philosophy in the Classroom*, 2nd ed. Philadelphia: Temple University Press, 1980

Lovell, B. *Adults Learning*. New York: John Wiley and Sons, 1980.

MacShane, J. *Learning to Talk*. Cambridge: Cambridge University Press, 1980.

Marcy, C. *The Prairie Traveler*. Originally printed 1859. Alexandria, VA: Time-Life Books, 1981.

Martin, N., P. Medway, and H. Smith. "What Children do with New Ideas." In *Writing Across the Curriculum Pamphlets*. N. Martin, ed, Upper Montclair, NJ: Boynton/Cook Pub, 1976.

Matthews, G. *Philosophy and the Young Child*. Cambridge: Harvard University Press, 1980.

Matthews, K. "A Child Composes." In *Understanding Writing: Ways of Observing, Learning, and Teaching,*" T. Newkirk & N. Atwell, eds. Portsmouth, NH: Heinemann, 1988.

Mayher, J., and R. Brause. "Learning through Teaching: Is Your Classroom Like Your Grandmother's?" Language Arts, 63, 6, October 1986, pp. 617–620.

Moffett, J. *Teaching the Universe of Discourse*. Portsmouth, NH: Boynton/Cook & Heinemann, 1968.

Murray, D. "Writing to Think." Article for *New Hampshire Register*, 1984.

National Council of Teachers of Mathematics. *Curriculum and Evaluation Standards for School Mathematics*. Reston, VA: NCTM, 1989.

Newkirk, T., and N. Atwell. *Understanding Writing*. Portsmouth, NH: Heinemann, 1988.

Newman, D., P. Griffin, and M. Cole. *The Construction Zone: Working for Cognitive Change in School*. Cambridge, Eng.: Cambridge University Press, 1989.

Paley, V. *The Boy who Would be a Helicopter*. Cambridge: Harvard University Press, 1990.

Pappas, I., B. Kiefir, and S. Levstik. *An Integrated Language Perspective in Elementary School*. New York: Longman, 1990.

Parry, J., and D. Hornsby. *Write on: A Conference Approach to Writing*. Portsmouth, NH: Heinemann, 1985.

Passmore, J. *The Philosophy of Teaching*. Cambridge: Harvard University Press, 1980.

Penrose, R. *The Emperor's New Mind: Concerning Computers, Minds, and the Laws of Physics*. New York: Oxford University Press, 1989.

Piaget, J. *The Moral Judgement of the Child (1932)*. New York: The Free Press, 1965.

Polacco, P. *Thundercake*. New York: Philomel, 1991.

Polya, G. *How to Solve it: A New Aspect of Mathematical Method*. Princeton NJ: Princeton University Press, 1945.

Rawls, W. *Where the Red Fern Grows*. Garden City, NJ: Doubleday, 1961.

Reason, J. "Skill and Error in Everyday Life." In Howe, J. *Adult Learning: Psychological Research and Applications*. New York: John Wiley & Sons, 1977.

Renner, A. *How to Build a Better Mousetrap Car: And Other Experimental Science Fun.* NY: Dodd, Mead, 1977.

Rief, L. *Seeking Diversity: Language Arts with Adolescents.* Portsmouth, NH: Heinemann, 1991.

―――. "Finding the Value in Evaluation: Self-Assessment in a Middle School Classroom" in *Educational Leadership*, March 1990, pp. 24–29.

Rogers, J. *Adults Learning.* Middlesex, Eng: Penguin, 1971.

Roth, A. *Iceberg Hermit.* NY: Scholastic, 1976.

Routman, R. *Invitations: Changing as Teachers and Learners K–12.* Portsmouth, NH: Heinemann, 1991.

―――. *Transitions: From Literature to Literacy.* Portsmouth, NH: Heinemann, 1988.

Rowe, J. "Framework for Infused Critical and Creative Thinking Instruction." Provincetown, MA: Revised 1991.

―――. "Learning to Teach Thinking: One School's Story." *Educational Leadership*, November 1990, pp. 43–44.

Russell, D. *Literature for Children: A Short Introduction.* New York: Longman, 1991.

Scardamalia, M., and C. Bereiter. "Writing." In *Cognition and Instruction.* R. Dillon & R. Sternberg, eds. Orlando: Academic Press, 1986.

Schlissel, L. *Women's Diaries of the Westward Journey.* New York: Schocken Books, 1982.

School Journals, various issues. New York: Richard C. Owen, Pub.

Smith, F. *Joining the Literacy Club: Further Essays into Education.* Portsmouth, NH: Heinemann, 1988.

Snow, C., and C. Ferguson, eds. *Talking to Children.* Cambridge: Cambridge University Press, 1977.

Stenmark, J. *Assessment Alternatives in Mathematics.* Berkeley, CA: Univ. of California, 1989.

Stenmark, J., V. Thompson and R. Cossey. *Family Math.* Berkeley, CA: Univ. of California, 1986.

Stewig, J., and S. Sebesta. *Using Literature in the Elementary Classroom.* Urbana, IL: NCTE, 1989.

Stratton, J. *Pioneer Women: Voices from the Kansas Frontier.* New York: Simon and Schuster, 1981.

Stratton, R. *Captivity of the Oatman Girls.* Originally printed 1857. Alexandria, VA: Time-Life Books, 1982.

Swartz, R. Personal communication, Center for Teaching Thinking, Andover, MA. 1989.

Swartz, R., and D. Perkins. *Teaching Thinking: Issues and Approaches.* Pacific Grove, CA: Midwest, 1989.

Tchudi, S. "The Hidden Agendas in Writing Across the Curriculum." *English Journal*, 75:7 1986.

Torrance, E. *Rewarding Creative Behavior.* Englewood Cliffs, NJ: Prentice-Hall, 1965.

Vygotsky, L. *Mind in Society: The Development of Higher Psychological Processes.* M. Cole, V. John-Steiner, S. Scribner, and E. Souberman, eds. Cambridge: Harvard University Press, 1978.

——. *Thought and Language.* E. Hanfmann and G. Vakar, eds. Cambridge: M.I.T. Press, 1962.

Walter, M. *Boxes, Squares and Other Things: A Teacher's Guide for a Unit in Informal Geometry.* Washington, D.C.: National Council of Teachers of Mathematics, 1971.

Watson, D. *Ideas and Insights.* Urbana, IL: National Council of Teachers of English, 1987.

Weaver C. *Reading Process and Practice: From Socio-Linguistics to Whole Language.* Portsmouth, NH: Heinemann, 1988.

——. *Understanding Whole Language: From Principles to Practice.* Portsmouth, NH: Heinemann, 1990.

——. "Welcoming Errors as Signs of Growth." *Language Arts*, 59, 1982, pp. 438–444.

Wesley, J. "Pioneers: A Simulation of Decision-Making on a Wagon Train." Published by Interact Company, Box 997, Lakeside, CA 92040. 1974.

Whole Language Teachers Association. "Principles of Whole Language." In Whole Language Teachers Association membership brochure. Massachusetts. 1989.

Wright, J. *Letters from the West: or a Caution to Emigrants: Being Facts and Observations Respecting the States of Ohio, Indiana, Illinois and Some Part of New York, Pennsylvania and Kentucky.* U.S.A.: Readex Microprint Corporation, 1966.

Bibliography of Picture Storybooks in Content Areas

Baylor, B., and P. Parnall. *The Other Way to Listen*. New York: Scribners, 1978. (Also, *I'm in Charge of Celebrations*, 1986; *Hawk, I'm Your Brother*, 1976, and others.)

Baylor, B., and P. Parnall. *If You Are a Hunter of Fossils*. New York: Macmillan, 1980.

Berger, B. *Grandfather Twilight*. New York: Philomel Books, 1984.

Bjork C., and L. Anderson. *Linnea in Monet's Garden*. New York: Farrar, Strauss, Giroux, 1985.

Branley, F. *The Moon Seems to Change*. New York: Thomas Y. Crowell or Harper Row, 1987.

Brett, J. *Annie and the Wild Animals*. Boston: Houghton Mifflin, 1985.

———. *Goldilocks and the Three Bears*. New York: Dodd, Mead & Co, 1987.

———. *The Mitten*. New York: G.P. Putnam, 1989.

Climo, S. *Egyptian Cinderella*. New York: Thomas Y. Crowell, 1989.

Coats, L. *Marcella and the Moon*. New York: Macmillan, 1986.

Cole, J. *The Magic School Bus at the Waterworks*. New York: Scholastic, 1986. (Also, *The Magic School Bus Inside the Earth*, 1987; and *The Magic School Bus Inside the Human Body*, 1989.)

Cooney, B. *Miss Rumphius*. New York: Viking Penguin, 1982; Puffin 1985 (pbk.).

dePaola, T. *Charlie Needs a Cloak*. New York: Simon and Schuster, 1973.

Dunrea, O. *Skara Brae: The Story of a Prehistoric Village*. New York: Holiday House, 1985.

Eisler, C. *Cats Know Best*. New York: Dial Books, 1988.

Fair, S. *The Bedspread*. New York: Morrow Junior, 1982.

Gantshev, I. *The Moon Lake*. USA: Picture Book Studio, 1985.

Gibbons, G. *The Seasons of Arnold's Apple Tree*. San Diego: Voyager/HBJ Book, 1984.

Goffstein, M. *A Writer*. New York: Harper & Row, 1984.

Goldin, A. *Ducks Don't Get Wet*. New York: Harper & Row, 1965.

Goodall, J. *The Story of an English Village*. New York: Atheneum, 1978.

Heller, R. *A Cache of Jewels*. New York: Grosset & Dunlap, 1987. (Also, *Kites, Sail High*, 1988; and *Many Luscious Lollipops*, 1989.)

Hines, A. *Sky All Around*. New York: Clarion Books, 1989.

Innocenti, R. *Rose Blanche*. Markato, MN: Creative Education, 1985.

Johnston, T. *Yonder*. New York: Dial, 1988.

Kitamura, A. *UFO Diary*. New York: Farrar, Strauss & Giroux, 1989.

Kitchen, B. *Tenrec's Twigs*. New York: Philomel Books, 1989.

Krupp, E. *The Big Dipper and You*. New York: Morrow Junior, 1989.

Lawson, R. *Ben and Me*. Boston: Little, Brown, 1988.

Livingston, M. *Sea Songs*. New York: Holiday House, 1986.

Martin, B., and J. Archambault. *Knots on a Counting Rope*. New York, Henry Holt, 1987.

Maruki, T. *Hiroshima No Pika*. New York: Lothrop, Lee & Shepard, 1980.

McCloskey, R. *Make Way for Ducklings*. New York: Viking Press, 1941.

Mitchell, A., and P. Lamont. *Our Mammoth*. New York: Harcourt, Brace, Javanovitch, 1987.

Nunes, S. *Coyote Dreams*. New York: Atheneum, 1988.

Pasley, L., and M.S. Pasley *The Adventures of Madalene and Louisa*. New York: Random House, 1980.

Pryor, B., and B. Peck. *The House on Maple Street*. New York: William Morrow, 1987.

Ryder, J. *The Snail's Spell*. New York: Viking Penguin Books, 1982; Puffin Books, 1982. (Also, *Chipmunk Song*, 1987.)

Ryder, J. *Catching the Wind*. New York: Morrow Junior, 1989. (Also, *Lizard in the Sun*, 1990.)

Ryder, J. *Under the Moon*. New York: Random House, 1989.

Rylant, C. *When I was Young in the Mountains*. New York: E.P. Dutton, 1982.

Schwartz, D. *How Much is a Million?* New York: Lothrop, Lee and Shepard, 1985. (Also, *If You Made a Million*, 1989.)

Sharmat, M. *Gila Monsters Meet you at the Airport*. New York: Aladdin Books, 1980.

Siebert, D. *Mohave*. New York: Thomas Crowell, 1988.

Spier, P. *People*. New York: Doubeday, 1980.

Steptoe, J. *The Story of Jumping Mouse*. New York: Mulberry Books, 1972.

Thomas, E., and J. White. *Hedgerow*. New York: William Morrow, 1980.

Turner, A. *Dakota Dugout*. New York: Aladdin Books, 1985.

Van Allsburg, Chris. *Two Bad Ants*. Boston: Houghton Mifflin, 1988.

Wheatley, N., and D. Rawlins. *My Place*. Long Beach, CA: Australia in Print, 1987.

Williams, V. *Stringbean's Trip to the Shining Sea*. New York: Scholastic, 1988.

Yolen, J. *Owl Moon*. New York: Philomel, 1987.

Pop-up Books

Hawkey, R. *Evolution*. New York: G.P. Putnam's, 1987.

Van der Meer, R. *Majesty in Flight*. Abbeville Press, 1984.

Big Books

Baker, J. *Where the Forest Meets the Sea*. New York: Scholastic, 1987.

Cowley, J. *Quack, Quack, Quack*. San Diego: The Wright Group, 1987.

Drew, D. *Postcards from the Planets*. Crystal Lake IL: Rigby, 1988. (Also, *Tadpole Diary*, 1988; *Somewhere in the Universe*, 1988; *Millions of Years Ago*, 1988; *Hidden Animals*, 1988.)

Heller, R. *The Reason for a Flower*. New York: Scholastic, 1983. (Also, *Chickens Aren't the Only Ones*, 1981.)

Mathews, L. *Bunches and Bunches of Bunnies*. New York: Scholastic, 1985.

Munsch, R. *Love you Forever*. Ontario, Can: Firefly, 1986.

Numeroff, L. *If you Give a Mouse a Cookie*. New York: Scholastic, 1988.

Ridpath, I. *The Children's Giant Atlas of the Universe*. Stamford CT: Longmeadow Press, 1989.

Schwartz, D. *How Much is a Million?* New York: Scholastic, 1985.

Tsuchiya, Y. *Faithful Elephants*. Boston,: Houghton, Mifflin, 1988.

White, E.B. *Charlotte's Web*. New York: Harper & Row, 1952.

Varley, S. *Badger's Parting Gifts*. New York: Lothrop, Lee & Shepard, 1984.

Viorst, J. *The Tenth Good Thing about Barney*. New York: Aladdin, 1971.

Appendix

Appendix 1

Dr. Patricia Cordeiro
Royal Archeological Institute
1111 Pharoahs Boulevard
Cairo, Egypt
8 January 1990

Alexandria Van der Linde
103 Sunshine Road
Orlando FL 07590

Dear Alexandria,

This is to inform you that you have been accepted as a member of one of
the 1990 Royal Archeological Institute Teams which will be working in
Egypt. This placement begins immediately.

You will receive assignments over the next 2-3 weeks to prepare you for
this research project. Please return these promptly so that your team
will not be slowed down.

Each member of each team will be expected to write a research paper on a
subject that is appropriate to doing archeology in Egypt. This paper
will be due at the beginning of February and will become a part of book
on Modern Egypt.

Please be sure that you have your identification ready by Wednesday.
This should include a driver's license, and possibly two other credit
cards. Also, you must show proof that you have $2000 credit or $2000 in
a bank account before you plan on making this trip.

For your first assignment, please write an essay on what you know of life
in modern Egypt. Use at least one source and cite it. This essay should
be as long as you need to make it. Your team will receive traveling
points for each essay.

You will receive the names of your team members shortly. The Institute
is impressed with the credentials of all the applicants and will match
them up as carefully as possible.

Looking forward to working with you,

Sincerely,

Dr. Patricia Cordeiro
Director, Royal Archelogical Institute

Appendix 2

Dr. Patricia Cordeiro
Royal Archeological Institute
1111 Pharoahs Boulevard
Cairo, Egypt
8 January 1990

Dear

This is to notify you that our departure date is January 26, 1990.
Please be sure that your passport and medical records are in order by
that time.

Teams will be assigned by January 19, 1990. Members are still telling
the Institute what they are experts at. The Institute hopes to arrange
balanced teams. So far we know that we have 2 experts on the art of
mumification, 2 experts on modern technology and mummification, and one
expert on diseases of the Middle East.

Please notify us of what you are an expert at as soon as possible.

By Tuesday, please provide a list of items you will be taking. Plan on
staying for 2-3 weeks. Plan on a hot, dusty climate, and a lot of
hiking. Bring with you any prescription medicines you will need for 2-3
weeks. Sometimes you must dress formally for dinner. Such things as
refills for ball point pens are hard to find in the area we are going to.
Women should plan on wearing long sleeves on blouses and dresses. No
shorts or halters, please. Hats are suggested for everyone but can be
purchased in Cairo. Bring suntan lotion.

Each passenger is limited to 40 pounds of luggage.

Sincerely,

Dr. Patricia Cordeiro
Director, Royal Archelogical Institute

Appendix 3

Dr. Patricia Cordeiro
Royal Archeological Institute
1111 Pharoahs Boulevard
Cairo, Egypt
8 January 1990

Dr. Aurelia T. Laschenova
22660 Pacific Coast Highway
Malibu CA 90265

Dear Aurelia,

Thank you for the fine work you have done so far for the Institute. Here
is your next assignment.

By Thursday, January 25, 1990, please submit a bibliography of five (5)
books or articles you may be using in your final report. As you know the
Institute requires a research report from each Fellow at the end of the
project. A bibliography is a complete list of books or articles you
might use. Here is the form the Institute requires:

For Books:
Author's last name, first initial. Title. Place of publication:
Publisher, year.

Like this:
    Watercat, Max. Sinks and Tubs. New York: Doubleday, 1990.

For articles.
Author's last name, first initial. "Article Title." In Book or Magazine
Title, year, pages xx-xx.

Like this:
   Crocker, Betty. "Egyptian Flatbreads I Have Eaten," In National
Geographic, 1990, pp. 222-223.

These bibliographies will be graded according to your careful choice of
sources, your use of the correct form, and neatness.

Sincerely,

Dr. Patricia Cordeiro
Director, Royal Archelogical Institute

Appendix 4

Dr. Patricia Cordeiro
Royal Archeological Institute
1111 Pharoahs Boulevard
Cairo, Egypt

7 March 1990

To all Visiting Scholars

The Royal Archeological Institute of Cairo cordially invites you to a
formal meeting of the 1989-90 Institute Scholars. The meeting will be
held on March 7, 1990, at 1:00 P.M.

This is a pre-publication meeting to review Fellows' Final Reports. At
this meeting, Fellows will present formal summaries of each others'
recent research. Fellows have been involved in selected projects
regarding Ancient and Modern Egypt. All Fellows have visited Egyptian
artifact collections and reviewed current thinking on Ancient Egyptian
history. All Fellows have filed preliminary final reports. These
reports are currently being prepared for publication.

This years' Fellows represent a wide range of interests and backgrounds.
Many come fully prepared to take part in projects such as this. Many
have participated in other archeological projects. All have published
formal research reports. Their letters of application are available at
the Institute if you care to review them. The Royal Archeological
Institute is proud to have had the opportunity to work with such
qualified Fellows.

We of the Royal Archeological Institute realize that travel arrangements
to these meetings are often difficult. We appreciate your interest in
our projects and publications.

Sincerely,

Patricia Cordeiro

Dr. Patricia Cordeiro
Director, Royal Archeological Institute
for, Institute Fellows 1989-90

cc. All 1989-90 Institute Fellows

Appendix 5

Dr. Patricia Cordeiro
Royal Archeological Institute
1111 Pharoahs Boulevard
Cairo, Egypt
8 January 1990

Dr. Aurelia T. Laschenova
22660 Pacific Coast Highway
Malibu CA 90265

Dear Aurelia,

You are cordially invited to a meeting of the Institute Fellows to be
held on March 7, 1990 at 1:00 P.M.

At this time, Fellows will present the results of each other's work. The
Institute requests that you present a summary of the research of:

Tracy Lynn Myer, Institute Fellow 1989-90

Looking forward to your report.

Sincerely,

Patricia Cordeiro

Dr. Patricia Cordeiro
Director, Royal Archelogical Institute

Appendix 6

Dr. Patricia Cordeiro
Royal Archeological Institute
1111 Pharoahs Boulevard
Cairo, Egypt

Dr. Aurelia T. Laschenova
22660 Pacific Coast Highway
Malibu CA 90265

Appendix 7

Royal Trading Exploration Company

1600 Trevarney Square
London, England
British Empire

Sailing under the Protection of
Her Royal Highnesss Queen Mary II,

Queen of England, Scotland, Ireland, protector of thr Faith;

21 May 1691   and, His Royal Highness William III,
King of England, Stadholder of Holland

To Loyal English Citizens applying for Emigration to the Colonies:-

Your name has been selected from the Lottery for those loyal English
Citizens applying for Emigration to the Colonies. In order to Qualify
for this long and arduous Journey, please provide the Royal Trading and
Exploration Company with information as follows, :-

   -Letter of Introduction:- Please inform the Royal Trading and
   Information about you and your Family, your present
   Address, Ages, State of Health, & etc.

   -Chosen Destination:- Please inform the Royal Trading and

   Exploration Company as to which Colony you prefer for your
   Emigration. Include Information that proves that you know
   enough about this Colony to make it your Home.

   -Trade or Profession:- Please make Clear what Trade or
   Profession you will Pursue when you are settled in your
   Chosen Colony.   State your background and qualifications
   for this Trade or Profession.   If you were an Apprentice
   give the Name of Your Master. If he is still living, have
   him write a Letter testifying to your Good Performance as
   an Apprentice.

   The Royal Trading and Exploration Company cannot allow any
   Citizens to Emigrate if they are unable to support
   Themselves and their Families.

The Sailing Ship, Her Majesty's Sailing Ship "Henry VIII," will be
sailing on the Tide before May 30, when Wind, Tide and Weather permit.
Therefore, do not Delay to Notify us of this Information.

We remind you that Their Gracious Majesties, Queen Mary II and King
William III, support this Voyage. Therefore, Passage for you and your
Family is Paid in Advance.   Please respond without delay.
God Bless Their Royal Majesties, Queen Mary II and William III, and
Preserve the Royal Empire,

Your Faithful Servant,

Sir Johnathan Hyphen-Smythe, Esquire
Director, Royal Trading and Exploration Company

Appendix 8

1600 Trevarney Square
London, England
British Empire

Sailing under the Protection of

Her Royal Highness Queen Mary II,
Queen of England, Scotland, Ireland, protector of the Faith;

24 May 1691

and, His Royal Highness William III,
King of England, Stadholder of Holland

NOTICE:

HER MAJESTY'S SAILING SHIP HENRY VIII

SAILS ON THE TIDE

MAY 26, 1691

GOD, WIND, AND WEATHER PERMITTING

DO NOT FAIL TO MEET THE TIDE.

THE ROYAL TRADING AND EXPLORATION COMPANY

RESPECTFULLY RECOMMENDS THAT ALL EMIGRANTS
DRAW UP THEIR LAST WILL AND TESTAMENT AND
PUT THEIR BUSINESS AND FAMILY AFFAIRS IN ORDER
BEFORE SAILING; -

LAWYERS ARE AVAILABLE THROUGH THIS FIRM
FOR THOSE REQUIRING LEGAL ASSISTANCE IN THESE MATTERS
FOR A SMALL FEE

THIS VOYAGE WILL TAKE AT LEAST NINETY DAYS

ALL EMIGRANTS MUST PROVIDE ALL FOOD AND SUSTENANCE
FOR THEIR OWN FAMILIES AND DEPENDENTS,
SERVANTS, & ETC.; -

ALL PASSENGERS SHOULD APPEAR BEFORE THE
MASTER OF THE SHIP
ON THE DAY BEFORE SAILING TO CONFIRM RESERVATIONS
AND TAKE UP THEIR ASSIGNED PLACES

God Bless Their Royal Majesties, Queen Mary II and King William III, and
Preserve the Royal Empire,

Sir Johnathan Hyphen-Smythe, Esquire
Director, Royal Trading and Exploration Company

Appendix 9

Please provide to the Good Captain, Captain Bartholomew Wentworthly
Hatt, alist of all the Provision and Goods, Livestock and personal Effects
You have with you on this Voyage. Include All Items for Each Passenger
Traveling with you. Know Ye that your Traveling Compartment Measures
6 Feet by 6 Feet by 6 Feet, Including Sleeping Space, Not Including Space for

Your Cooking Fire.

This List is Provided to the Captain for

Insurance Purposes.

Please do not Fail to Provide it Posthaste.

Signed,

Mortimer Squirrely,First Mate and Company Clark

Appendix 10

KILLINGLY, JOHOSOPHAT & SNYDELY, ESQs.

BROKERS AT LARGE -,

17 Plumbottom Road
London, England

BONDED AND LICENSED BROKERS
FOR INDENTURED SERVANTS, APPRENTICES & LAYMEN

SERVING FAITHFULLY SINCE THE YEAR OF OUR LORD, 1655

We have available through our brokerage House the Names of several Indentured Servants interested in securing Passage to the Colonies;

They are all of the Highest Reputation and are Possessed of Good Work Habits; - Many have been in the Trades and have in their possession Recommendations from the Finest of Trade Masters;

All are of Sound Mind and Body, and are Sworn against the Taking of Strong Spirits and other Bad Habits;

If any Emigrating Loyal English Citizens are able to Support an Indentured Servants, the terms are, to wit: -

> One-half the Passage to be paid by Their Royal Majesties, Queen Mary II and King William III

> One-Half the Passage to be Paid by the Emigrant

> All Fees and Taxes to be Paid by the Emigrant

> Board and Room for the Indentured Servant for a Period of Seven Years to be provided by the Emigrant

> At the end of Seven Years, a Severance Pay of 5 Pounds to be paid by the Emigrant to the Indentured Servant to assist in establishing a New Home

> For a Period of Seven Years, the Indentured Servant will perform agreed-on services for the Emigrant as according to a Signed and Sworn Contract drawn up by this Brokeage House

> IF YOU ARE ABLE TO SUPPORT AN INDENTURED SERVANT,
> PLEASE CONTACT US AT
> 17 PLUMBOTTOM ROAD
> FOR FURTHER DETAILS.

Appendix 11

```
                    NOTICE TO ALL  PASSENGERS
                 SAILING ABOARD H.M.S.S. KING HENRY VIII


    WE WILL BE ENCOUNTERING THE SAILING PACKET, "WINDSWIFT,"
                 IN TWO DAYS TIME.
    ANY PASSENGERS DESIRING TO SEND LETTERS TO THOSE AT HOME  IN  ENGLAND
            SHOULD PROVIDE THEM TO THE CAPTAIN NO LATER
                 THAN 2:00 P.M. TOMORROW FOR
                    THE MAIL SACK.

    THE CHARGE FOR THIS SERVICE IS 1 SHILLING.


            Mortimer Squirelly, First Mate and Company Clark
```

Appendix 12

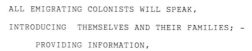

TO ALL LOYAL ENGLISH SUBJECTS SELECTED

FOR EMIGRATION TO THE COLONIES: -,

ON THURSDAY NEXT, MAY 23, 1691,

A GENERAL MEETING WILL BE HELD.

ALL EMIGRATING COLONISTS WILL SPEAK,

INTRODUCING THEMSELVES AND THEIR FAMILIES; -

PROVIDING INFORMATION,

TO WIT : -

COLONIAL DESTINATION

TRADE OR PROFESSION AND NAME OF MASTER

TOWN OR VILLAGE OF ORIGIN

ANY AND ALL GENERAL BACKGROUND INFORMATION

SUFFICIENT TO AQUAINT OTHER TRAVELERS

WITH ALL TRAVELING TOGETHER

DO NOT FAIL TO BE PREPARED TO SPEAK.

PREPARED BY MY HAND, THIS 22 DAY OF MAY 1691 -

SIR JOHNATHAN HYPHEN-SMYTHE, ESQ.

FOR THE ROYAL TRADING AND EXPLORATION COMPANY, LONDON

Index

Academic writing, 196
Ad hoc groups, 22, 40
Adams, Ansel, 134
Administration, 24
Adult
  characteristics, 39
  learning, 221
  performance model, 224
Alternative hypotheses, 58
Altwerger, Bess, 10, 11, 17
American civics, 31
Appropriateness, 24, 43
Approximation, 9, 60, 226, 229
Arthur, Pamela, 154
Articulation in writing, 49, 205
Assessment, 236
Atwell, Nancie, 10, 70, 114, 168,
  194
Authenticity, 9, 17, 40, 57, 75, 77,
  78, 79, 85, 112, 161, 169,
  170, 224, 246, 252, 257
Author Dialogues, 159

Baker, Ann, 154
Baker, Dave, 154
Baker, Johnny, 154
Bamberger, Jeanne, 253
Barnes, Douglas, 30
Barton, John, 49
Bash, Barbara, 195
Baskiwell, Jane, 248
Baylor, Byrd, 179, 180
Bellanoff, P., 248
Bereiter, Carl, 197
Bezuska, Stanley, 151
Big Ideas, 18, 138, 147, 149
Bissex, Glenda, 182
Bixby, Mary, 10, 114
Bizarre writing habits, 47
Blending, 22, 25
Bodanis, David, 117
Brause, Rita, 44
Brown, Ann, 140, 197
Brown, Mary, 195
Bruner, Jerome, 222, 227

Bunting, Eve, 195
Burke, Carolyn, 71, 168, 180
Burns, Marilyn, 154
Butzow, Carol, 135
Butzow, John, 135

Calkins, Lucy, 71, 180, 182
Cambourne, Brian, 8, 10, 12, 22,
  221, 222, 223, 224, 230
Cazden, Courtney, 7, 8, 58, 155,
  173, 231, 247
Chaos, 152
Charting, 118, 131
Cherry, Lynn, 195
Child-centered, 9, 10
Choice reading, 161
Christie, Agatha, 165, 167, 213
Christopher, Matt, 163
Classifying, 19
Classroom climates, 36, 43, 253
Classroom configuration, 37, 44
Classroom talk, 4, 22
Clay, Marie, 8, 155
Climate of trust, 141
Clyne, Margaret, 154
Cognitive connections, 199, 201
Cole, Joanna, 117, 131, 190
Cole, Michael, 153, 173, 233
Coles, Robert, 56
Collaborative learning, 22
Communication in writing, 49, 205
Community, 37, 43, 78, 79, 252, 257
Community-building, differences at
  upper level, 38
Compartmentalization, 6, 180, 194,
  198
Conceptual development, 17, 227,
  229, 234
Conferencing, 51, 67, 203, 233, 238
"Construction zone," 153, 173, 233
Content areas, viii, ix, 14, 21, 23, 26,
  28, 29, 64, 169, 172, 183,
  199, 203, 205
Continuity in learning process, 16
Conventions in writing, 49

Cooperation, 37, 76, 224, 248
Cooperative competitiveness, 22
Copy-delete, 197
Cordeiro, Marty, 74, 200
Cordeiro, Pat, 18, 21, 58, 75, 129,
    142, 148, 151
Correcting by consensus, 141
Cowley, Joy, 161
Creativity, 179, 180, 181, 254
Crenshaw, Shirley, 10, 114
Critical and creative thinking, infused,
    19
Critical thinking, 67, 75, 215
Cross, Patricia, 225, 227, 229
Cross-cultural awareness, 81
Crowley, Paul, 10, 114
Culminating activities, 31, 86, 96
Curriculum
    coordinated, 29
    developmental, 29, 218
    directives, 19
    generative, 28, 29, 30, 218, 253
    integrated, 29
    levels of, 29
    reading, 167
    segregated, 29
    teacher developed, 23, 75
Curtis, E.S., 80

Daiute, Colette, 228
Davidson, Neil, 154
Davidson, Patricia, 140, 148, 154
Day, Jeanne, 140, 197
Decentering, 160
Decision-making, 41, 76, 79, 86, 219
Delano, A., 80
Demi, 195
Demonstration, 38
"Dense print," 117, 176, 185
Dialogue journals, 162–3
Dickinson, Terence, 130
Dickson, M., 248
Dillard, Annie, 178
Discovery-based environment, 41
"Doing what scientists do," 117,
    128, 135
Donaldson, Margaret, 58, 142
Doodling, 207
Doris, Ellen, 135

Double entry, 146
Drawing and writing, 182
Drew, David, 190
Duckworth, Eleanor, 26, 38, 128,
    129, 134, 135, 221, 231, 256

Edelsky, Carole, 10, 11
Edge of adulthood, 221
Educational Testing Service, 143
Egg Drop Contest, 127
Egypt
    simulation, 85
    theme, 25, 41, 43, 85, 170, 258
Ehlert, Lois, 195
Elbow, Peter, 198
Emergent
    literacy, 9, 227
    mathematicians, 25
    readers, 167
    writers, 63, 182
Ennis, Robert, 67
Erdmann, Linda, 157
Error analysis, 142
Errors in math, 142
Escher, M.C., 149
Evaluation and assessment, ix, 236
Everyday life in Early America, 44,
    96
Expert model, 21, 24, 31, 37, 86, 88,
    91, 96, 114, 124, 170–173,
    202, 208

Farmer's almanac, 119, 129, 131
Faults, 256
Ferguson, C., 222
Final reports, Egypt, 91
Finn, Jackie, 9
Fisher, Bobbi, 7, 10, 218, 224
Flexibility, 27, 29, 85
Flexible reality, 40–42, 78, 113
Flores, Barbara, 10, 11
Focused freewriting, 201
Formal writing, 205
"Fourth grade slump," 183–4
Fractions and decimals, 140
Freewriting, 198

Gallo, Delores, 181, 185, 194
Gamow, George, 18, 148
Generalists, 28

Generative, 148, 257
  curriculum, 28, 29, 30, 35
Genre, 193
Giacobbe, Mary Ellen, 58, 177
Gilles, Carol, 10, 114
Gilligan, Carol, 217
Gleick, M., 148, 152
Goble, Paul, 195
Goodman, Ken, 6, 9, 10, 58, 248
Goodman, Yetta, 9, 10, 79, 237, 247,
  248
Gordon, Karen, 57
Grammar games, 53
Graphing, 118
Graves, Donald, 28, 57, 59, 67, 69,
  70, 168, 174, 180–182, 186,
  244
Greenfield, Patricia, 222
Grifalconi, Ann, 195
Griffin, Peg, 153, 173, 233
Griffiths, Rachel, 154
Grotz, Ben, 40, 51, 64, 81, 82, 96
Group theory, 151
Groups
  ad hoc, 22, 40
  heterogeneous, 22, 40, 167
  homogeneous, 157, 167
  reading, 157, 164
  TAWL, 254

Hall, Susan, 187, 194
Halliday, Michael, 222
Harp, B., 248
Harste, Jerry, 71, 168, 180, 257
Hawkey, Ron, 178
Hawkins, David, 26, 28, 152, 253
Heald-Taylor, G., 248
Heathcote, Dorothy, 5, 25, 76, 77,
  114, 219, 253
Heller, Ruth, 192
Henrichs, Margaret, 10, 114
Herbert, Phyl, 25, 114
Hines, Anna, 130
Historical fiction, 179
Holdaway, Don, 8, 29, 30, 43, 60,
  222, 223, 230, 231, 247, 250
Holly, Mary, 253
Holubec, E., 37
Homer, Winslow, 201

Honesty, 214
Hood, Wendy, 9, 10, 248
Hornsby, David, 6, 71, 168, 180, 225
Howard, Vernon, 49, 227
Hoyt-Goldsmith, Diane, 195
Hyde, Arthur, 154
Hypothesis revision, 58

Ideas in school, 207
Independent study, 21
Inductive learning, 6
Infinity, a theme, 18, 21, 149
Informal writing, 205
Infusion, 19
Integrated day, 18, 28
Integrated learning, 234, 235
Integration, 75, 144, 161, 194
Interaction, 5, 26, 49, 52, 148, 153,
  162, 163, 172–3, 212, 231,
  234, 235, 247, 255, 257
Internal versus external criteria, 240
International Reading Association,
  169, 195
Interpsychological, 232
Intersections for literacy, 25, 35
Intrapsychological, 52, 232
Intuitive knowledge, 252
  teachers', 253

John-Steiner, Vera, 151
Johnson, D., 37
Johnson, R., 37
Jotting, 200, 206, 224
Journals
  reading, 162–3
  teachers', 254
Journey-maker, 5, 77, 114
"Joy and laughter," 230
Junior editors, 59

Kagan, J., 183
Kamii, Constance, 253
Kenney, Margaret, 151
Kidd, J., 225–229
Kidwatching, 79, 247
Kinesthetics, 134, 140
Knowledge
  telling, 197
  transforming, 197
Knowles, Malcolm, 229

Knox, S., 228–230
Kohlberg, Lawrence, 217
Kolczynski, Richard, 178

Lab reports, 127
Labinowicz, E., 154
Language acquisition, 222
Language arts, 237
    infused, 52
Language, oral, 8
Lawson, Robert, 179
Learner-centered, 9, 10, 17, 23, 44
Learners on the edge of adulthood, 11
Learners with a history, 11, 221
Learning centers, 33
"Life themes," 218
Linguistics, 59
Linquist, Mary, 138
Lipman, A., 213
Listening, 255
    to learners, 33
Lists, 108
    in simulation, 91
Literacy, 28, 86, 101, 208
    in math, 145
Literature Circles, 164
Living diagrams, 133–4
Locke, Betty, 39, 74, 116, 138, 156,
    237, 251, 254, 256
Locke, Jim, 115
Lovell, B., 225–229
Lucretia Crocker Fellowship Program,
    43

Mantle of the Expert, 25, 114
Mapwork and literacy, 81
Marcy, Captain, 80
Martin, Nancy, 172
Math manipulatives, 4, 139, 232
Math/science, ix
Mathematics, ix, 21, 22, 136
Mathews, Gareth, 213, 218
Matthews, Kathy, 182
May, Sandra, 39, 116, 207, 255
Mayher, John, 44
McCloskey, Robert, 187
McShane, J., 222
Measurement, 137
Mediated learning, 233, 234

Medway, Peter, 172
Memorization in social studies, 74
Metacognition, 64
Millman, Arthur, 214
Modeling, 32, 38, 44, 75, 227, 254
Modular mathematics, 152
Moffett, James, 205
Moldy Bread Contest, 124
Moon in the daytime, 129, 131
"Moonday," 122, 132
Moonwatching, 128
Motto, Helen, 127
Murray, Don, 48

National Council of Teachers of
    English, 148, 244
National Council of Teachers of
    Mathematics, 138
National Geographic, 117, 163, 191
Native Americans, 80
Negotiated settlements, 15
Networking, 254
Newkirk, Tom, 10
Newman, Denis, 153, 173, 233
Newspaper, in science, 119

Observation, 116, 117, 127, 129, 190
Open classroom movement, 33, 36
Optimal conditions for learning, 8,
    12, 22, 153, 221, 222, 224,
    230, 253, 257
Oscanyon, F.S., 213
Ownership, 24, 59

Paley, Vivian, 257
Panofsky, Carolyn, 151
Parent involvement in simulations, 96,
    109
Parnell, Peter, 180
Parry, Jo-Ann, 71, 168, 180
Partially adequate strategies, 197
Passmore, John, 116, 254
Peer bonding, 39
Penrose, Robert, 147
Perkins, David, 19
Philosophy in the classroom, 211
Phrases, writing in, 203
Piaget, Jean, 139, 160, 217, 231
Picture storybooks, 130, 176, 187
    with a difference, 192

"Pioneers," 75, 77, 219, 251, 257
Polacco, Patricia, 195
Polya, G., 144
Ponce de Leon, 200
Portfolio assessment, 237, 238
Portugal, a theme, 17, 30
"Positive prophecy," 231, 248, 254
Powell, Whitney, 121
Practical knowledge, teachers', 253
Pre-Revolutionary America, 96
Predictions, 122
Pretending, 40, 112
Prior knowledge, 83
Problem-based thematic simulations, 75
Problem posing, 137, 143
Problem-solving, 19, 41, 75, 79, 86, 96, 101, 145
Problem-solving framework, 21, 65
Problem-solving, infused, 19
Process learning, 4, 6
Process writing, 48, 180
Publishing, 51, 59, 68, 161, 180–1
Punctuation, 49, 101, 203
Pyle, Donelle, 10, 114

Readarounds, 24, 199, 208
Readers' workshop, ix, 155, 161
Reading, content material, 168
Reading groups, 157, 164
Reading process, infused, 21
Reason, J., 227
Recess, learning at, 230
Reffe, Candice, 131
Reliability of source, 24, 132
Renner, Al, 127
Report cards, 249
Research, 170, 189
Responsibility, 14
Reynolds, Francis, 10, 114
Rich contexts, 18
Rief, Linda, 10, 236, 240, 241
Rogers, J., 227
Role playing, 41, 75, 76, 112
Rothman, Michael, 180, 189
"Roundrobin" reading, 156
Routman, Regie, 9, 10, 159
Rowe, Jane, 19, 65, 137
Roy, P., 37

Royal Archeological Institute of Cairo, 85, 170
Russell, David, 194
Ryder, Joanne, 117, 131, 179, 180, 187, 189

Safety net, 11, 252
Scardamalia, Marlene, 197
Schedule, viii, 6, 13, 16, 21, 25, 33, 157
  fall daily, 14
  in my mind, 25
Schlissel, Lillian, 80, 252
School Journals, 159
Science, ix, 21, 115
Scientific method, 118
Scientific versus spontaneous, 129, 153, 232, 234
Sebesta, Sam, 168, 178
Self-contained classroom, viii, 14, 196
Self-correction, 43
Self-esteem, 31, 174
Self-evaluation, 237, 244, 249, 250
Self-regulation, 60, 223, 247
Semple, Cheryl, 154
Sentences, 203
Shared competencies, viii, 11
Sharp, A.M., 213
Shifting dimensions, 132
Short, Kathy, 71, 168, 180
Silent reading, 162
Silvey, Linda, 151
Simon, Seymour, 130
Simulations, 31, 41, 75, 143, 213
  and integration, 112
  creating original, 85
  early life in America, 96
  Egypt, 85, 170
  Westward movement, 77
Smith, Frank, 156, 168, 228
Smith, Harold, 172
Smith, J., 222
Smith, Larry, 151
Snow, Catherine, 222
Social studies, viii, 73, 164
Socratic dialogue, 214–5, 217
"Southeast Explorers," 200
Speaking, public, 79, 91, 109

Spelling tests, 52
Standardizations in writing, 49
State Chart, 217
Stead, Tony, 154
Stenmark, J., 154
Stewig, John, 168, 178
Stratton, Joanna, 81
Stratton, R.B., 80
Structure, 248
    classroom, 13
Students with a history, 142
Sub-communities, 39
Sukarnah, Deborah, 168
Summary writing, 170
Swartz, Robert, 19, 63

TAWL groups, 254
Tchudi, Stephen, 61
Teacher
    as learner, 25
    proof, 24, 34
Text models, 178, 187
Textbooks, 24, 73, 116, 156–158
Thematic learning, 75
Theme, westward movement, 40, 75
Themes, viii, 17, 33, 202
    and philosophy, 218
Theoretical perspectives, ix
Theories, 221
    teachers, 220
Three-dimensions, 132, 134
Tolkien, J.R.R., 162
Torrance, E., 183–4
Tours of a million, 151
Trade books, 175, 176
Transcribing, 56
Transliterating, 81, 117
Triangulating, 133
Turner, Ann, 177
Twain, Mark, 167, 179
Two dimensions, 132, 211

Units, 18, 21, 31, 202, 204

Van Der Meer, Ron, 178
Venn circle, 249
    grammar game, 53
Vision, 252, 254–5, 257
Vocabulary work, 202
Voice, in writing, 55
Volume, in mathematics, 138
Voyage of the Mimi, 117
Vygotsky, Lev, 16, 22, 34, 52, 129,
    153, 173, 182, 226, 227, 229,
    231–5, 255

Walter, Marion, 151
War and philosophy, 211
War books, 192
Watson, Dorothy, ix, 6, 168
Weaver, Connie, 58, 168
Westward migration, 251
    as a theme, 40, 75, 77, 219
White, Sheldon, 233
Whitman, P., 248
Whole language, 222, 254
    grass roots, 9
    philosophy, 7
Whole Language Teachers
    Association, 7
Whole Language Umbrella, 257
Women's diaries, 80, 81, 219, 252
Wright, J., 80
Writing
    as problem-solving, 65
    editing, 50
    finding time, 52
    planning, 61
    process in content, infused, 21
    teacher as publishing house, 57
    teacher demonstration, 57
    Time, viii, 15, 23, 47
    what they know, 54
    with·learners with a history, 55
    working with experienced writers,
        60

Zone of proximal development, 34,
    153, 173, 232, 233